SO-CFR-676

GREAT AMERICAN PROSE POEMS

❦

From Poe to the Present

EDITED BY

DAVID LEHMAN

SCRIBNER POETRY

NEW YORK   LONDON   TORONTO   SYDNEY   SINGAPORE

SCRIBNER POETRY
1230 Avenue of the Americas
New York, NY 10020

SCRIBNER POETRY and design are trademarks of Macmillan Library Reference USA,
Inc., used under license by Simon & Schuster, the publisher of this work.

For information about special discounts for bulk purchases,
please contact Simon & Schuster Special Sales:
1-800-465-6798 or business@simonandschuster.com

DESIGNED BY ERICH HOBBING

Text set in Stempel Garamond

Manufactured in the United States of America

1 3 5 7 9 10 8 6 4 2

B+7 30.00 4/03
Library of Congress Cataloging-in-Publication Data is available.

ISBN 0-7432-2989-4
0-7432-4350-1 (Pbk)

It is even in
prose, I am a real poet.

—Frank O'Hara,
—"Why I Am Not a Painter"

CONTENTS

INTRODUCTION

by David Lehman

In December 1978, two members of a three-person committee voted to give the year's Pulitzer Prize in poetry to Mark Strand for his book *The Monument*. It was a bold move. *The Monument* was anything but a conventional book of verse. It comprised short prose musings on the subject of death, with the author's sentences presented in counterpoint to quotations from Shakespeare, Unamuno, Sir Thomas Browne, Nietzsche, Wallace Stevens, and other experts on mortality. In the end, however, Strand didn't win the prize, because the third judge—the committee chair, Louis Simpson—adamantly opposed the choice. Simpson objected to *The Monument* on the grounds that it is predominantly in prose. He argued that the prestigious award is designed expressly to honor verse, and the argument prevailed with the Pulitzer higher-ups who act on the committee's recommendations. To an admirer of *The Monument* it was as if the very qualities that distinguished this quirky, unfamiliar, hard-to-classify sequence worked against it when it came time to distribute accolades. It was clear then that prose had not yet gained acceptance as a medium for writing poetry. The poets who had been doing it were still working in advance of official recognition and in some cases (the Ashbery of *Three Poems*, the Merwin of *The Miner's Pale Children*) despite their own misgivings about the terms "prose poem" and "prose poetry." Such terms implied a link to a modern French tradition with which the American poets were familiar but from which they meant to keep a respectful distance. "The prose poem has the unusual distinction of being regarded with suspicion not only by the usual haters of poetry, but also by many poets themselves," Charles Simic observed.

So when Simic won the Pulitzer for *The World Doesn't End* in 1991 it seemed doubly significant, marking an event not only in Simic's reputation but in the place of the prose poem itself. Its validity as a form or genre with a specific appeal to American poets could no longer be denied. For Simic's Pulitzer volume, like Strand's jinxed volume thirteen years earlier, consisted mainly of prose poems, and it was defiantly as prose poems that they succeeded. In neither case was the prose tarted up to ape the supposed prettiness of verse. The writing was not self-consciously "poetic." On the contrary, the prose of these poems — one might say their "prosaic" nature if a pejorative valence did not hang over that word — was a crucial dimension of their being.

The prose poems in *The World Doesn't End* are brief, spare, sometimes chilling, dark. Many evoke Simic's childhood in Belgrade during World War II. A strange whimsy makes a grim memory of smoke and fog no less grim but perhaps more haunting. One untitled prose poem begins:

> I was stolen by the gypsies. My parents stole me right back. Then the gypsies stole me again. This went on for some time.

This succession of sentences, not lines, moves at a speed faster than verse. Then comes the formulaic last sentence to slow down the action. The effect is to make the extraordinary seem somehow routine, and it has everything to do with the rhythms of narrative prose. In another poem the opening sentence introduces a metaphor, and the rest of the piece elaborates it in an effort to sustain the epiphany:

> We were so poor I had to take the place of the bait in the mousetrap.

As it happens, the opening part of the sentence scans perfectly as blank verse. But it owes its force to the tension between the flatness of the delivery and the macabre twist in the plot. By putting his understated prose style at the service of the fantastic and surreal, Simic had found a way to capture the foreignness of his boyhood experience in war-torn Yugoslavia. His use of simple, declarative sentences, sometimes at a staccato pace, recalls the prose style of his fellow Oak Park High School alumnus, Ernest Hemingway, himself a prose poem pioneer.

It is possible to read Simic's prose poems as dream narratives that end abruptly, enigmatically. You might almost treat them as prose fiction, except for their extreme brevity, the ambiguous ways they achieve resolution, and their author's unmistakably poetic intent. Simic told an interviewer that his book originated as "quick notations," "ideas for poems," written haphazardly and on the run. They came, he said, from a place where "the impulses for prose and those for poetry collide." What made them poems? "What makes them poems is that they are self-contained, and once you read one you have to go back and start reading it again. That's what a poem does."

What is a prose poem? The best short definition is almost tautological. The prose poem is a poem written in prose rather than verse. On the page it can look like a paragraph or fragmented short story, but it acts like a poem. It works in sentences rather than lines. With the one exception of the line break, it can make use of all the strategies and tactics of poetry. Just as free verse did away with meter and rhyme, the prose poem does away with the line as the unit of composition. It uses the means of prose toward the ends of poetry.

The prose poem is, you might say, poetry that disguises its true nature. In the prose poem the poet can appropriate such unlikely models as the newspaper article, the memo, the list, the parable, the speech, the dialogue. It is a form that sets store by its use of the demotic, its willingness to locate the sources of poetry defiantly far from the spring on Mount Helicon sacred to the muses. It is an insistently modern form. Some would argue further that it is, or was, an inherently subversive one. Margueritte Murphy's *A Tradition of Subversion* (1992) contends that an adversarial streak characterizes the genre. Others are drawn to the allegorical formula that would align the prose poem with "working-class discourse" undermining the lyric structures of the upper bourgeosie. Many examples and precedents elude or combat this facile notion, and commentators have begun to stress the inclusiveness of the genre and not its putatively subversive properties. While it sometimes seems that the only generalization you can safely make about the prose poem is that it resists generalization, certain terms recur in essays and critical discussions. The prose poem is a *hybrid* form, an *anomaly* if not a *paradox* or *oxymoron*. It offers the enchantment of *escape* whether from the invisible chains of the superego, or from the oppressive reign of the alexandrine line, from which Charles Baudelaire broke vehemently in his *Petits Poèmes en prose* (1862), which inaugurated the genre in France. Sooner or later in the discussion it will be said that the prose poem, born in rebellion against *tradition,* has itself become a tradition. It will be noted approvingly that the prose poem *blurs boundaries*. "My own formal literary education had not accorded much regard to what in English are referred to as 'prose poems,' and I am not at all sure what the genre is supposed to entail," W. S. Merwin wrote in a 1994 reprinting of *The Miner's Pale Children* (1970). "I recalled what I thought were precedents—fragments, essays, journal entries, instructions and lists, oral tales, fables. What I was hoping for as I went was akin to what made a poem seem complete. But it was prose that I was writing, and I was pleased when the pieces raised questions about the boundary between prose and poetry, and where we think it runs."

The words *poetry* and *prose* seem to be natural antagonists. The French Renaissance poet Pierre Ronsard said they were "mortal enemies." Matthew Arnold, thinking to damn the poets Dryden and Pope, called them "classics of our prose." Oscar Wilde subtly refined the insult: "Meredith is a prose Browning, and so is Browning. He used poetry as a medium for writing in prose." In these examples, it is *prose* that has the negative charge, but the opposite can sometimes be true. Not every poet accused of writing *poetic prose* today will feel complimented, though to Baudelaire in Paris in 1862 it represented an ideal. No doubt *poetry* and *prose* will continue to exist in an antithetical relationship if only because they, and *poetry* in particular, are not neutrally descriptive but have an evaluative meaning. This complicates any discussion of the prose poem and assures that it will probably always retain its oxymoronic status. Nevertheless, there is a way to cut to the quick. As soon as you admit the possibility that verse is an adjunct of poetry and not an indispensable quality, the prose poem ceases to be a contradiction in terms. *Verse* and *prose* are the real antonyms, and the salient difference between them is that verse occurs in lines of a certain length determined by the poet whereas prose continues to the end of the page. In Richard Howard's formulation, verse reverses—the reader turns at the end of the line—while prose proceeds. The form of a prose poem is not an absence of form. It is just that the sentence and the paragraph must act the part of the line and the stanza, and there are fewer rules and governing traditions to observe, or different ones, because the prose poem has a relatively short history and has enjoyed outsider status for most of that time. Writing a prose poem can therefore seem like accepting a dare to be unconventional. It is a form that invites the practitioner to reinvent it.

In an aphorism contest, the winning definition would come from Charles Simic. "The prose poem is the result of two contradictory impulses, prose and poetry, and therefore cannot exist, but it does," he writes. "This is the sole instance we have of squaring the circle." Elsewhere Simic proposes a gastronomic analogy for this "veritable literary hybrid," this "impossible amalgamation of lyric poetry, anecdote, fairy tale, allegory, joke, journal entry, and many other kinds of prose." Prose poems "are the culinary equivalent of peasant dishes, like paella and gumbo, which bring together a great variety of ingredients and flavors, and which in the end, thanks to the art of the cook, somehow blend. Except, the parallel is not exact. Prose poetry does not follow a recipe. The dishes it concocts are unpredictable and often vary from poem to poem." Sticking with kitchen metaphors, James Richardson comments that the prose poem's shifty position is akin to that of the tomato, which may be a fruit in botany class but is a vegetable if you're making fruit salad.

The problem of nomenclature is—as Marianne Moore observed of attempts to differentiate poetry from prose—"a wart on so much happiness." Amy Hempel summed up some of the options in her title for a lecture she and I planned to give together at Bennington College: "Prose poem, short short, or couldn't finish?" There will always be exceptions, prose pieces that defy category or fit into more than one, but a practical way of proceeding is to make a division between work that the writer conceives as fiction and work that is conceived as poetry. Writers are under no obligation to classify their writing for us. But their intentions, if articulated, could be thought decisive. For the fiction writer, the prose poem (or "short short") may be exhilarating because it allows an escape from the exigencies of the novel, novella, and short story. But that writer may nevertheless conceive the result to be not poetry but fiction. For the poet, writing in prose gains one entry into a world of formal possibility—the poem as anecdote, as letter, as meditation, as plot summary—but what is produced is still conceptually a poem. (Editorial intervention can complicate matters. The late Kenneth Koch, pleased that three pieces from his book *Hotel Lambosa* were chosen for this anthology, asked me nevertheless to note that he regards them not as prose poems but as stories in the manner of Yasunari Kawabata's *Palm-of-the-Hand Stories*). Of terms now in use, "short short" sounds like an undergarment, "flash fiction" evokes the image of an unshaved character in a soiled raincoat, and "poem in prose" sounds a bit tweedy. That leaves the poet with "prose poem," which has at least the virtues of simplicity and directness. Perhaps the prose poem's ironic motto could come from the moment in *Citizen Kane* when the newspaper magnate, played by Orson Welles, receives a telegram from a reporter in the field: "Girls delightful in Cuba STOP Could send you prose poems about scenery but don't feel right spending your money STOP There is no war in Cuba." And Kane wires back: "You provide the prose poems, I'll provide the war."

* * *

15

Baudelaire wasn't the first to write prose poems in French. Aloysius Bertrand beat him to the punch with his remarkable and still underrated *Gaspard de la nuit* in 1842. But it was Baudelaire who launched the genre, giving it a local habitation and a name. He gave his book alternate titles. One was *Spleen de Paris*, the other *Petits Poèmes en prose* (*Little Prose Poems*). In a letter to a friend, Baudelaire wrote a sentence that scholars have quoted ever since: "Who among us has not, in his ambitious moments, dreamed of the miracle of a poetic prose, musical without meter or rhyme, supple enough and rugged enough to adapt itself to the lyrical impulses of the soul, the undulations of the psyche, the jolts of consciousness?" Liberated from the implacable requirements of formal French verse, Baudelaire wrote with a sort of infernal energy that the prose medium helped to release. He employed a cruel irony that joined suffering to laughter. Paris is the setting and sometimes the subject, and man is not a wonder but a creature of vanity, lust, disgust, and gratuitous nastiness.

Writing prose poems may have been cathartic for Baudelaire. They were the agency by which he could transform ennui and daydreams into symbolic action. The imp of the perverse, on loan from Edgar Allan Poe, makes its way out of the shadows like an unrepentant id. The impulse results variously in an argumentative prose poem counseling that it's better to beat up a beggar than to give him alms; a sort of drinking song in prose advising the reader to "be always drunk" ["Toujours être ivre"] whether "on wine, on poetry, or on virtue"; and a prankish narrative ["Le Mauvais vitrier," or "The Bad Glazier"], in which the narrator yields to the spontaneous urge to abuse a seller of window glass who has done him no harm. From a high window he drops a pot of flowers on the glazier's head, and shouts: "Make life beautiful! Make life beautiful!" The narrator acknowledges that such antics may exact a price. But he won't let that stand in the way. He summons the amoral didacticism of a fallen angel when he concludes: "But what is an eternity of damnation compared to an infinity of pleasure in a single second?"

"The Stranger," the first poem in Baudelaire's sequence, establishes the poet and artist as an outsider, almost an alien: a disillusioned city dweller, who feels his aloneness most acutely in a crowd, and who might, under different circumstances, pack a gun and set himself up as a hard-boiled gumshoe. "The Stranger" takes the form of a brief dialogue, and so we learn nothing about the man other than what he says in reply to a friendly if persistent interlocutor, perhaps in a railway car or café, a neutral place where strangers meet and feel obliged to converse. He reveals that he is indifferent to the claims of family, the pleasures of friendship, the duty demanded by God or country, the perquisites of money. What does he, the "enigmatic stranger," love? And here he bursts into a lyric exclamation: "The clouds passing by . . . over there . . . over there . . . the marvelous clouds!" Why are they marvelous? Presumably it's because they constantly change shape, are perpetually in motion, and are far from the sphere of human sorrow. Baudelaire gave an English title to another of his prose poems, "Anywhere Out of This World," which embodies the romantic wish to escape. It begins with a characteristic assertion: "Life is a hospital and all the patients keep wanting to change beds." Equally romantic, equally epigrammatic, is the conclusion of "The Confiteor of the Artist": "The study of Beauty is a duel in which the artist cries out in fright before being vanquished."

If Baudelaire set the prose poem in motion with his anecdotes, parables, short essays, and aphorisms, Arthur Rimbaud provides the great counterexample in *Illuminations* and *Une Saison en enfer* [*A Season in Hell*]. The precocious Rimbaud—"You're not too serious when you're seventeen years old," he wrote when he was fifteen—renounced poetry and headed to Africa for a more "serious" career in the munitions trade. But before he was twenty, he had created the "visionary" prose poem or, in Martha Kinney's phrase, "the prose poem as a lantern, an illuminated container, casting images and phrases needed but barely understood." The prose poems in *Illuminations* are like dream landscapes and journeys, visionary fragments, brilliant but discontinuous. They represent a considerable advance in abstraction and compression, and they are revolutionary, too, in recommending a breakdown in order, "a willful derangement of the senses," as a necessary regimen.

Rimbaud, the poet as youthfully debauched seer, will take a romantic theme and render it in idiosyncratic and abstract terms. Consider his prose poem "Guerre" ["War"] from *Illuminations*:

When I was a child, certain skies sharpened my vision: all their characters were reflected in my face. The Phenomena were aroused.—At present the eternal inflection of moments and the infinity of mathematics drive me through this world where I meet with every public honor, adored by children with their prodigious affections.—I dream of a War, of might and of right, of unanticipated logic.

It is as simple as a musical phrase.

17

At its heart, this is a reworking of a familiar Wordsworthian trajectory (There was a time "when like a roe I bounded o'er the mountains. . . . That time is past, and all its aching joys are now no more. . . . Other gifts have followed. . . . Therefore am I still a lover of the meadows and the woods"). The structure is the same in Rimbaud: a movement from childhood to the present, great loss and a new compensatory resolution. In Rimbaud, however, to get from one clause to the next requires a long leap. The clauses themselves are like free-floating fragments, and the conclusion has an air of revolutionary menace very far from the consolation Wordsworth found in nature.

In France, the prose poem quickly became a genre. Prose represented freedom from the alexandrine, the tyrannical twelve-syllable line that ruled over French poetry with an inflexibility that made English blank verse seem positively libertine in comparison. For Stéphane Mallarmé, the prose poem afforded a pretext to digress or pursue a detour; "La Pipe" ["The Pipe"] is a fine pre-Proustian exploration of the involuntary memory. Max Jacob, in *The Dice Cup* (1917), crafted fables that unfold with an absurd logic, with a comic edge sometimes and a non sequitur where we expected to find an epiphany. There is beauty in the inconclusive anecdote terminating in ellipses—as when we're told, in "The Beggar Woman of Naples," that the person thus described, to whom the narrator had tossed some coins every day, was "a wooden case painted green which contained some red earth and a few half-rotten bananas. . ." Henri Michaux made a cunning use of personae ("I like to beat people up") and ironic protagonists (the hapless Plume, who is arrested in a restaurant for eating an item not on the menu). Francis Ponge "took the side of objects" in poems that spurned the self-conscious ego and discovered themselves as studies of things. The achievement of these poets and others (Pierre Reverdy, René Char) made Paris the indisputable capital of the prose poem.

In the English-speaking world, the prose poem never quite graduated to the status of a genre. But then it didn't really have to. The opportunity to write prose poetry, by whatever name, had long existed. The King James Bible, as Shelley observes, was a triumph of prose as a vehicle for "astonishing" poetry. Coleridge singles out "the writings of Plato, and Bishop Taylor, and the *Theoria Sacra* of Burnet" as furnishing "undeniable proofs that poetry of the highest kind may exist without metre, and even without the contra-distinguishing objects of a poem." No list of English precursors of modern prose poetry would be complete without Shakespeare's prose (in *Hamlet*, for example, the "quintessence of dust" speech, and "the readiness is all"), John Donne's sermons, Thomas Traherne's *Centuries of Meditation*, James MacPherson's hoax translation of the Scottish bard Ossian, and the "Proverbs of Hell" and "memorable fancies" of Blake's "Marriage of Heaven and Hell": a list so diverse that it resists any effort at codification.

The American prose poem owes much to the French but veers off decisively to accommodate the sui generis work that transcends category. In 1959, the French scholar Suzanne Bernard could stipulate that there were four requirements that every prose poem had to fulfill. It had to embody the poet's intention, it had to have an organic unity, it had to be its own best excuse for being, and it had to be brief. In other words, a prose poem was a short poem that happened to be written in prose. There may be something in the Gallic temperament that gravitates toward systematic classification, but it seems anathema to poets who identify prose with the wish to escape from strictures and injunctions. Brevity is not a requirement for an American poet. I think immediately of wonderful prose poems that are too long to be represented in this book, such as W. H. Auden's "Caliban to the Audience" and John Ashbery's "The System." In 1848, Poe, whose influence on Baudelaire and Mallarmé was so great, wrote a 150–page treatise on the nature and origin of the universe, in which he intuitively grasped the Big Bang theory of cosmic creation. Poe called this lengthy work *Eureka* and subtitled it *A Prose Poem*, despite his own earlier declaration that a long poem is a "flat contradiction in terms."

Some prose poem enthusiasts approach the subject in a self-deprecatory manner. Simic depicts the poet in mad pursuit of a fly in a dark room: "The prose poem is a burst of language following a collision with a large piece of furniture." Russell Edson, a master of the comic surreal fable, likens the prose poem to the offspring of a giraffe and an elephant that may look grotesque but is hailed nonetheless as a "beautiful animal." Or perhaps the prose poem is "a cast-iron aeroplane that can actually fly, mainly because its pilot doesn't seem to care if it does or not." When Louis Jenkins compares the writing of a prose poem to throwing a crumpled piece of paper into a wastebasket ("a skill that, though it may improve hand-eye coordination, does not lead necessarily to an ability to play basketball"), it's as if failure were a premise of the enterprise. Perhaps it is, or perhaps the fellows are being impish as much as diffident. Jenkins would rather chuck paper into basket than listen to the teacher "drone on about the poetry of Tennyson." Edson jovially stresses the capaciousness of the genre. "You could call the pieces in *Tender Buttons* prose poems," he tells an interviewer who has asked about Gertrude Stein. "Heck, one can call most anything a prose poem. That's what's great about them, anything that's not something else is probably a prose poem." The interviewer persists. How about "the 70's when you, Bly, Tate, and others were writing prose poems"? And Edson, sensing the hunger for a myth, obligingly concocts one. There was a time when "prose poems were illegal" and he, Jim [Tate], and the Captain [Bly, after the stern Captain Bligh in *Mutiny on the Bounty*] began their clandestine activities. "After long evenings of talking prose poems we'd relax by trying to guess who was ghostwriting all the stuff that was appearing in all the poetry magazines. It looked like the work of a single hack."

In the 1970s, the prose poem afforded a means to depart or dissent from what that "single hack" was producing. The prose poem as surreal fable, in the manner of Edson or Maxine Chernoff, seemed a compelling option. "There is a shorter distance from the unconscious to the Prose Poem than from the unconscious to most poems in verse," Michael Benedikt said. There was never any danger of a new orthodoxy, but someone quipped that if you said *prose poem* in a word association game the next word to come to everyone's mind would be *surrealist* or *surreal*. Certainly the prose poem in the United States today is not as predictably unpredictable, in part because it has loosened its ties to the French tradition. There is a renewed sense that the homemade American prose poem is a thing that could not exist without the idea of America preceding it. This is not entirely a new story. In a 1957 prologue to his early *Kora in Hell: Improvisations*, William Carlos Williams took pains to distinguish the book from "the typically French prose poem," whose "pace was not my own"—despite the debt, evident in the title, to Rimbaud's *Season in Hell*. The question "what is American about the American prose poem" remains second to "what is American about American poetry" as a topic that can be debated and discussed endlessly without any prospect of a resolution. But surely Joe Wenderoth's *Letters to Wendy's*, which he composed on a fast food chain's customer comment cards, is but one recent instance of a rule-breaking prose poem that is saturated with American culture and the American vernacular.

Experimental writers have invested much energy in prose as a poetic medium while at the same time often repudiating or resisting the narrative impulse. In 1980 the Language poet Ron Silliman wrote a manifesto under the heading "the New Sentence." He argued that the sentence—the liberated sentence in prose that works like poetry—is not a unit of logic but an independent entity that relates to the sentences before and after it in multiple, complex, and ambiguous ways. As Marjorie Perloff remarks about works by Silliman (*Tjanting*), Lyn Hejinian (*My Life*), and Rosmarie Waldrop *(The Reproduction of Profiles)*, "In these prose compositions, a given sentence, far from following its predecessor or preparing the way for the sentence that follows, remains relatively autonomous, continuity being provided by word and sound repetition as well as by semantic transfer, in what the Russian Formalists called the 'orientation toward the neighboring word.'" If poems resemble paintings, the prose poem could as easily correspond to a Mondrian abstraction as to a Flemish street scene.

That this argument can be derived from a reading of Gertrude Stein is but one reason for considering her the mother of the American prose poem (as Poe, through his influence on Baudelaire, was an uncle of the French prose poem). The prose poems that constitute Stein's *Tender Buttons* initiate a tradition of experimentation. Stein had a revolutionary poetic intent, and *Tender Buttons* is a sustained effort at treating words as objects in their own right rather than as symbolic representations of things. To this day no one has better captured the abstract music of sentences and paragraphs. Nor has anyone departed so radically from the conventions of making sense while making such richly evocative poetry. Consider "A Dog" from *Tender Buttons*. Here it is in its entirety:

> A little monkey goes like a donkey that means to say that means to say that more sighs last goes. Leave with it. A little monkey goes like a donkey.

At first this seems a sort of riddle, as if the writer's task were to suggest a thing without naming it (except in the title). It has charm, its rhymes are spirited, but it has something else as well. There is drama in the sentences and between them, the stock phrase ("that means to say") repeated to lend urgency, then the four accented monosyllables in a row ("more sighs last goes"), and finally the appearance of a resolution ("Leave with it"), with closure achieved by recapitulation of the initial theme. In a sense this prose poem has, in Walter Pater's famous formulation, aspired to the condition of music. It has achieved abstractness. But what "A Dog" also shows us is the abstract structure of syntax that precedes content and helps create meaning, charging common words like "sighs" and "goes" with a power of signification we didn't know they had.

In verse, the tension between the line and the sentence can be fruitful. The canonical example is the opening of *Paradise Lost*, where Milton isolates the word *fruit* at the end of line one, and the word acquires triple or even quadruple meanings. In prose the poet gives up the meaning-making powers of the line break. The poet in prose must use the structure of the sentence itself, or the way one sentence modifies the next, to generate the surplus meaning that helps separate poetry in prose from ordinary writing. W. H. Auden, who habitually subdivided people into classes and types, favored antithesis as a syntactical principle in "Vespers" where he presents himself, a partisan of Eden, squaring off against an advocate of utopian socialism:

> In my Eden a person who dislikes Bellini has the good manners not to get born: In his New Jerusalem a person who dislikes work will be very sorry he was born.

The antithesis creates balance but also invites the reader to weigh the scales. The repetition of clauses allows for significant variation, so when we're told that the shirker in the New Jerusalem "will be very sorry he was born," the locution itself exemplifies the sort of "good manners" that make Auden's Eden a more attractive place.

John Ashbery seems to incorporate self-contradiction as an operating principle in his prose poem "A Nice Presentation." He enacts within the sentence a mazy motion:

> Most things don't matter but an old woman of my acquaintance is always predicting gloom and doom and her prophecies matter though they may never be fulfilled. That's one reason I don't worry too much but I like to tell her she is right but also wrong because what she says won't happen.

The sentences embody reversal and hesitation; they suggest a kind of logic but mostly they reveal that logic is an illusion. They enact a paradox: that one can be in perpetual motion while remaining stationary, as the mind of a perennial fence-sitter may race from one thought to the next.

Writing in prose you give up much, but you gain in relaxation, in the possibilities of humor and incongruity, in narrative compression, and in the feeling of escape or release from tradition or expectation. The prose poem can feel like a holiday from the rigors of verse, as is sometimes the case in Shakespeare's plays. In *Hamlet*, for example, prose can serve the purposes of the "antic disposition" the prince affects to make people think he is mad. In *Much Ado About Nothing*, on the other hand, prose stands for plain sense, verse for hyperbole, ornament; Benedick is an inept rhymester, but his love for Beatrice and hers for him has a chance to endure because it is founded not on the fantastical language of romantic courtship but on the sallies and scorn of prose wit. The prose poem can have this antipoetical, down-to-earth quality, can stand as a corrective to the excesses to which verse is susceptible.

Russell Edson is attracted to the idea of "a poetry freed from the definition of poetry, and a prose free of the necessities of fiction." Robert Bly associates prose with "the natural speech of a democratic language." For James Tate, the prose poem is an effective "means of seduction. For one thing, the deceptively simple packaging: the paragraph. People generally do not run for cover when they are confronted with a paragraph or two. The paragraph says to them: I won't take much of your time, and, if you don't mind my saying so, I am not known to be arcane, obtuse, precious, or high-falutin'. Come on in." Robert Hass explains that he was happy with one of his efforts because it "was exactly what the prose poem wasn't supposed to be. It was too much like the sound of expository prose." At the time of writing it seemed to Hass that he was exploring unknown territory. And in retrospect? "It seems a sort of long escape."

Any of the forms of prose can serve, from traditional rhetorical models to newfangled concoctions. Mark Jarman writes an "Epistle" and Joe Brainard writes "mini-essays" in the form of one-sentence poems. James Richardson specializes in what he calls "Vectors," which are aphorisms and "ten-second essays." Paul Violi's "Triptych" takes its form from *TV Guide* and Charles Bernstein taps the same source for the content of "Contradiction turns to rivalry." Tyrone Williams's "Cold Calls" consists of a sequence of footnotes to an absent text. There are prose poems in the form of journal entries (Harry Mathews's *20 Lines a Day*), radically foreshortened fictions

(Lydia Davis's "In the Garment District"), a fan letter (Amy Gerstler's "Dear Boy George"), a rant (Gabriel Gudding's "Defense of Poetry"), a linguistic stunt (Fran Carlen's "Anal Nap," in which only one vowel is used), an essay (Fanny Howe's "Doubt"), a political parable (Carolyn Forché's "The Colonel"), and other inventions, some of which can't be easily summarized. Mark Strand's "Chekhov: A Sestina" demonstrates that prose can accommodate the intricacies of that verse form, just as "Woods" in Emerson's journals can serve as a "prose sonnet." The appearance of such a poem as Tom Whalen's "Why I Hate Prose Poems" indicates that the prose poem has, for all the talk of its "subversive" nature, itself become a self-conscious genre inviting spoofery.

The prose poem has achieved an unprecedented level of popularity among American poets. The evidence is abundant to one who closely monitors literary magazines. There are excellent journals devoted exclusively to prose poems. Both *Key Satch(el)* and *Untitled* yielded work you will find in this anthology. So did a quartet of magazines that seem to have sectioned off parts of the territory. *Quarterly West* specializes in the prose poem as short fiction. *The Seneca Review* favors the prose poem as lyric essay. *Quarter After Eight* announces that its editorial mission is to "provide a space for work that fits neither genre: a space that demonstrates the tension between poetry and prose," while the Rhode Island–based magazine whose title is the diacritical sign for a paragraph considers the single block of text to be the prose poem's ideal shape or default structure. There are magazines whose whole existence is based on advocacy. Brian Clements has just started *Sentence: A Journal of Prose Poetics.* Founded in 1992 by Peter Johnson, *The Prose Poem: An International Journal* recently went under but not before proclaiming a prose poem renaissance and articulating a strong case for the form. Fascinating adventures in the prose poem have turned up in many other magazines as well. I found poems for this book—poems I wanted to spread the news about—in *The Hat* and *The Germ* and *Shiny*, in *New American Writing* and *Conjunctions* and *Another Chicago Magazine*, *American Poetry Review* and *Conduit* and *Verse*, *Hambone* and *Ploughshares* and *American Letters and Commentary*, and this is not an exhaustive list.

Seven of the poets who have served as guest editors of *The Best American Poetry*—Simic, Strand, Ashbery, Robert Bly, Robert Hass, John Hollander, and James Tate—have championed the prose poem or done some of their best work in that form (if it is a form) or genre (if that's what it is). As many prose poems as sonnets—more probably—have been chosen for *The Best American Poetry* since the inception of the annual anthology in 1988. And certainly signs of the prose poem's belated respectability abound. Several "international" anthologies were published in the 1990s, the first since Michael Benedikt's in 1976. One was the culminating issue of *The Prose Poem* (2000), the other Stuart Friebert and David Young's valuable *Models of the Universe* (1995). Recent academic studies, such as Steven Monte's *Invisible Fences* (2000) and Michel Delville's *The American Prose Poem* (1998), overlap surprisingly little, so fertile and various is the field. The issue of *TriQuarterly* that is current as I write, with Campbell McGrath as guest editor, includes a section called "Prose Poetics." I've just read provocative articles on the subject in *Rain Taxi* and the *Antioch Review*. Undoubtedly the conference on the prose poem, replete with "craft lectures," that was held in Walpole, New Hampshire, in August 2001, was the first of many to come. This is all a far cry from the situation in 1978 when *The Monument* was denied the Pulitzer, excellent prose poems were being written but it still seemed a secret, and the editor of this volume, then a thesis candidate at Columbia University, defended his dissertation on the prose poem in English, choosing Oscar Wilde, Gertrude Stein, W. H. Auden, and John Ashbery as four exemplars.

All anthologies are partial in one and sometimes two senses, though I'd rather sin on the side of ecumenicism than exclusivity. I wanted to present the prose poem in its American context, showing what Elizabeth Bishop did with the form, and how Delmore Schwartz handled it, and what poets ranging from James Wright and Robert Bly to Terence Winch and Andrei Codrescu were doing in the 1970s, and what young writers such as Sarah Manguso and Anselm Berrigan are up to today. Every anthology is also a personal statement. I had a few rules. Excerpts from long works had to be self-contained to warrant inclusion. Though dating poems is a notoriously approximate art, the gain in our historical understanding make it well worth doing, and I have followed each poem with the year of either composition or publication. I have ordered the contents chronologically by year of the poet's birth but arranged the contributor's notes alphabetically for the reader's ease. Poe, born after Emerson, precedes him in the subtitle for reasons that may seem self-evident. For the purposes of this anthology, both T. S. Eliot and W. H. Auden qualify as "American," and the same goes for such Canadian poets as Margaret Atwood and Anne

Carson. There are always more poems than you have room for, but the final criterion is the most important one: Do I love it? Is it something I can't bear to do without? You have no choice but to trust your instincts and, in Frank O'Hara's phrase, to "go on your nerve."

There is a moment in O'Hara's poem "Why I Am Not a Painter" when the poet—urbane, bohemian buddy of avant-garde painters that he is—exultantly says of his latest poetic effort: "It is even in / prose, I am a real poet." There is an ambiguity here that readers may not notice at first. If the excerpt were shortened to "even in prose, I am a real poet," it would mean "I am a real poet even when I write prose," and *prose* would be counted not a virtue but a defect. But of course we read the line to mean, "It is even in prose, [and therefore] I am a real poet"—the act of writing a prose poem certifies me as an authentic one hundred percent avant-garde American poet (though at this moment I happen to be writing in verse). While we shouldn't overlook the characteristically ironic spin O'Hara gave to his words, they retain their element of truth and their larger element of ambiguity, and their bravado is exactly what readers should have in mind as they prepare to encounter the American prose poem in all its glorious variety.

RALPH WALDO EMERSON (1803–1882)

∾

Woods, A Prose Sonnet

Wise are ye, O ancient woods! wiser than man. Whoso goeth in your paths or into your thickets where no paths are, readeth the same cheerful lesson whether he be a young child or a hundred years old. Comes he in good fortune or bad, ye say the same things, & from age to age. Ever the needles of the pine grow & fall, the acorns on the oak, the maples redden in autumn, & at all times of the year the ground pine & the pyrola bud & root under foot. What is called fortune & what is called Time by men—ye know them not. Men have not language to describe one moment of your eternal life. This I would ask of you, o sacred Woods, when ye shall next give me somewhat to say, give me also the tune wherein to say it. Give me a tune of your own like your winds or rains or brooks or birds; for the songs of men grow old when they have been often repeated, but yours, though a man have heard them for seventy years, are never the same, but always new, like time itself, or like love.

(1839)

EDGAR ALLAN POE (1809–1849)

~

Shadow—A Parable

Yea, though I walk through the valley of the Shadow.
—Psalm of David.

Ye who read are still among the living; but I who write shall have long since gone my way into the region of shadows. For indeed strange things shall happen, and secret things be known, and many centuries shall pass away, ere these memorials be seen of men. And, when seen, there will be some to disbelieve, and some to doubt, and yet a few who will find much to ponder upon in the characters here graven with a stylus of iron.

The year had been a year of terror, and of feelings more intense than terror for which there is no name upon the earth. For many prodigies and signs had taken place, and far and wide, over sea and land, the black wings of the Pestilence were spread abroad. To those, nevertheless, cunning in the stars, it was not unknown that the heavens wore an aspect of ill; and to me, the Greek Oinos, among others, it was evident that now had arrived the alternation of that seven hundred and ninety-fourth year when, at the entrance of Aries, the planet Jupiter is conjoined with the red ring of the terrible Saturnus. The peculiar spirit of the skies, if I mistake not greatly, made itself manifest, not only in the physical orb of the earth, but in the souls, imaginations, and meditations of mankind.

Over some flasks of the red Chian wine, within the walls of a noble hall, in a dim city called Ptolemais, we sat, at night, a company of seven. And to our chamber there was no entrance save by a lofty door of brass: and the door was fashioned by the artisan Corinnos, and, being of rare workmanship, was fastened from within. Black draperies, likewise, in the gloomy room, shut out from our view the moon, the lurid stars, and the peopleless streets—but the boding and the memory of Evil they would not be so excluded. There were things around us and about of which I can render no distinct account—things material and spiritual—heaviness in the atmosphere—a sense of suffocation—anxiety—and, above all, that terrible state of existence which the nervous experience when the senses are keenly living and awake, and meanwhile the powers of thought lie dormant. A dead weight hung upon us. It hung upon our limbs—upon the household furniture—upon the goblets from which we drank; and all things were depressed, and borne down thereby—all things save only the flames of the seven lamps which illumined our revel. Uprearing themselves in tall slender lines of light, they thus remained burning all pallid and motionless; and in the mirror which their lustre formed upon the round table of ebony at which we sat, each of us there assembled beheld the pallor of his own countenance, and the unquiet glare in the downcast eyes of his companions. Yet we laughed and were merry in our proper way—which was hysterical; and sang the songs of Anacreon—which are madness; and drank deeply—although the purple wine reminded us of blood. For there was yet another tenant of our chamber in the person of young Zoilus. Dead, and at full length he lay, enshrouded; the genius and the demon of the scene. Alas! he bore no portion in our mirth, save that his countenance, distorted with the plague, and his eyes, in which Death had but half extinguished the fire of the pestilence, seemed to take such interest in our merriment as the dead may haply take in the merriment of those who are to die. But although I, Oinos, felt that the eyes of the departed were upon me, still I forced myself not to perceive the bitterness of their expression, and gazing down steadily into the depths of the ebony mirror, sang with a loud and sonorous voice the songs of the son of Teios. But gradually my songs they ceased, and their echoes, rolling afar off among the sable draperies of the chamber, became weak, and undistinguishable, and so faded away. And lo! from among those sable draperies where the sounds of the song departed, there came forth a dark and undefined shadow—a shadow such as the moon, when low in heaven, might fashion from the figure of a man: but it was the shadow neither of man nor of God, nor of any familiar thing. And quivering awhile among the draperies of the room, it at length rested in full view upon the surface of the door of brass. But the shadow was vague, and formless, and indefinite, and was the shadow neither of man nor of God—neither God of Greece, nor God of Chaldaea, nor any Egyptian God. And the shadow rested upon the brazen doorway, and under the arch of the entablature of the door, and moved not, nor spoke any word, but there became stationary and remained. And the door whereupon the shadow rested was, if I remember aright, over against the feet of the young Zoilus enshrouded. But we, the seven there assembled, having seen the shadow as it came out from among the draperies, dared not steadily behold it, but cast down our eyes, and gazed continually into the depths of the mirror of ebony. And at length I, Oinos, speaking some low words, demanded of the shadow its dwelling and its appellation. And the shadow answered, "I am SHADOW, and my dwelling is near to the Catacombs of Ptolemais, and hard by those dim plains of Helusion which border upon the foul Charonian canal." And then did we, the seven, start from our seats in horror, and stand trembling, and shuddering, and aghast, for the tones in the voice of the shadow were not the tones of any one being, but of a multitude of beings, and, varying in their cadences from syllable to syllable fell duskly upon our ears in the well-remembered and familiar accents of many thousand departed friends.

(1835)

EMMA LAZARUS (1849–1887)

∽

The Exodus (August 3, 1492)

1. The Spanish noon is a blaze of azure fire, and the dusty pilgrims crawl like an endless serpent along treeless plains and bleached high-roads, through rock-split ravines and castellated, cathedral-shadowed towns.

2. The hoary patriarch, wrinkled as an almond shell, bows painfully upon his staff. The beautiful young mother, ivory-pale, well-nigh swoons beneath her burden; in her large enfolding arms nestles her sleeping babe, round her knees flock her little ones with bruised and bleeding feet. "Mother, shall we soon be there?"

3. The youth with Christ-like countenance speaks comfortably to father and brother, to maiden and wife. In his breast, his own heart is broken.

4. The halt, the blind, are amid the train. Sturdy pack-horses laboriously drag the tented wagons wherein lie the sick athirst with fever.

5. The panting mules are urged forward with spur and goad; stuffed are the heavy saddlebags with the wreckage of ruined homes.

6. Hark to the tinkling silver bells that adorn the tenderly-carried silken scrolls.

7. In the fierce noon-glare a lad bears a kindled lamp; behind its network of bronze the airs of heaven breathe not upon its faint purple star.

8. Noble and abject, learned and simple, illustrious and obscure, plod side by side, all brothers now, all merged in one routed army of misfortune.

9. Woe to the straggler who falls by the wayside! no friend shall close his eyes.

10. They leave behind, the grape, the olive, and the fig; the vines they planted, the corn they sowed, the garden-cities of Andalusia, and Aragon, Estremadura and La Mancha, of Granada and Castile; the altar, the hearth, and the grave of their fathers.

11. The townsman spits at their garments, the shepherd quits his flock, the peasant his plow, to pelt with curses and stones; the villager sets on their trail his yelping cur.

12. Oh the weary march, oh the uptorn roots of home, oh the blankness of the receding goal!

13. Listen to their lamentation: *They that ate dainty food are desolate in the streets; they that were reared in scarlet embrace dunghills. They flee away and wander about. Men say among the nations, they shall no more sojourn there; our end is near, our days are full, our doom is come.*

14. Wither shall they turn? for the West hath cast them out, and the East refuseth to receive.

15. O bird of the air, whisper to the despairing exiles, that to-day, to-day, from the many-masted, gayly-bannered port of Palos, sails the world-unveiling Genoese, to unlock the golden gates of sunset and bequeath a Continent to Freedom!

(1887)

❧

Red Slippers

Red slippers in a shop-window; and outside in the street, flaws of gray, windy sleet!

Behind the polished glass the slippers hang in long threads of red, festooning from the ceiling like stalactites of blood, flooding the eyes of passers-by with dripping color, jamming their crimson reflections against the windows of cabs and tram-cars, screaming their claret and salmon into the teeth of the sleet, plopping their little round maroon lights upon the tops of umbrellas.

The row of white, sparkling shop-fronts is gashed and bleeding, it bleeds red slippers. They spout under the electric light, fluid and fluctuating, a hot rain—and freeze again to red slippers, myriadly multiplied in the mirror side of the window.

They balance upon arched insteps like springing bridges of crimson lacquer; they swing up over curved heels like whirling tanagers sucked in a wind-pocket; they flatten out, heelless, like July ponds, flared and burnished by red rockets.

Snap, snap, they are cracker sparks of scarlet in the white, monotonous block of shops.

They plunge the clangor of billions of vermilion trumpets into the crowd outside, and echo in faint rose over the pavement.

People hurry by, for these are only shoes, and in a window farther down is a big lotus bud of cardboard, whose petals open every few minutes and reveal a wax doll, with staring bead eyes and flaxen hair, lolling awkwardly in its flower chair.

One has often seen shoes, but whoever saw a cardboard lotus bud before?

The flaws of gray, windy sleet beat on the shop-window where there are only red slippers.

(1916)

GERTRUDE STEIN (1874–1946)

~

22 Objects from *Tender Buttons*

A CARAFE, THAT IS A BLIND GLASS

A kind in glass and a cousin, a spectacle and nothing strange a single hurt color and an arrangement in a system to pointing. All this and not ordinary, not unordered in not resembling. The difference is spreading.

A BOX

Out of kindness comes redness and out of rudeness comes rapid same question, out of an eye comes research, out of selection comes painful cattle. So then the order is that a white way of being round is something suggesting a pin and is it disappointing, it is not, it is so rudimentary to be analysed and see a fine substance strangely, it is so earnest to have a green point not to red but to point again.

DIRT AND NOT COPPER

Dirt and not copper makes a color darker. It makes the shape so heavy and makes no melody harder.

It makes mercy and relaxation and even a strength to spread a table fuller. There are more places not empty. They see cover.

NOTHING ELEGANT

A charm a single charm is doubtful. If the red is rose and there is a gate surrounding it, if inside is let in and there places change then certainly something is upright. It is earnest.

A cause and no curve, a cause and loud enough, a cause and extra a loud clash and an extra wagon, a sign of extra, a sac a small sac and an established color and cunning, a slender grey and no ribbon, this means a loss a great loss a restitution.

A METHOD OF A CLOAK

A single climb to a line, a straight exchange to a cane, a desperate adventure and courage and a clock, all this which is a system, which has feeling, which has resignation and success, all makes an attractive black silver.

A RED STAMP

If lilies are lily white if they exhaust noise and distance and even dust, if they dusty will dirt a surface that has no extreme grace, if they do this and it is not necessary it is not at all necessary if they do this they need a catalogue.

A LONG DRESS

What is the current that makes machinery, that makes it crackle, what is the current that presents a long line and a necessary waist. What is this current.

What is the wind, what is it.

Where is the serene length, it is there and a dark place is not a dark place, only a white and red are black, only a yellow and green are blue, a pink is scarlet, a bow is every color. A line distinguishes it. A line just distinguishes it.

A RED HAT

A dark grey, a very dark grey, a quite dark grey is monstrous ordinarily, it is so monstrous because there is no red in it. If red is in everything it is not necessary. Is that not an argument for any use of it and even so is there any place that is better, is there any place that has so much stretched out.

A BLUE COAT

A blue coat is guided guided away, guided and guided away, that is the particular color that is used for that length and not any width not even more than a shadow.

A FRIGHTFUL RELEASE

A bag which was left and not only taken but turned away was not found. The place was shown to be very like the last time. A piece was not exchanged, not a bit of it, a piece was left over. The rest was mismanaged.

A PURSE

A purse was not green, it was not straw color, it was hardly seen and it had a use a long use and the chain, the chain was never missing, it was not misplaced, it showed that it was open, that is all that it showed.

A MOUNTED UMBRELLA

What was the use of not leaving it there where it would hang what was the use if there was no chance of ever seeing it come there and show that it was handsome and right in the way it showed it. The lesson is to learn that it does show it, that it shows it and that nothing, that there is nothing, that there is no more to do about it and just so much more is there plenty of reason for making an exchange.

A LITTLE CALLED PAULINE

A little called anything shows shudders.

Come and say what prints all day. A whole few watermelon. There is no pope.

No cut in pennies and little dressing and choose wide soles and little spats really little spices.

A little lace makes boils. This is not true.

Gracious of gracious and a stamp a blue green white bow a blue green lean, lean on the top.

If it is absurd then it is leadish and nearly set in where there is a tight head.

A DOG

A little monkey goes like a donkey that means to say that means to say that more sighs last goes. Leave with it. A little monkey goes like a donkey.

A WHITE HUNTER

A white hunter is nearly crazy.

A LEAVE

In the middle of a tiny spot and nearly bare there is a nice thing to say that wrist is leading. Wrist is leading.

SUPPOSE AN EYES

Suppose it is within a gate which open is open at the hour of closing summer that is to say it is so.

All the seats are needing blackening. A white dress is in sign. A soldier a real soldier has a worn lace a worn lace of different sizes that is to say if he can read, if he can read he is a size to show shutting up twenty-four.

Go red go red, laugh white.

Suppose a collapse in rubbed purr, in rubbed purr get.

Little sales ladies little sales ladies little saddles of mutton.

Little sales of leather and such beautiful beautiful, beautiful beautiful.

BOOK

Book was there, it was there. Book was there. Stop it, stop it, it was a cleaner, a wet cleaner and it was not where it was wet, it was not high, it was directly placed back, not back again, back it was returned, it was needless, it put a bank, a bank when, a bank care.

Suppose a man a realistic expression of resolute reliability suggests pleasing itself white all white and no head does that mean soap. It does not so. It means kind wavers and little chance to beside beside rest. A plain.

Suppose ear rings that is one way to breed, breed that. Oh chance to say, oh nice old pole. Next best and nearest a pillar. Chest not valuable, be papered.

Cover up cover up the two with a little piece of string and hope rose and green, green.

Please a plate, put a match to the seam and really then really then, really then it is a remark that joins many many lead games. It is a sister and sister and a flower and a flower and a dog and a colored sky a sky colored grey and nearly that nearly that let.

PEELED PENCIL, CHOKE

Rub her coke.

IT WAS BLACK, BLACK TOOK

Black ink best wheel bale brown.

Excellent not a hull house, not a pea soup, no bill no care, no precise no past pearl pearl goat.

THIS IS THIS DRESS, AIDER

Aider, why aider why whow, whow stop touch, aider whow, aider stop the muncher, muncher munchers.

A jack in kill her, a jack in, makes a meadowed king, makes a to let.

(1914)

WILLIAM CARLOS WILLIAMS (1883–1963)

❧

Three Improvisations
from *Kora in Hell*

VIII

1

Some fifteen years we'll say I served this friend, was his valet, nurse, physician, fool and master: nothing too menial, to say the least. Enough of that: so.

Stand aside while they pass. This is what they found in the rock when it was cracked open: this fingernail. Hide your face among the lower leaves, here's a meeting should have led to better things but — it is only one branch out of the forest and night pressing you for an answer! Velvet night weighing upon your eye-balls with gentle insistence; calling you away: Come with me, now, tonight! Come with me! now tonight . . .

———————

In great dudgeon over the small profit that has come to him through a certain companionship a poet addresses himself and the loved one as if it were two strangers, thus advancing himself to the brink of that discovery which will reward all his labors but which he as yet only discerns as a night, a dark void coaxing him whither he has no knowledge.

2

You speak of the enormity of her disease, of her poverty. Bah, these are the fiddle she makes tunes on and its tunes bring the world dancing to your house-door, even on this swamp side. You speak of the helpless waiting, waiting till the thing squeeze her windpipe shut. Oh, that's best of all, that's romance — with the devil himself a hero. No my boy. You speak of her man's callous stinginess. Yes, my God, how can he refuse to buy milk when it's alone milk that she can swallow now? But how is it she picks market beans for him day in, day out, in the sun, in the frost? You understand? You speak of so many things, you blame me for my indifference. Well, this is you see my sister and death, great death is robbing her of life. It dwarfs most things.

Filth and vermin though they shock the over-nice are imperfections of the flesh closely related in the just imagination of the poet to excessive cleanliness. After some years of varied experience with the bodies of the rich and the poor a man finds little to distinguish between them, bulks them as one and bases his working judgements on other matters.

3

Hercules is in Hacketstown doing farm labor. Look at his hands if you'll not believe me. And what do I care if yellow and red are Spain's riches and Spain's good blood. Here yellow and red mean simply autumn! The odor of the poor farmer's fried supper is mixing with the smell of the hemlocks, mist is in the valley hugging the ground and over Parsippany—where an oldish man leans talking to a young woman—the moon is swinging from its star.

XI

1

Why pretend to remember the weather two years back? Why not? Listen close then repeat after others what they have just said and win a reputation for vivacity. Oh feed upon petals of edelweiss! one dew drop, if it be from the right flower, is five years' drink!

Having once taken the plunge the situation that preceded it becomes obsolete which a moment before was alive with malignant rigidities.

2

When beldams dig clams their fat hams (it's always beldams) balanced near Tellus' hide, this rhinoceros pelt, these lumped stones — buffoonery of midges on a bull's thigh — invoke, — what you will: birth's glut, awe at God's craft, youth's poverty, evolution of a child's caper, man's poor inconsequence. Eclipse of all things; sun's self turned hen's rump.

3

Cross a knife and fork and listen to the church bells! It is the harvest moon's made wine of our blood. Up over the dark factory into the blue glare start the young poplars. They whisper: It is Sunday! It is Sunday! But the laws of the county have been stripped bare of leaves. Out over the marshes flickers our laughter. A lewd anecdote's the chase. On through the vapory heather! And there at banter's edge the city looks at us sidelong with great eyes, — lifts to its lips heavenly milk! Lucina, O Lucina! beneficent cow, how have we offended thee?

Hilariously happy because of some obscure wine of the fancy which they have drunk four rollicking companions take delight in the thought that they have thus evaded the stringent laws of the county. Seeing the distant city bathed in moonlight and staring seriously at them they liken the moon to a cow and its light to milk.

XXVI

1

Doors have a back side also. And grass blades are double-edged. It's no use trying to deceive me, leaves fall more by the buds that push them off than by lack of greenness. Or throw two shoes on the floor and see how they'll lie if you think it's all one way.

41

There is no truth—sh!—but the honest truth and that is that touch-me-nots mean nothing, that daisies at a distance seem mushrooms and that—your Japanese silk today was not the sky's blue but your pajamas now as you lean over the crib's edge are and day's in! Grassgreen the mosquito net caught over your head's butt for foliage. What else? except odors—an old hallway. Moresco. Salvago.—and a game of socker. I was too nervous and young to win—that day.

All that seem solid: melancholias, *idees fixes,* eight years at the academy, Mr. Locke, this year and the next and the next—one like another—whee!—they are April zephyrs, were one a Botticelli, between their chinks, pink anemones.

―――――――――

Often it happens that in a community of no great distinction some fellow of superficial learning but great stupidity will seem to be rooted in the earth of the place the most solid figure imaginable impossible to remove him.

(1920)

H. D. (1886–1961)

∾

Strophe

. . . I love you would have no application for the moment. I love you waits with cold wings furled, stands a cold angel shut up like cherry-buds; cherry-buds not yet half in blossom. The cold rain and the mist and the scent of wet grass is in the unpronounceable words, I love you.

. . . I love you would have no possible application. It would tear down the walls of the city and abstract right and grace from the frozen image that might have right and grace painted upon its collar bones. The Image has no right decoration for the moment, is swathed in foreign and barbaric garments, is smothered out in the odd garments of its strange and outlandish disproportion.

. . . the Nordic image that stands and is cold and has that high mark of queen-grace upon its Nordic forehead is dying . . . is dying . . . it is dying, its buds are infolded. If once the light of the sheer beauty of the Initiate could strike its features, it would glow like rare Syrian gold; the workmanship of the East would have to be astonishingly summoned to invent new pattern of palm branch, new decoration of pine-bud and the cone of the Nordic pine that the Eastern workman would so appropriately display twined with the Idaian myrtle. The Idaian myrtle would be shot with the enamel of the myrtle-blue that alone among workmen, the Idaian workmen fashioned in glass and in porphyry, stained to fit separate occasion and the right and perfect slicing of the rose-quartz from the Egyptian quarry.

. . . the Nordic Image is my Image and alone of all Images I would make it suitable so that the South should not laugh, so that the West should be stricken, so that the East should fall down, bearing its scented baskets of spice-pink and little roses.

Antistrophe

. . . flowers fall, unreasonable, out of space and counter point of time beaten by the metronome of year and year, century on century. The metronome is wound up, will go on, go on beating for our life span; a metronome tick of year, year, year; life for life; heart beat on heart beat, beats the metronome holding us to the music that is the solid rhythm of the scale of the one, two, three, four; one, two, three, four, I am here, you are there; tell me I am here and I will tell you, you are there; but the metronome ticks a metronome music and the voice flinging its challenge to all music in the teeth of Reason stays for no tick, tick; the heart that springs to the feet of Love with all unreason, stays no moment to listen to the human tick and tick of the human metronome heart-beat.

. . . heart you are beating, heart you are beating, I am afraid to measure my heart beat by your heart beat for I am afraid with the shame of a child struck across fingers by the master that says play soft, play loud, play one-two-three-four again, again. I am struck across the fingers and across the mouth. My mouth aches with the unutterable insult of one-two-three-four.

. . . O, friend or enemy. Why can't I cry out, fall at your feet or you at my feet, one or the other overcome by the beauty of the metronome whose beauty is unassailable, or overwhelmed, overcome by the fragrance, dripped, ripped, sputtered, spread or split!

Epode

... voiceless, without a voice, seeking areas of consciousness without you. Seeking with you areas of consciousness that without you would no more be plausible. Set up choros against acted drama, the high boot, the gilt wreath of ivy for some dramatic deity; set him forth, crown him with pasteboard pomegranates ... pasteboard pomegranates have nothing to do with this reality. Out of the air, into the air, the colour flames and there is pulse of thyme, fire-blue that leads me across a slab of white-hot marble. My feet burn there and the wet garment clings so that I am a nymph risen from white water. So you overseeing, burn into my flesh until my bones are burnt through and attacking the marrow of my singular bone-structure, you light the flame that makes me cry toward Delphi. Were pasteboard pomegranates of any worth or plums stitched on to a paper crown? Listen ... men recounted your valour, shut you up in strophes, collected you in pages whose singular letters are still laced across your spirit. The Greek letters are an arabesque shutting you in, away, away; you are shut in from the eyes that read Greek letters. Take away the gold and manifest chryselephantine of your manifest decoration and you are left ... seeping into wine-vats, creeping under closed doors, lying beside me ...

(1921)

T. S. ELIOT (1888–1965)

෴

Hysteria

As she laughed I was aware of becoming involved in her laughter and being part of it, until her teeth were only accidental stars with a talent for squad-drill. I was drawn in by short gasps, inhaled at each momentary recovery, lost finally in the dark caverns of her throat, bruised by the ripple of unseen muscles. An elderly waiter with trembling hands was hurriedly spreading a pink and white checked cloth over the rusty green iron table, saying: 'If the lady and gentleman wish to take their tea in the garden, if the lady and gentleman wish to take their tea in the garden . . .' I decided that if the shaking of her breasts could be stopped, some of the fragments of the afternoon might be collected, and I concentrated my attention with careful subtlety to this end.

(1917)

e. e. cummings (1894–1962)

∽

i was sitting in mcsorley's.   outside it was New York and beautifully snowing.

Inside snug and evil.   the slobbering walls filthily push witless creases of screaming warmth chuck pillows are noise funnily swallows swallowing revolvingly pompous a the swallowed mottle with smooth or a but of rapidly goes gobs the and of flecks of and a chatter sobbings intersect with which distinct disks of graceful oath, upsoarings the break on   ceiling-flatness

the Bar.tinking luscious jigs dint of ripe silver with warmlyish wetflat splurging smells waltz the glush of squirting taps plus slush of foam knocked off and a faint piddle-of-drops she says I ploc spittle what the lands thaz me kid in no sir hopping sawdust you kiddo he's a palping wreaths of badly Yep cigars who jim him why gluey grins topple together eyes pout gestures stickily point made glints squinting who's a wink bum-nothing and money fuzzily mouths take big wobbly foot-steps every goggle cent of it get out ears dribbles soft right old feller belch the chap hic summore eh chuckles skulch. . . .

and i was sitting in the din thinking drinking the ale, which never lets you grow old blinking at the low ceiling my being pleasantly was punctuated by the always retchings of a worthless lamp.

when With a minute terrif   iceffort one dirty squeal of soiling light yanKing from bushy obscurity a bald greenish foetal head established It suddenly upon the huge neck around whose unwashed sonorous muscle the filth of a collar hung gently.

(spattered) by this instant of semiluminous nausea A vast wordless nondescript genie of trunk trickled firmly in to one exactly-mutilated ghost of a chair,

a;domeshaped interval of complete plasticity, shoulders, sprouted
the extraordinary arms through an angle of ridiculous velocity com-
menting upon an unclean table, and, whose distended immense Both
paws slowly loved a dinted mug

gone Darkness   it was so near to me, i ask of shadow won't you
have a drink?

(the eternal perpetual question)

Inside snugandevil.   i was sitting in mcsorley's   It, did not
answer.

outside. (it was New York and beautifully, snowing. . . .

(1922)

JEAN TOOMER (1894–1967)

~

Calling Jesus

Her soul is like a little thrust-tailed dog that follows her, whimpering. She is large enough, I know, to find a warm spot for it. But each night when she comes home and closes the big outside storm door, the little dog is left in the vestibule, filled with chills till morning. Someone . . . eoho Jesus . . . soft as a cotton boll brushed against the milk-pod cheek of Christ, will steal in and cover it that it need not shiver, and carry it to her where she sleeps upon clean hay cut in her dreams.

When you meet her in the daytime on the streets, the little dog keeps coming. Nothing happens at first, and then, when she has forgotten the streets and alleys, and the large house where she goes to bed of nights, a soft thing like fur begins to rub your limbs, and you hear a low, scared voice, lonely, calling, and you know that a cool something nozzles moisture in your palms. Sensitive things like nostrils, quiver. Her breath comes sweet as honeysuckle whose pistils bear the life of coming song. And her eyes carry to where builders find no need for vestibules, for swinging on iron hinges, storm doors.

Her soul is like a little thrust-tailed dog, that follows her, whimpering. I've seen it tagging on behind her, up streets where chestnut trees flowered, where dusty asphalt had been freshly sprinkled with clean water. Up alleys where niggers sat on low door-steps before tumbled shanties and sang and loved. At night, when she comes home, the little dog is left in the vestibule, nosing the crack beneath the big storm door, filled with chills till morning. Someone . . . eoho Jesus . . . soft as the bare feet of Christ moving across bales of southern cotton, will steal in and cover it that it need not shiver, and carry it to her where she sleeps: cradled in dream-fluted cane.

(1922)

49

THORNTON WILDER (1897–1975)

◡

Sentences

1

In the Italian quarter of London I found a group of clerks, waiters and idealistic barbers calling itself The Rosicrucian Mysteries, Soho Chapter, that met to read papers on the fabrication of gold and its metaphysical implications, to elect from its number certain Arch-adepts and *magistri hieraticorum,* to correspond with the last of the magi, Orzinda-mazda, on Mt. Sinai, and to retell, wide-eyed, their stories of how some workmen near Rome, breaking by chance into the tomb of Cicero's daughter, Tulliola, discovered an everburning lamp suspended in mid-air, its wick feeding on Perpetual Principle; of how Cleopatra's son Caesarion was preserved in a translucent liquid, "oil of gold," and could be still seen in an underground shrine at Vienna; and of how Virgil never died, but was alive still on the Island of Patmos, eating the leaves of a peculiar tree.

2

In Rome I encountered a number of people who for one reason or another were unable to sleep between midnight and dawn, and when I tossed sleepless, or when I returned late to my rooms through the deserted streets—at the hour when the parricide feels a cat purring about his feet in the darkness—I pictured to myself old Baldassare in the Borgo, former Bishop of Shantung and Apostolic Visitor to the Far East, rising at two to study with streaming eyes the Fathers and the Councils, marvelling, he said, at the continuous blooming of the rose-tree of Doctrine; or of Stasia, a Russian refugee who had lost the habit of sleeping after dark during her experience as nurse in the War, Stasia playing solitaire through the night and brooding over the jocose tortures to which her family had been subjected by the soldiers of Taganrog; and of Elizabeth Grier who, like some German prince of the Eighteenth Century, owned her own band of musicians, listening the length over her long shadowed room to some new work that D'Indy had sent her, or bending over the score while her little troupe revived the overture to *Les Indes Galantes*.

(1922)

HART CRANE (1899–1932)

∽

Havana Rose

Let us strip the desk for action—now we have a horse in Mexico.
. . . That night in Vera Cruz—verily for me "the True Cross"—let us
remember the Doctor and my thoughts, my humble, fond remem-
brances of the great bacteriologist. . . . The wind that night, the clam-
our of incessant shutters, trundle doors, and the cherub
watchman—tiptoeing the successive patio balconies with a typical pis-
tol—trying to muffle doors—and the pharos shine—the mid-wind
midnight stroke of it, its milk-light regularity above my bath partition
through the lofty, dusty glass—*Cortez—Cortez*—his crumbled palace
in the square—the typhus in a trap, the Doctor's rat trap. Where?
Somewhere in Vera Cruz—to bring—to take—to mix—to ransom—
to deduct—*to cure*. . . . The rats played ring around the rosy (in their
basement basinette)—the Doctor *supposedly* slept, supposedly in
#35—thus in my wakeful watches at least—the lighthouse flashed
. . . whirled . . . delayed, and struck—*again, again.* Only the Mayans
surely slept—whose references to typhus and whose records spurred
the Doctor into something nigh those metaphysics that are typhoid
plus and had engaged him once before to death's beyond and back
again—antagonistic wills—into immunity. Tact, horsemanship,
courage were germicides to him. . . . Poets may not be doctors, but
doctors are rare poets when roses leap like rats—and too, when rats
make rose nozzles of pink death around white teeth. . . .

And during the wait over dinner at La Diana the Doctor had
said—who was American, also—"You cannot heed the negative—so
might go on to undeserved doom . . . must therefore loose yourself
within a pattern's mastery that you can conceive, that you can yield
to—by which also you win and gain mastery and happiness which is
your own from birth.["]

(1933)

ERNEST HEMINGWAY (1899–1961)

Montparnasse

There are never any suicides in the quarter among people one
    knows
No successful suicides.
A Chinese boy kills himself and is dead.
(They continue to place his mail in the letter rack at the Dome)
A Norwegian boy kills himself and is dead.
(No one knows where the other Norwegian boy has gone)
They find a model dead
Alone in bed and very dead.
(It made almost unbearable trouble for the concierge)
Sweet oil, the white of eggs, mustard and water soapsuds and
    stomach pumps rescue the people one knows.
Every afternoon the people one knows can be found at the cafe.

(Paris, 1923)

❧

News

A crowd of twenty-three thousand coy mistresses is expected to turn out this morning for the forty-four day ruby-finding meet by the Indian Ganges' side. Eighth race on the card is scheduled for quaint honor to succumb to the tide at 4.35 P.M. and will be telecast. Thus while her willing soul transpires, she who wins shall take her due except she come up with the same bruised thigh that put her out of action last week.

*

"This measure," the Attorney-General stated, "This legislation—which I endorse—requires some thirty thousand skylarks to register for the first time with my office." And he left the room.

*

"Cuckoo cuckoo cuckoo," president of the Young Cuckoo's Christian Association board said today during the appointment of a married man as general chairman of the YCCA's local $800,000 building and expansion campaign. "When daisies pied and violets blue," the president continued, "Cuckoo cuckoo cuckoo cuckoo." The president's speech will be repeated again tonight in a nationwide broadcast.

*

Miss Diana Palmer went roaring through a ceremony tonight of white lace whips waving wild and hurtling with winds of eighty miles an hour or more over the top of the Wedding March straight to the bottom of Christ Church (Baptist) with Mr. Theodore Van Huston. This was her maiden voyage.

*

A young man in scanty contemplation clad was picked up yesternight while suffering a dialect change at the junction of Eighth and Grant Streets. He is said to be the first of the season.

(1961)

❧

Aaron

Aaron had a passion for the lost chord. He looked for it under the newspapers at the Battery, saying to himself, "So many things have been lost." He was very logical and preferred to look when nobody was watching, as anyone would have, let us add. He was no crank, though he was funny somehow in his bedroom. He was so funny that everybody liked him, and hearing this those who had been revolted by him changed their minds. They were right to be pleasant, and if it hadn't been for something making them that way, they wouldn't have been involved in the first place. Being involved of course was what hurt. "It's a tight squeeze," Aaron was saying in his bedroom, and let us suppose he was quite right. He closed his eyes and shivered, enjoying what he did. And he went on doing it, until it was time for something else, saying, "I like it." And he did. He liked a good tune too, if it lasted. He once remarked to somebody, "Tunes are like birds." He wanted to say it again, but he couldn't remember, so the conversation became general, and he didn't mind. What was Aaron's relationship to actuality? I think it was a very good relationship.

(1948)

W. H. AUDEN (1907–1973)

~

Vespers

If the hill overlooking our city has always been known as Adam's Grave, only at dusk can you see the recumbent giant, his head turned to the west, his right arm resting for ever on Eve's haunch,

can you learn, from the way he looks up at the scandalous pair, what a citizen really thinks of his citizenship,

just as now you can hear in a drunkard's caterwaul his rebel sorrows crying for a parental discipline, in lustful eyes perceive a disconsolate soul,

scanning with desperation all passing limbs for some vestige of her faceless angel who in that long ago when wishing was a help mounted her once and vanished:

For Sun and Moon supply their conforming masks, but in this hour of civil twilight all must wear their own faces.

And it is now that our two paths cross.

Both simultaneously recognize his Anti-type: that I am an Arcadian, that he is a Utopian.

He notes, with contempt, my Aquarian belly: I note, with alarm, his Scorpion's mouth.

He would like to see me cleaning latrines: I would like to see him removed to some other planet.

Neither speaks. What experience could we possibly share?

Glancing at a lampshade in a store window, I observe it is too hideous for anyone in their senses to buy: He observes it is too expensive for a peasant to buy.

Passing a slum child with rickets, I look the other way: He looks the other way if he passes a chubby one.

I hope our senators will behave like saints, provided they don't reform me: He hopes they will behave like *baritoni cattivi*, and, when lights burn late in the Citadel,

I (who have never seen the inside of a police station) am shocked and think: "Were the city as free as they say, after sundown all her bureaus would be huge black stones.":

He (who has been beaten up several times) is not shocked at all but thinks: "One fine night our boys will be working up there."

You can see, then, why, between my Eden and his New Jerusalem, no treaty is negotiable.

In my Eden a person who dislikes Bellini has the good manners not to get born: In his New Jerusalem a person who dislikes work will be very sorry he was born.

In my Eden we have a few beam-engines, saddle-tank locomotives, overshot waterwheels and other beautiful pieces of obsolete machinery to play with: In his New Jerusalem even chefs will be cucumber-cool machine minders.

In my Eden our only source of political news is gossip: In his New Jerusalem there will be a special daily in simplified spelling for non-verbal types.

In my Eden each observes his compulsive rituals and superstitious tabus but we have no morals: In his New Jerusalem the temples will be empty but all will practice the rational virtues.

One reason for his contempt is that I have only to close my eyes, cross the iron footbridge to the tow-path, take the barge through the short brick tunnel and there I stand in Eden again, welcomed back by the krumhorns, doppions, sordumes of jolly miners and a bob major from the Cathedral (romanesque) of St. Sophie (*Die Kalte*):

One reason for my alarm is that, when he closes his eyes, he arrives, not in New Jerusalem, but on some august day of outrage when hellikins cavort through ruined drawing-rooms and fish-wives intervene in the Chamber or

some autumn night of delations and noyades when the unrepentant thieves (including me) are sequestered and those he hates shall hate themselves instead.

So with a passing glance we take the other's posture: Already our steps recede, heading, incorrigible each, towards his kind of meal and evening.

Was it (as it must look to any god of cross-roads) simply a fortuitous intersection of life-paths, loyal to different fibs,

or also a rendezvous between accomplices who, in spite of themselves, cannot resist meeting

to remind the other (do both, at bottom, desire truth?) of that half of their secret which he would most like to forget,

forcing us both, for a fraction of a second, to remember our victim (but for him I could forget the blood, but for me he could forget the innocence)

on whose immolation (call him Abel, Remus, whom you will, it is one Sin Offering) arcadias, utopias, our dear old bag of a democracy, are alike founded:

For without a cement of blood (it must be human, it must be innocent) no secular wall will safely stand.

(June 1954)

∾

12 O'Clock News

gooseneck lamp

As you all know, tonight is the night of the full moon, half the world over. But there the moon seems to hang motionless in the sky. It gives very little light; it could be dead. Visibility is poor. Nevertheless, we shall try to give you some idea of the lay of the land and the present situation.

typewriter

The escarpment that rises abruptly from the central plain is in heavy shadow, but the elaborate terracing of its southern glacis gleams faintly in the dim light, like fish scales. What endless labor those small, peculiarly shaped terraces represent! And yet, on them the welfare of this tiny principality depends.

pile of mss.

A slight landslide occurred in the northwest about an hour ago. The exposed soil appears to be of poor quality: almost white, calcareous, and shaly. There are believed to have been no casualties.

typed sheet

Almost due north, our aerial reconnaissance reports the discovery of a large rectangular "field," hitherto unknown to us, obviously man-made. It is dark-speckled. An airstrip? A cemetery?

envelopes

In this small, backward country, one of the most backward left in the world today, communications are crude and "industrialization" and its products almost nonexistent. Strange to say, however, signboards are on a truly gigantic scale.

We have also received reports of a mysterious, oddly shaped, black structure, at an undisclosed distance to the east. Its presence was revealed only because its highly polished surface catches such feeble moonlight as prevails. The natural resources of the country being far from completely known to us, there is the possibility that this may be, or may contain, some powerful and terrifying "secret weapon." On the other hand, given what we *do* know, or have learned from our anthropologists and sociologists about this people, it may well be nothing more than a *numen,* or a great altar recently erected to one of their gods, to which, in their present historical state of superstition and helplessness, they attribute magical powers, and may even regard as a "savior," one last hope of rescue from their grave difficulties.

ink-bottle

At last! One of the elusive natives has been spotted! He appears to be—rather, to have been—a unicyclist-courier, who may have met his end by falling from the height of the escarpment because of the deceptive illumination. Alive, he would have been small, but undoubtedly proud and erect, with the thick, bristling black hair typical of the indigenes.

typewriter eraser

From our superior vantage point, we can clearly see into a sort of dugout, possibly a shell crater, a "nest" of soldiers. They lie heaped together, wearing the camouflage "battle dress" intended for "winter warfare." They are in hideously contorted positions, all dead. We can make out at least eight bodies. These uniforms were designed to be used in guerrilla warfare on the country's one snow-covered mountain peak. The fact that these poor soldiers are wearing them *here,* on the plain, gives further proof, if proof were necessary, either of the childishness and hopeless impracticality of this inscrutable people, our opponents, or of the sad corruption of their leaders.

ashtray

(1976)

CZESLAW MILOSZ (1911–)

❧

Esse

I looked at that face, dumbfounded. The lights of métro stations flew by; I didn't notice them. What can be done, if our sight lacks absolute power to devour objects ecstatically, in an instant, leaving nothing more than the void of an ideal form, a sign like a hieroglyph simplified from the drawing of an animal or bird? A slightly snub nose, a high brow with sleekly brushed-back hair, the line of the chin—but why isn't the power of sight absolute?—and in a whiteness tinged with pink two sculpted holes, containing a dark, lustrous lava. To absorb that face but to have it simultaneously against the background of all spring boughs, walls, waves, in its weeping, its laughter, moving it back fifteen years, or ahead thirty. To have. It is not even a desire. Like a butterfly, a fish, the stem of a plant, only more mysterious. And so it befell me that after so many attempts at naming the world, I am able only to repeat, harping on one string, the highest, the unique avowal beyond which no power can attain: I am, she is. Shout, blow the trumpets, make thousands-strong marches, leap, rend your clothing, repeating only: is!

She got out at Raspail. I was left behind with the immensity of existing things. A sponge, suffering because it cannot saturate itself; a river, suffering because reflections of clouds and trees are not clouds and trees.

(Brie-Comte-Robert, 1954)
Translated by Czeslaw Milosz and Robert Pinsky

Be Like Others

Wherever you lived—in the city of Pergamum at the time of the Emperor Hadrian, in Marseilles under Louis XV, or in the New Amsterdam of the colonists—be aware that you should consider yourself lucky if your life followed the pattern of life of your neighbors. If you moved, thought, felt, just as they did; and, just as they, you did what was prescribed for a given moment. If, year after year, duties and rituals became part of you, and you took a wife, brought up children, and could meet peacefully the darkening days of old age.

Think of those who were refused a blessed resemblance to their fellow men. Of those who tried hard to act correctly, so that they would be spoken of no worse than their kin, but who did not succeed in anything, for whom everything would go wrong because of some invisible flaw. And who at last for that undeserved affliction would receive the punishment of loneliness, and who did not even try then to hide their fate.

On a bench in a public park, with a paper bag from which the neck of a bottle protrudes, under the bridges of big cities, on sidewalks where the homeless keep their bundles, in a slum street with neon, waiting in front of a bar for the hour of opening, they, a nation of the excluded, whose day begins and ends with the awareness of failure. Think, how great is your luck. You did not even have to notice such as they, even though there were many nearby. Praise mediocrity and rejoice that you did not have to associate yourself with rebels. For, after all, the rebels also were bearers of disagreement with the laws of life, and of exaggerated hope, just like those who were marked in advance to fail.

(1998)
Translated by Czeslaw Milosz and Robert Hass

KENNETH PATCHEN (1911–1972)

∾

In Order To

Apply for the position (I've forgotten now for what) I had to marry the Second Mayor's daughter by twelve noon. The order arrived three minutes of.

I already had a wife; the Second Mayor was childless: but I did it.

Next they told me to shave off my father's beard. All right. No matter that he'd been a eunuch, and had succumbed in early childhood: I did it, I shaved him.

Then they told me to burn a village; next, a fair-sized town; then, a city; a bigger city; a small, down-at-heels country; then one of "the great powers"; then another (another, another) — In fact, they went right on until they'd told me to burn up every man-made thing on the face of the earth! And I did it, I burned away every last trace, I left nothing, nothing of any kind whatever.

Then they told me to blow it all to hell and gone! And I blew it all to hell and gone (oh, didn't I!) . . .

Now, they said, put it back together again; put it all back the way it was when you started.

Well . . . it was my turn then to tell *them* something! Shucks, I didn't want any job that bad.

(1954)

Delighted with Bluepink

Flowers! My friend, be delighted with what you like; but with *something*.

Be delighted with something. Yesterday for me it was watching sun on stones; wet stones.

I spent the morning lost in the wonder of that. A delight of god's size.

The gods never saw anything more enchanting than that. Gorgeous! the sun on wet stones.

But today what delights me is thinking of bluepink flowers! Not that I've seen any . . .

Actually there isn't a flower of any kind in the house. —Except in my head.

But, my friend, oh my friend! what wonderful bluepink flowers! Delight in my bluepink flowers!

(1954)

The Famous Boating Party

Instead of remaining in "C-grade survellesession to Mr. Blaskett" ... ah, dear, dear little Yellow Hat, I hear you talking but my hands are tied, I'd help you out if I could, believe me, ah poor dear cork abob on life's troubled waters I always say. *However—*

"You are so oh I don't know so so sort of like they—Goddam Mr. Blaskett and Mrs. Blaskett and all the goddam little Blasketts. Without the tea this time."

"I beg your pardon."

"I say I'll just take the milk and sugar this round. And lemon. Yes, I think it might be nice, the lemon, oh all right no lemon."

"It's five after eight already. You know what—"

The Announcer: Ladies and gents, your attention please. It is now exactly two and sixty-four minutes past seven. Thank you, thank you, I was coming to that if you will be so kindly. But wait! Things are beginning to do! I'm afraid that something has gone amiss! I will thank you not to panic ... The management stands behind its usual rights in cases of this kind. I—excuse me—Sam! Hey, Sam! over here. . ! (Aside: No, no, no, *no* . . . Sam, look, I know you think I did. But I don't want no mustard on my frank. You know I never take it except plain—no pickle, no relish, no onion, no catsup, no mustard, no nothin!)

What the fellow said was murder, Sam—not mustard. Uh-huh, that's right—blew the ship skyhigh . . . Over seven hundred people—just like that, *poof-poof.*

(1954)

DELMORE SCHWARTZ (1913–1966)

❦

Justice

What! The same voluble fellow again—such is your speech with
yourself, I suppose, upon seeing me again, though this time in a
dress suit with a top hat (as if to appeal to the snob and fop in every
man, or at least to the upper-class sentiments in all of the lower and
middle class). Yes! What a buttonholing mariner! What a jack-in-the-
box I am, but truly with a decent motive—to entertain, to be useful—
and also to arrive at a point. What point? I do not actually know,
except that there must be a point and when I get there I will recognize
it, though I scarcely expect to get there very soon, and one who did
would equal all the seven wonders of nature of the ancients—the
camel, the rainbow, the echo, the cuckoo, the Negro, the volcano, and
the sirocco.

I have been thinking about justice. Naturally: look at what sur-
rounds us. Justice: a fine word and immediately suggesting how
beautiful a thing the fact must be, if there is such a fact, either possi-
ble or actual. A round, complete, self-contained datum, like an enor-
mous globe radiating a dazzling light which illuminates every corner,
subterfuge, and mystery *between* human beings, not creating, as the
sun does (being like all natural things involved in the dialectic of
nature) so many morbid shadows, and the black broom of night at
once with the bright bloom of day.

What could I think of, desiring to amuse as well as instruct, also to
be pleased and to learn myself—of what but the ancient short story
made known to me in childhood by my crippled father, a brief his-
tory which has prepossessed me to this day, even with the archness in
which my poor father attempted to hide the essential viciousness
and despair of the narrative.

"Once upon a time," said my father, seated in his wheel chair, and
summoning unknowingly in that traditional opening the continuous
present necessary to the interest of any story, "Once upon a time," he
repeated, "an old farmer named Schrecklichkeitunendlich" (a name
chosen to tickle me) "and his young son Hans, aged ten, went to town

67

taking with them their brown pony named Ego." "Ego, Father?" I asked. "That is a strange name for a pony or anyone else." "No, no," said my bitter father, "it is a well-known name." "I have never heard of anyone with that name," I said stubbornly. "Please," said my father, angered, "if you continue to interrupt me, I will never finish the story, which you begged me to tell you. Father, son, and pony," my father continued, "started for the market place, and Hans rode the pony. It was a beautiful blue-and-gold day in the month of June, and all three were pleased with all things, the father because he was going to sell the pony and with the proceeds buy a gun with which to kill deer, the son because he had been promised a pair of boxing gloves by the father, and the pony merely glad because he was exercising himself and the weather was fine.

"The three travelers had gone but a mile—the town being four miles distant—when a man with a whip came along from the opposite direction, and seeing them, said indignantly: 'O pitiless boy! You who are young and strong ride the pony, while your father, the weak old man, walks beside you and by such exertion shortens his days. Get down from the pony, let your father ride, honor your father, remember his weakness.' Intimidated by this, father and son said nothing, the traveler went on his way absentmindedly, Hans dismounted, and his father mounted the pony."

"But they should have had two ponies," I said to my father. "They had only one," my father replied. "The number of ponies is not infinite. Many people have only one pony, and as for us, as you know, we have none," said my father in his embittered voice and continued.

"They went forward another mile and another stranger approached, holding a gun in his hand, stopped them, took the pony by the halter, standing there as if he were an official authority: 'Evil old man,' he said. 'Selfish father! The young boy must walk while the father rides, as if he were a king and would like to live forever.' "

"A king, Father?" I inquired. "Kings do not live forever. No one does." "By king, I meant an important person," he said annoyed and impatient. "Do not, please, interrupt me so often.

"The stranger stood there so threateningly that the father dismounted. Satisfied, the stranger passed on, leaving father and son completely perplexed, not knowing at all what to do. Suddenly Hans was inspired: 'Father, Father!' he said. 'We will both ride the pony.' The father saw how intelligent this idea was and said with pride: 'Hans, you are a smart boy,' and soon both were mounted on the pony and jogging toward town. The pony's pace slowed up a bit, but not otherwise did he show himself troubled by the additional weight.

"But soon a third stranger came along, saw them and stopped them. This one brandished a sword and said, in a tone of the greatest moral indignation and self-righteousness: 'O heartless humans! Both of you riding one weak and young pony! What ruthless cruelty toward the dumb and inoffensive beast! Dismount before you kill him, or I will report you to both the civil and sacred authorities!' Both father and son dismounted hurriedly, and clumsily (for it is difficult for two to dismount from a horse at the same time). 'Something is always wrong,' said the father aloud, as he dismounted and the stranger, satisfied, departed.

" 'Hans,' said the father, 'we will both walk and the pony will walk beside us. Then perhaps all will be content.' No sooner had he said this than a fourth stranger appeared. Hans drew back and wished to hide in the wood until the stranger passed, especially since the newcomer carried a whip, *and* a gun, *and* a sword. But the father decided against hiding. 'What is wrong with you?' said the stranger in a voice whose kindliness stunned them with surprise. 'Why don't you ride the pony? Why are you so stupid? What is a pony for, if not to ride?' Then the stranger passed on, before they could tell him of the difficulties involved in riding the pony.

"Desperate by this time, the farmer said: 'Son, only one choice remains. If either of us ride the pony, we will remain at the mercy of these denunciations of the first, second, and third class. We must carry the pony, then perhaps all sides will be satisfied.' 'The pony may not like it, Father.' 'He is silent. If he says anything, we will whip him.' And so they lifted the pony on their backs, although it was a difficult and clumsy thing to do."

"Father," I said at this point, in disbelief, "you are inventing this story. You ought not to tell me falsehoods. No one carries a pony upon his back. That is ridiculous." My father was greatly angered and slapped me savagely, making me howl with pain. "Don't ever call your father a liar," he said. "It's enough that your mother does so."

"Finish the story, Father, please," I said meekly, weeping.

"After a slow and painful effort, the farmer and Hans managed to reach the market place, carrying the pony upon their backs and looking very strange. In the market place, idlers were congregated, who, when they saw this sight, began to laugh and their laughter increased in intensity and volume. 'What are you good-for-nothings laughing about?' said the father, challenging them, while Hans in shame hid his head in his father's sleeve. The leader, the biggest wiseacre of all, answered: 'Why, you damned fool! Whoever heard of carrying a pony? A pony is supposed to carry you.' Their laughter increased still more at this sally, and the farmer felt completely helpless—at the end of his rope—and besides he could not stand being laughed at, being very sensitive. So he took out his revolver, which he had had in his pocket all the while, and—bang! bang! bang!—shot the pony, shot his son, and, shrugging his shoulders, and brushing the hair back from his forehead, shot himself."

My mother entered at this moment and began to argue with my father for telling the child such a story, and soon all the hate between them made each bring up past wrongs on each other's part, and in their heat they forgot my presence and spoke shamelessly and brutally, while I wept loudly, watching them, weeping because of the sad end of the story, because they were denouncing each other and because I had been slapped for calling my father a liar.

(1938)

DAVID IGNATOW (1914–1997)

I sink back upon the ground, expecting to die. A voice speaks out of my ear, You are not going to die, you are being changed into a zebra. You will have black and white stripes up and down your back and you will love people as you do not now. That is why you will be changed into a zebra that people will tame and exhibit in a zoo. You will be a favorite among children and you will love the children in return whom you do not love now. Zoo keepers will make a pet of you because of your round, sad eyes and musical bray, and you will love your keeper as you do not now. All is well, then, I tell myself silently, listening to the voice in my ear speak to me of my future. And what will happen to you, voice in my ear, I ask silently, and the answer comes at once: I will be your gentle, musical bray that will help you as a zebra all your days. I will mediate between the world and you, and I will learn to love you as a zebra whom I did not love as a human being.

(1978)

The Story of Progress

The apple I held and bit into was for me. The friend who spoke to me was for me. My father and mother were for me. The little girl with brown hair and brown eyes who looked and smiled shyly and ran away was for me, although I never dared follow her because I feared she would not understand that she was for me alone.

The bed I slept in was for me. The clothes I wore were for me. The kindness I showed a dead bird one winter by placing it in my warm pocket was for me. The time I went to the rescue of my sister from a bully was to prove myself, for me. The music on the radio, the books I was beginning to read, all were for me.

I had hold of a good thing, me, and I was going to give of my contentment to others, for me, and when I gave, it was taken with a smile that I recognized as mine, when I would be given. I had found that for me was everybody's way, and I became anxious and uncertain. I held back a bit when I exchanged post card pictures of baseball players, with a close look at what I was getting in return to make sure I was getting what I could like, and when my parents bought me a new pair of gloves after I had lost the first pair I was sure that for me was not as pure in feeling as the first time, because I was very sorry that my parents had to spend an extra dollar to replace my lost gloves, and so when I looked up at the night stars, for me remained silent, and when my grandmother died, for me became a little boy sent on an errand of candles to place at the foot and head of her coffin.

(1998)

BARBARA GUEST (1920–)

❧

Color

He believed if the woman on the right moved over to the left he could place her into the frame where a meadow lay beyond her. But it did not work out that way. The moon came up too early. The glow the moon cast lit up the shadow behind the wheelbarrow. No one could advance in the shattering moonlight. The film begins to take the shape of a milk bottle with the heavy cream on top.

He blamed everything on the use of color. The heavy woman who played the woodcutter's wife wanted to lay some emeralds on her bosom. They are the color of trees, she says. The skin of the leading actor was the color of ferns which do not blend with the pastel process that turns the clouds to pastel. The girl's knee is supposed to be grey when she bends it, not the color of blood. The voice coming from the elderberries is colorless, indicating melancholy. He remembers the alluring depths in film without color when tears were dark as drops falling from a raven's mouth. Once again his efforts have been emptied of meaning.

(1999)

JAMES SCHUYLER (1923–1991)

∾

Two Meditations

Gladioli slant in the border as though stuck not growing there and around the square white wood beehive the bees drone like the layers of a bulb at the center of which is a viscous shoot. Small green apples hang from the small trees and under the skinny boughs ducks a skinny boy in wool swim trunks steering a lawn mower. Damp blades of chopped off grass and clover leaves stick to his shins. The mower ceases, the bees whirl their routes higher and he drinks from the nozzle of a hose. The gravel spurts under the wheels of a car, which, coming from between the lilac hedges, discloses itself as a laundry truck.

Out of the gray bay gray rocks, close spaced and each a little black green north tree forest. This became denser until it was the color of a hole. The trawler anchored and they scrambled ashore in an inlet closed by a little white sand beach like a Negro's very white palm, the guide experienced and dignified last in laced boots with moccasin bottoms. The clarity of the water reliced a dead tree while he boiled great lake trout in a galvanized bucket on a resinous fire. A green flame. Everyone planned to change his 'way of life' until he tasted the fish, which was tasteless. Scales on the dull sand like garbage, or rain. It began raining, a drop at a time, big as cod liver oil capsules. The two boys' knees lichened and their shrills faded high and out into the falls of shot grouse curving into a November wet match stick field. Burrs, unfinished houses.

(1953)

Wonderful World

for Anne Waldman
July 23, 1969

"I," I mused, "yes, I," and turned to the fenestrations of the night beyond one of Ada and Alex Katz's windows. Deep in Prince Street lurked thin sullen fumes of Paris green; some great spotty Danes moved from room to room, their tails went whack whack in a kindly way and their mouths were full of ruses (roses). Flames in red glass pots, unlikely flowers, a spot of light that jumped ("Don't fret") back and forth over a strip of moulding, the kind of moulding that spells low class dwelling—I, I mused, take no interest in the distinction between amateur and pro, and despise the latter a little less each year. The spot of light, reflected off a cup of strong blue coffee, wasn't getting anywhere but it wasn't standing still. They say a lot of gangsters' mothers live around here, so the streets are safe. A vast and distant school building made chewing noises in its sleep. Our Lady of someplace stood up in a wood niche with lots and lots of dollar bills pinned around her. The night was hot, everybody went out in the street and sold each other hot sausages and puffy sugared farinaceous products fried in deep fat ("Don't put your fingers in that, dear") while the band played and the lady in the silver fox scarf with the beautiful big crack in her voice sang about the young man and how he ran out in front of the stock exchange and drank a bottle of household ammonia: "Ungrateful Heart." Big rolls of paper were delivered, tall spools of thread spun and spelled Jacquard, Jacquard. Collecting the night in her hand, rolling its filaments in a soft ball, Anne said, "I grew up around here," where, looking uptown on summer evenings, the Empire State Building rears its pearly height.

(1969)

Footnote

The bluet is a small flower, creamy-throated, that grows in patches in New England lawns. The bluet (French pronunciation) is the shaggy cornflower, growing wild in France. "The Bluet" is a poem I wrote. *The Bluet* is a painting of Joan Mitchell's. The thick hard blue runs and holds. All of them, broken-up pieces of sky, hard sky, soft sky. Today I'll take Joan's giant vision, running and holding, staring you down with beauty. Though I need reject none. Bluet. "Bloo-ay."

(1980)

KENNETH KOCH (1925–2002)

❧

On Happiness

It was distressing to think that Kawabata had committed suicide. It wasn't distressing, however, to find out that he had defined happiness as drinking a scotch and soda at the Tokyo Hilton Hotel. An acquaintance of mine thought this was a terrible thing to say, to such an extent that for him it seemed almost to destroy the value of Kawabata's work.

Sitting on the terrace of the Hilton!

What's wrong with that?

A friend of mine, a woman, once explained happiness to me.

We were sitting in the Place de la République in Paris, an unlikely spot for happiness. We were tired, had walked a lot, had sat down at a large, generic big-square café. Dear though it may be to its proprietors and its habitués, it seemed ordinary enough to us. So we sat there and she ordered a Beaujolais and I, a beer. After two swallows of the beer, I was overcome by a feeling of happiness. I told her and I told her again about it later.

She had a theory about a "happiness base." Once, she said, you had this base, at odd times, moments of true happiness could occur.

Without the base, however, they would not.

The base was made of good health, good work, good friendship, good love. Of course, you can have all these and not be "happy."

You have to have the base, and then be lucky, she said. That's why you were happy at the café.

Kawabata asked my acquaintance in turn: How would you define happiness? He told me his answer: "I said 'How can anyone answer a question like that?' "

(1993)

The Allegory of Spring

The blossoming cherry trees were quarreling. She thought this when she was fifty yards away and when she was closer, right in amongst them, she imagined she heard them. One tree said to another: I am prettier than you. And the other said: It is impossible for you to see yourself. But I see you. And I tell you you're wrong. The first tree disputed the illogic of this remark. And so on. She went on walking, and when she came out of the cherry grove, she had been through a lot. She hated quarreling. Dietrich was standing by his boat. Come, can you go out with me? he said. I don't want to quarrel, she said. He didn't understand. Well, will you or not? he said. Yes, she said. Then she said, No.

(1993)

The Wish to Be Pregnant

A bird just sat on a tree branch outside my living room window and when it opened its beak, bubbles came out. They looked like soap bubbles. But I have no idea what they actually were.

Serenity was not a main subject or even concern of the New York painters. A big bully of a guy, named Haggis Coptics, was strutting around the bars.

It was spring, and the alloys in the earth were melting. I saw my wife with the pot in which a chestnut soup was cooking. Right after our marriage she began to cook exotic and flavorsome foods. I half-expected quickly to grow fat in this marriage, as L. Tagenquist had in his, but I did not. It was only a few years after this that mildly excessive eating began to cause me to put on some weight. One morning I looked in the glass—"You are much too fat!"

A valentine was exchanged for a handclasp then a kiss and then finally another valentine from the shop. Held hands veered downstreet together. For one, the holiday had not replaced feeling at all. But this one was a dog.

Hello, said Jerry, coming up from behind me with a blindfold in his hand that, he said, he had just tied around the eyes of a girl. I fucked her in the basement, he said. Well, that's better than doing nothing, huh?

My wife came in from the kitchen. Lunch is ready, she said. Then, Oh, how I want to have a child!

(1993)

79

ROBERT BLY (1926–)

The Hockey Poem

Duluth, Minnesota
For Bill Duffy

1
The Goalie

The Boston College team has gold helmets, under which the long black hair of the Roman centurion curls out.... And they begin. How weird the goalies look with their African masks! The goalie is so lonely anyway, guarding a basket with nothing in it, his wide lower legs wide as ducks'.... No matter what gift he is given, he always rejects it.... He has a number like 1, a name like Mrazek, sometimes wobbling on his legs waiting for the puck, or curling up like a baby in the womb to hold it, staying a second too long on the ice.

The goalie has gone out to mid-ice, and now he sails sadly back to his own box, slowly; he looks prehistoric with his rhinoceros legs; he looks as if he's going to become extinct, and he's just taking his time....

When the players are at the other end, he begins sadly sweeping the ice in front of his house; he is the old witch in the woods, waiting for the children to come home.

2
The Attack

They all come hurrying back toward us, suddenly, knees dipping like oil wells; they rush toward us wildly, fins waving, they are pike swimming toward us, their gill fins expanding like the breasts of opera singers; no, they are twelve hands practicing penmanship on the same piece of paper.... They flee down the court toward us like birds, swirling two and two, hawks hurrying for the mouse, hurrying down wind valleys, swirling back and forth like amoebae on the pale slide, as they sail in the absolute freedom of water and the body, untroubled by the troubled mind, only the body, with wings as if there were no grave, no gravity, only the birds sailing over the cottage far in the deep woods. . . .

Now the goalie is desperate . . . he looks wildly over his left shoulder, rushing toward the other side of his cave, like a mother hawk whose chicks are being taken by two snakes. . . . Suddenly he flops on the ice like a man trying to cover a whole double bed. He has the puck. He stands up, turns to his right, and drops it on the ice at the right moment; he saves it for one of his children, a mother hen picking up a seed and then dropping it. . . .

But the men are all too clumsy, they can't keep track of the puck . . . no, it is the *puck,* the puck is too fast, too fast for human beings, it humiliates them constantly. The players are like country boys at the fair watching the con man—The puck always turns up under the wrong walnut shell. . . .

They come down ice again, one man guiding the puck this time . . . and Ledingham comes down beautifully, like the canoe through white water, or the lover going upstream, every stroke right, like the stallion galloping up the valley surrounded by his mares and colts, how beautiful, like the body and soul crossing in a poem. . . .

3
The Fight

The player in position pauses, aims, pauses, cracks his stick on the ice, and a cry as the puck goes in! The goalie stands up disgusted, and throws the puck out. . . .

The player with a broken stick hovers near the cage. When the play shifts, he skates over to his locked-in teammates, who look like a nest of bristling owls, owl babies, and they hold out a stick to him. . . .

Then the players crash together, their hockey sticks raised like lobster claws. They fight with slow motions, as if undersea . . . they are fighting over some woman back in the motel, but like lobsters they forget what they're battling for; the clack of the armor plate distracts them, and they feel a pure rage.

Or a fighter sails over to the penalty box, where ten-year-old boys wait to sit with the criminal, who is their hero. . . . They know society is wrong, the wardens are wrong, the judges hate individuality. . . .

4
The Goalie

And this man with his peaked mask, with slits, how fantastic he is, like a white insect who has given up on evolution in this life; his family hopes to evolve after death, in the grave. He is ominous as a Dark Ages knight . . . the Black Prince. His enemies defeated him in the day, but every one of them died in their beds that night. . . . At his father's funeral, he carried his own head under his arm.

He is the old woman in the shoe, whose house is never clean, no matter what she does. Perhaps this goalie is not a man at all, but a woman, all women; in her cage everything disappears in the end; we all long for it. All these movements on the ice will end, the seats will come down, the stadium walls bare. . . . This goalie with his mask is a woman weeping over the children of men, that are cut down like grass, gulls that stand with cold feet on the ice. . . . And at the end, she is still waiting, brushing away before the leaves, waiting for the new children developed by speed, by war . . .

(1972)

82

Warning to the Reader

Sometimes farm granaries become especially beautiful when all the oats or wheat are gone, and wind has swept the rough floor clean. Standing inside, we see around us, coming in through the cracks between shrunken wall boards, bands or strips of sunlight. So in a poem about imprisonment, one sees a little light.

But how many birds have died trapped in these granaries. The bird, seeing freedom in the light, flutters up the walls and falls back again and again. The way out is where the rats enter and leave; but the rat's hole is low to the floor. Writers, be careful then by showing the sunlight on the walls not to promise the anxious and panicky blackbirds a way out!

I say to the reader, beware. Readers who love poems of light may sit hunched in the corner with nothing in their gizzards for four days, light failing, the eyes glazed . . .

They may end as a mound of feathers and a skull on the open boardwood floor . . .

(1990)

A Rusty Tin Can

Someone has stepped on this tin can, which now has the shape of a broken cheekbone. It has developed a Franciscan color out in the desert, perhaps some monk who planted apple trees in the absent pastures, near the graveyard of his friends. The can's texture is rough and reminds one of Rommel's neck. When the fingers touch it, they inquire if it is light or heavy. It is both light and heavy like Mrs. Mongrain's novel we just found in the attic, written seventy years ago. None of the characters are real but in any case they're all dead now.

(2001)

One Day at a Florida Key

Here we are at Whitehorse Key. It is early morning. The tide is out. Hints of "earlier and other creation" . . . And the sea, having slept all night, seems heated, immobile, uncenturied, robust, abundant, low-voiced. On a dead tree just offshore, fourteen pelicans are drying their wings and encouraging their stomach linings. Now they can look down and see the helpless shining fish once more.

The day has gone by; it is early dusk. The sun is setting down through a neighboring island. We see dark ragged lines of trees, braced behind shiny, coppery water, given a momentary further darkness by a leaping fish, given broad strokes of murder by a pelican lumbering shoreward, then diving with a splash like a car wreck, rising cradling a fish in his bill, and so emerging triumphant.

Just before dark, the rosy band left by the setting sun begins to evaporate. The sun disk is gone, leaving behind the solitary, funereal, obscure, Jesuitical, cloud-reflecting, cloud-worshipping, altar-mad, boat-strewn Florida waters.

(2002)

❧

A Supermarket in California

What thoughts I have of you tonight, Walt Whitman, for I walked down the sidestreets under the trees with a headache self-conscious looking at the full moon.

In my hungry fatigue, and shopping for images, I went into the neon fruit supermarket, dreaming of your enumerations!

What peaches and what penumbras! Whole families shopping at night! Aisles full of husbands! Wives in the avocados, babies in the tomatoes!—and you, García Lorca, what were you doing down by the watermelons?

I saw you, Walt Whitman, childless, lonely old grubber, poking among the meats in the refrigerator and eyeing the grocery boys.

I heard you asking questions of each: Who killed the pork chops? What price bananas? Are you my Angel?

I wandered in and out of the brilliant stacks of cans following you, and followed in my imagination by the store detective.

We strode down the open corridors together in our solitary fancy tasting artichokes, possessing every frozen delicacy, and never passing the cashier.

Where are we going, Walt Whitman? The doors close in an hour. Which way does your beard point tonight?

(I touch your book and dream of our odyssey in the supermarket and feel absurd.)

Will we walk all night through solitary streets? The trees add shade to shade, lights out in the houses, we'll both be lonely.

Will we stroll dreaming of the lost America of love past blue automobiles in driveways, home to our silent cottage?

Ah, dear father, graybeard, lonely old courage-teacher, what America did you have when Charon quit poling his ferry and you got out on a smoking bank and stood watching the boat disappear on the black waters of Lethe?

(1955)

Three Poems from "Prose of Departure"

River Trip

Short walk through fields to soft-drink stand where boats wait—all aboard! Creak of rope oarlock. One man pulls the single oar, another poles, a third steers, a fourth stands by to relieve the first. High-up shrine, bamboo glade. Woodland a cherry tree still in bloom punctuates like gun-smoke. Egret flying upstream, neck cocked. Entering the (very gentle) rapids everyone gasps with pleasure. The little waves break backwards, nostalgia con moto, a drop of fresh water thrills the cheek. And then? Woodland, bamboo glade, high-up shrine. Years of this have tanned and shriveled the boatmen. For after all, the truly exhilarating bits

> were few, far between
> —boulders goaded past, dumb beasts
> mantled in glass-green
>
> gush—and patently
> led where but to the landing,
> the bridge, the crowds. We

step ashore, in our clumsiness hoping not to spill these brief impressions.

Sanctum

Another proscenium. At its threshold we sit on our heels, the only audience. Pure bell notes, rosaries rattled like dice before the throw. Some young priests—the same who received us yesterday, showed us to our rooms, served our meal, woke us in time for these matins—surround a candlelit bower of bliss. The abbot briskly enters, takes his place, and leads them in deep, monotonous chant. His well-fed back is to us. He faces a small gold pagoda flanked by big gold lotus trees overhung by tinkling pendants of gold. Do such arrangements please a blackened image deep within? To us they look like Odette's first drawing room (before Swann takes charge of her taste) lit up for a party, or the Maison Dorée he imagines as the scene of her infidelities. Still, when the abbot turns, and with a gesture invites us to place incense upon the brazier already full of warm, fragrant ash, someone—myself perhaps—tries vainly

> to hold back a queer
> sob. Inhaling the holy
> smoke, praying for dear

life—

In the Shop

Out came the most fabulous kimono of all: dark, dark purple traversed by a winding, starry path. To what function, dear heart, could it possibly be worn by the likes of—

Hush. Give me your hand. Our trip has ended, our quarrel was made up. Why couldn't the rest be?

Dyeing. A homophone deepens the trope. Surrendering to Earth's colors, shall we not *be* Earth before we know it? Venerated therefore is the skill which, prior to immersion, inflicts upon a sacrificial length of crêpe de Chine certain intricate knottings no hue can touch. So that one fine day, painstakingly unbound, this terminal gooseflesh, the fable's whole eccentric

> star-puckered moral—
> white, never-to-blossom buds
> of the mountain laurel—

may be read as having emerged triumphant from the vats of night.

(1988)

FRANK O'HARA (1926–1966)

⌘

Meditations in an Emergency

Am I to become profligate as if I were a blonde? Or religious as if I were French?

Each time my heart is broken it makes me feel more adventurous (and how the same names keep recurring on that interminable list!), but one of these days there'll be nothing left with which to venture forth.

Why should I share you? Why don't you get rid of someone else for a change?

I am the least difficult of men. All I want is boundless love.

Even trees understand me! Good heavens, I lie under them, too, don't I? I'm just like a pile of leaves.

However, I have never clogged myself with the praises of pastoral life, nor with nostalgia for an innocent past of perverted acts in pastures. No. One need never leave the confines of New York to get all the greenery one wishes—I can't even enjoy a blade of grass unless I know there's a subway handy, or a record store or some other sign that people do not totally *regret* life. It is more important to affirm the least sincere; the clouds get enough attention as it is and even they continue to pass. Do they know what they're missing? Uh huh.

My eyes are vague blue, like the sky, and change all the time; they are indiscriminate but fleeting, entirely specific and disloyal, so that no one trusts me. I am always looking away. Or again at something after it has given me up. It makes me restless and that makes me unhappy, but I cannot keep them still. If only I had grey, green, black, brown, yellow eyes; I would stay at home and do something. It's not that I'm curious. On the contrary, I am bored but it's my duty to be attentive, I am needed by things as the sky must be above the earth. And lately, so great has *their* anxiety become, I can spare myself little sleep.

Now there is only one man I love to kiss when he is unshaven. Heterosexuality! you are inexorably approaching. (How discourage her?)

St. Serapion, I wrap myself in the robes of your whiteness which is like midnight in Dostoevsky. How am I to become a legend, my dear? I've tried love, but that hides you in the bosom of another and I am always springing forth from it like the lotus—the ecstasy of always bursting forth! (but one must not be distracted by it!) or like a hyacinth, "to keep the filth of life away," yes, there, even in the heart, where the filth is pumped in and slanders and pollutes and determines. I will my will, though I may become famous for a mysterious vacancy in that department, that greenhouse.

Destroy yourself, if you don't know!

It is easy to be beautiful; it is difficult to appear so. I admire you, beloved, for the trap you've set. It's like a final chapter no one reads because the plot is over.

"Fanny Brown is run away—scampered off with a Cornet of Horse; I do love that little Minx, & hope She may be happy, tho' She has vexed me by this Exploit a little too.—Poor silly Cecchina! or F:B: as we used to call her.—I wish She had a good Whipping and 10,000 pounds."—Mrs. Thrale.

I've got to get out of here. I choose a piece of shawl and my dirtiest suntans. I'll be back, I'll re-emerge, defeated, from the valley; you don't want me to go where you go, so I go where you don't want me to. It's only afternoon, there's a lot ahead. There won't be any mail downstairs. Turning, I spit in the lock and the knob turns.

(1954)

Schoenberg

In a fever of style, having slaughtered the false Florimells of harmonious thought and their turgid convincements, he marshalled lightning and the beautiful stench of signed clouds. Some sneered: him a silly Quixote! but he laid waste Central Europe and painted with the salt of Jenghiz the wounds of World War I. Not enough women rubbed their breasts against trees while waiting for big nightingales, so he pushed these ladies, intelligent refugees from Weimar, into a Pierrotless sea, and everywhere the frontiers of a sensibility whose left foot was only then fearfully emerging trembled like the rim of the sun under his hot clothes. The classic grace of a spirit resting on broken glass informed the shell of his virgin Muse with pink echoes from the newspapers, at the mercy of every fresh breath from the tradewinds.

(1977)

JOHN ASHBERY (1927–)

❧

Whatever It Is, Wherever You Are

The cross-hatching technique which allowed our ancestors to exchange certain genetic traits for others, in order to provide their off-spring with a way of life at once more variegated and more secure than their own, has just about run out of steam and has left us wondering, once more, what there is about this plush solitude that makes us think we will ever get out, or even want to. The ebony hands of the clock always seem to mark the same hour. That is why it always seems the same, though it is of course changing constantly, subtly, as though fed by an underground stream. If only we could go out in back, as when we were kids, and smoke and fool around and just stay out of the way, for a little while. But that's just it—don't you see? We are "out in back." No one has ever used the front door. We have always lived in this place without a name, without shame, a place for grownups to talk and laugh, having a good time. When we were children it seemed that adulthood would be like climbing a tree, that there would be a view from there, breathtaking because slightly more elusive. But now we can see only down, first down through the branches and fur-ther down the surprisingly steep grass patch that slopes away from the base of the tree. It certainly is a different view, but not the one we expected.

What did *they* want us to do? Stand around this way, monitoring every breath, checking each impulse for the return address, wonder-ing constantly about evil until necessarily we fall into a state of torpor that is probably the worst sin of all? To what purpose did they cross-hatch so effectively, so that the luminous surface that was underneath is transformed into another, also luminous but so shifting and so alive with suggestiveness that it is like quicksand, to take a step there would be to fall through the fragile net of uncertainties into the bog of certainty, otherwise known as the Slough of Despond?

Probably they meant for us to enjoy the things they enjoyed, like late summer evenings, and hoped that we'd find others and thank them for providing us with the wherewithal to find and enjoy them. Singing the way they did, in the old time, we can sometimes see through the tissues and tracings the genetic process has laid down between us and them. The tendrils can suggest a hand; or a specific color—the yellow of the tulip, for instance—will flash for a moment in such a way that after it has been withdrawn we can be sure that there was no imagining, no auto-suggestion here, but at the same time it becomes as useless as all subtracted memories. It has brought certainty without heat or light. Yet still in the old time, in the faraway summer evenings, they must have had a word for this, or known that we would someday need one, and wished to help. Then it is that a kind of purring occurs, like the wind sneaking around the baseboards of a room: not the infamous "still, small voice" but an ancillary speech that is parallel to the slithering of our own doubt-fleshed imaginings, a visible soundtrack of the way we sound as we move from encouragement to despair to exasperation and back again, with a gesture sometimes that is like an aborted movement outward toward some cape or promontory from which the view would extend in two directions—backward and forward—but that is only a polite hope in the same vein as all the others, crumpled and put away, and almost not to be distinguished from any of them, except that *it knows we know,* and in the context of not knowing is a fluidity that flashes like silver, that seems to say a film has been exposed and an image will, most certainly will, not like the last time, come to consider itself within the frame.

It must be an old photograph of you, out in the yard, looking almost afraid in the crisp, raking light that afternoons in the city held in those days, unappeased, not accepting anything from anybody. So what else is new? I'll tell you what is: you are accepting this now from the invisible, unknown sender, and the light that was intended, you thought, only to rake or glance is now directed full in your face, as it in fact always was, but you were squinting so hard, fearful of accepting it, that you didn't know this. Whether it warms or burns is another matter, which we will not go into here. The point is that you are accepting it and holding on to it, like love from someone you always thought you couldn't stand, and whom you now recognize as a brother, an equal. Someone whose face is the same as yours in the photograph but who is someone else, all of whose thoughts and feelings are directed at you, falling like a gentle slab of light that will ultimately loosen and dissolve the crusted suspicion, the timely self-hatred, the efficient cold directness, the horrible good manners, the sensible resolves and the senseless nights spent waiting in utter abandon, that have grown up to be you in the tree with no view; and place you firmly in the good-natured circle of your ancestors' games and entertainments.

(1984)

Haibun 6

To be involved in every phase of directing, acting, producing and so on must be infinitely rewarding. Just as when a large, fat, lazy frog hops off his lily pad like a spitball propelled by a rubber band and disappears into the water of the pond with an enthusiastic plop. It cannot be either changed or improved on. So too with many of life's little less-than-pleasurable experiences, like the rain that falls and falls for so long that no one can remember when it began or what weather used to be, or cares much either; they are much too busy trying to plug holes in ceilings or emptying pails and other containers and then quickly pushing them back to catch the overflow. But nobody seems eager to accord ideal status to this situation and I, for one, would love to know why. Don't we realize that after all these centuries that are now starting to come apart like moldy encyclopedias in some abandoned, dusty archive that we have to take the bitter with the sweet or soon all distinctions will be submerged by the tide of tepid approval of everything that is beginning to gather force and direction as well? And when its mighty roar threatens in earnest the partially submerged bridges and cottages, picks up the floundering cattle to deposit them in trees and so on to who knows what truly horrible mischief, it will be time, then, to genuinely rethink this and come up with true standards of evaluation, only it will be too late of course, too late for anything but the satisfaction that lasts only just so long. A pity, though. Meanwhile I lift my glass to these black-and-silver striped nights. I believe that the rain never drowned sweeter, more prosaic things than those we have here, now, and I believe this is going to have to be enough.

Striped hair, inquisitive gloves, a face, some woman named Ernestine Throckmorton, white opera glasses and more

(1984)

A Nice Presentation

I have a friendly disposition but am forgetful, though I tend to forget only important things. Several mornings ago I was lying in my bed listening to a sound of leisurely hammering coming from a nearby building. For some reason it made me think of spring which it is. Listening I heard also a man and woman talking together. I couldn't hear very well but it seemed they were discussing the work that was being done. This made me smile, they sounded like good and dear people and I was slipping back into dreams when the phone rang. No one was there.

Some of these are perhaps people having to do with anything in the world. I wish to go away, on a dark night, to leave people and the rain behind but am too caught up in my own selfish thoughts and desires for this. For it to happen I would have to be asleep and already started on my voyage of self-discovery around the world. One is certain then to meet many people and to hear many strange things being said. I like this in a way but wish it would stop as the unexpectedness of it conflicts with my desire to revolve in a constant, deliberate motion. To drink tea from a samovar. To use chopsticks in the land of the Asiatics. To be stung by the sun's bees and have it not matter.

Most things don't matter but an old woman of my acquaintance is always predicting doom and gloom and her prophecies matter though they may never be fulfilled. That's one reason I don't worry too much but I like to tell her she is right but also wrong because what she says won't happen. Yet how can I or anyone know this? For the seasons do come round in leisurely fashion and one takes a pinch of something from each, according to one's desires and what it leaves behind. Not long ago I was in a quandary about this but now it's too late. The evening comes on and the aspens leaven its stars. It's all about this observatory a shout fills.

(2001)

Disagreeable Glimpses

After my fall from the sixteenth floor my bones were lovingly assembled. They were transparent. I was carried into the gorgeous dollhouse and placed on a fainting couch upholstered with brilliant poppies. My ship had come in, so to speak.

There were others, lovers, sitting and speaking nearby. "Are you the Countess of C.?," I demanded. She smiled and returned her gaze to the other. Someone brought in a tray of cakes which were distributed to the guests according to a fixed plan. "Here, this one's for you. Take it." I looked and saw only a small cat rolling in the snow of the darkened gutter. "If this is mine, then I don't want it." Abruptly the chords of a string quartet finished. I was on a shallow porch. The village movie palaces were letting out. I thought I saw a cousin from years back. Before I could call out she turned, sallow. I saw that this was not the person. Conversations continued streaming in the erstwhile twilight, I betook myself to the tollbooth. The pumpkin-yellow sun lit all this up, climbing slowly from ankles to handlebar.

He had shaved his head some seven years ago. The lovers were bored then. They no longer meandered by the brook's side, telling and retelling ancient secrets, as though this time of life were an anomaly, a handicap that had been foreseen. "In truth these labels don't go far. It was I who made a career in singing, but it could just as well have been somewhere else."

Indeed? The dust was sweeping itself up, making sport of the broom. The solar disk was clogged with the bristles of impending resolution. Which direction did he say to take? I'm confused now, a little. It was my understanding we would in joining hands be chastised, that the boss man would be sympathetic, the sly apprentice unresonant as a squatter's treehouse. See though, it wasn't me that dictated . . .

that dictated the orbits of the plants, the viburnum at the door. And just as I had called to you, the image decomposed. Restlessness of fish in a deodorant ad. By golly, Uncle Ted will soon be here. Until it happens you can catch your breath, looking about the walls of the familiar nest. But his flight was delayed for five hours. *Now* someone was interested. The travel mishaps of others are truly absorbing. He read from a large timetable and the helium balloon rose straight up out of the city, entered the region of others' indifference and their benighted cares. Can't that child be made to stop practicing?

In another life we were in a cottage made of thin boards, above a small lake. The embroidered hems of waves annoyed the shoreline. There were no boats, only trees and boathouses.

It's good to step off that steel carrousel. The woods were made for musicianly echoes, though not all at once. Too many echoes are like no echo, or a single tall one. Please return dishes to main room after using. Try a little subtlety in self-defence; it'll help, you'll find out.

The boards of the cottage grew apart and we walked out into the sand under the sea. It was time for the sun to exhort the mute apathy of sitters, hangers-on. Ballast of the universal dredging operation. The device was called candy. We had seen it all before but would never let on, not until the postman came right up to the door, borne on the noble flood. Racked by jetsam, we cry out for flotsam, anything to stanch the hole in the big ad.

We all came to be here quite naturally. You see we are the lamplighters of our criminal past, trailing red across the sidewalks and divided highways. Yes, she said, you most certainly can come here now and be assured of staying, of starving, forever if we wish, though we shall not observe the dark's convolutions much longer (sob). Utterly you are the under one, we are all neighbors if you wish, but don't under any circumstances go crawling to the barrel organ for sympathy, you would only blow a fuse and where's the force in that? I know your seriousness is long gone, facing pink horizons in other hemispheres. We'd all blow up if it didn't. Meanwhile it's nice to have a chair. A chair is a good thing to be. We should all know that.

The last trail unspools beyond Ohio.

(2001)

Meet Me Tonight in Dreamland

It was an hour ago. I walked upstairs to dreamland. Took a cab and got out and somebody else backed in. Now we weren't actually on the Dreamland floor. That would be for later. Look, these are the proper plans, plants. They used to have a Chautauqua here, far out into the lake. Now it's peeled. No one actually comes here. Yet there are people. You just hardly ever see them. No I wasn't being modest. Some get out on the floor, several a year, whose purple glass sheds an eldritch glow on the trottoirs, as Whitman called them. Or spittoons. Look, we are almost a half a mile later, it must link up. The Tennessee drifter smiled sharkly. Then it was on to native board games.

Je bois trop.

In one of these, called "Skunk," you are a weasel chasing a leveret back to its hole when Bop! the mother weasel, about ten stories tall, traps you with her apron string, patterned with poppies and rotted docks. You see, you thought every noun had to have an adjective, even "sperm," and that's where you made your first big mistake. Later it's raining and we have to take a car. But the game isn't over—there are sixteen thousand marble steps coming up, down which you glide as effortlessly as you please, as though on a bicycle, weasel in tow. It's an exercise bike. What a time to tell me, the solar wind has sandpapered everything as smooth as quartz. Now it's back to the finish line with you.

You're not quite out of the woods yet. Dreamland has other pastures, other melodies to chew on. Hummingbirds mate with dragonflies beneath the broken dome of the air, and it's three o'clock, the sun is raining mineral-colored candy. I'd like one of these. It's yours. Now I'm glad we came. I hate drafts though and the sun is slowly moving away. I'm standing on the poopdeck wiggling colored pennants at the coal-colored iceberg that seems to be curious about us, is sliding this

way and that, then turns abruptly back into the moors with their cor-
rect hills in the distance. If it was me I'd take a trip like this every day
of my life.

(2001)

❧

Humble Beginning

When he had learned how to kill his brother with a rock he learned how to use a rock to begin stairs. For both of which secrets he thanked the rock.

He considered the rock further. It had always been there keeping secret what it could do. It had never so much as hinted at what it had already done. Now it was keeping all of its other secrets. He fell on his knees facing it and touched it with his forehead, his eyes, his nose, his lips, his tongue, his ears.

He thought the rock had created him. He thought that.

(1970)

The Dachau Shoe

My cousin Gene (he's really only a second cousin) has a shoe he picked up at Dachau. It's a pretty worn-out shoe. It wasn't top quality in the first place, he explained. The sole is cracked clear across and has pulled loose from the upper on both sides, and the upper is split at the ball of the foot. There's no lace and there's no heel.

He explained he didn't steal it because it must have belonged to a Jew who was dead. He explained that he wanted some little thing. He explained that the Russians looted everything. They just took anything. He explained that it wasn't top quality to begin with. He explained that the guards or the kapos would have taken it if it had been any good. He explained that he was lucky to have got anything. He explained that it wasn't wrong because the Germans were defeated. He explained that everybody was picking up something. A lot of guys wanted flags or daggers or medals or things like that, but that kind of thing didn't appeal to him so much. He kept it on the mantelpiece for a while but he explained that it wasn't a trophy.

He explained that it's no use being vindictive. He explained that he wasn't. Nobody's perfect. Actually we share a German grandfather. But he explained that this was the reason why we had to fight that war. What happened at Dachau was a crime that could not be allowed to pass. But he explained that we could not really do anything to stop it while the war was going on because we had to win the war first. He explained that we couldn't always do just what we would have liked to do. He explained that the Russians killed a lot of Jews too. After a couple of years he put the shoe away in a drawer. He explained that the dust collected in it.

Now he has it down in the cellar in a box. He explains that the central heating makes it crack worse. He'll show it to you, though, any time you ask. He explains how it looks. He explains how it's hard to take it in, even for him. He explains how it was raining, and there weren't many things left when he got there. He explains how there wasn't anything of value and you didn't want to get caught taking anything of that kind, even if there had been. He explains how everything inside smelled. He explains how it was just lying out in the mud, probably right where it had come off. He explains that he ought to keep it. A thing like that.

You really ought to go and see it. He'll show it to you. All you have to do is ask. It's not that it's really a very interesting shoe when you come right down to it but you learn a lot from his explanations.

(1970)

Our Jailer

Our jailer is in the habit of placing a baited mouse trap in the cells of the condemned on their last night. Ours is a well-kept jail; mice are rare and not many stray into the occupied cells. The jailer watches the prisoners.

Surprisingly few, he says, remain completely indifferent to the presence of the trap throughout the whole night. A larger number become absorbed by it and sit staring at it, whether or not it occupies their thoughts consistently. A proportion which he has recorded releases the trap, either at once or after a period of varying length. He has other statistics for those who deliberately smash the trap, those who move it (presumably to a more likely spot), those who make a mark on the wall if a mouse is caught in the trap, and those who make one if none was caught, either to state the fact or to bequeath, as a tiny triumph, a lie.

Month after month, year after year, he watches them. And we watch him. And each other.

(1970)

The Lonely Child

The lonely child arranges all his toys in front of him.

"Come, play with me," he says to everyone who comes near. "Come and see all the toys I have."

But they go away.

So he smashes the first of the toys.

Then other children come to watch and help, and to fight over who can break his toys.

If a lonely child has no toys, he makes them.

(1977)

JAMES WRIGHT (1927–1980)

୬

On Having My Pocket Picked in Rome

These hands are desperate for me to stay alive. They do not want to lose me to the crowd. They know the slightest nudge on the wrong bone will cause me to look around and cry aloud. Therefore the hands grow cool and touch me lightly, lightly and accurately as a gypsy moth laying her larvae down in that foregone place where the tree is naked. It is only when the hands are gone, I will step out of this crowd and walk down the street, dimly aware of the dark infant strangers I carry in my body. They spin their nests and live on me in their sleep.

(1982)

Honey

My father died at the age of eighty. One of the last things he did in his life was to call his fifty-eight-year-old son-in-law "honey." One afternoon in the early 1930's, when I bloodied my head by pitching over a wall at the bottom of a hill and believed that the mere sight of my own blood was the tragic meaning of life, I heard my father offer to murder his future son-in-law. His son-in-law is my brother-in-law, whose name is Paul. These two grown men rose above me and knew that a human life is murder. They weren't fighting about Paul's love for my sister. They were fighting with each other because one strong man, a factory worker, was laid off from his work, and the other strong man, the driver of a coal truck, was laid off from his work. They were both determined to live their lives, and so they glared at each other and said they were going to live, come hell or high water. High water is not trite in southern Ohio. Nothing is trite along a river. My father died a good death. To die a good death means to live one's life. I don't say a good life.

I say a life.

(1982)

JOHN HOLLANDER (1929–)

◆

The Way We Walk Now

It was not that there were only the old ways of going from one chamber to another: we had learned to imitate the noble walk of those who had built, and dwelt in, the Great Palaces, moving gravely through the interconnecting rooms; aware of the painted ceilings and the import of the images there for their lives, but never needing to look up at them; free among their footmen; roaming their spaces and yet by no means imprisoned in the fragile grandeur to which, in the afternoon light, the rooms had fallen. We had learned thereafter to mock that stiff way of walking, and after that, to replace it with our own little dances and gallops; we roller-skated from room to room, or occasionally bicycled. Being confined by the layout was not the point, nor was it what may or may not have happened to the houses—whether they were indeed in ruins or merely in need of repair. We had all gone away somewhere: off to war, or to the city, or had shipped out for the East. And those of us who returned, or who had stayed wherever it was, came quite naturally to go about in the field, or among the hills or through the streets. At first, it was almost with memorized maps of the ways rooms opened off each other, and of just what courts it was on which the various windows gave; after that, with no recollected plan, but always moving the better for having started out in one of the great houses.

But then it almost ceased to matter where we were. What had become necessary that we do by way of amble, or of hop skip and jump, had so taken over power from mere place that it generated the shapes of space through which it moved, like a lost, late arrival at the start of a quest who had set out nonetheless, dreaming each new region into which he wandered. Pictures of the old places still had a certain pathos; but they were not of ourselves or of our lives. The distance that had been put between us and the houses crammed full of chambers was utter, like that between the starry heavens above and the text below us, on the opened page.

(1986)

106

Crocus Solus

A sigh? No more: a yellow or white rupture of the cold silent winter ground, the exclamation of such effort. Yet unaccompanied by the echoing multitudes that hope surveys; one only, and whether an accident or an example, too important in its uniqueness to be considered important for its meaning. O, spring will come, and one time it will not, but what we are to know we will know from all the various emblems crying, out of the grass, *vivace assai,* and waving in the soft wind, *ô Mort.* One swallow of water makes no summer of earth. One drop of darkness is no sign of wine. One flower points to nothing but itself, a signboard bravely hung outside the signpainter's. The crocus of all points, lying along the river, that speak for themselves is but one point of saffron or of snow. A sign? O, more . . .

(1986)

Not Something for Nothing

What he had begun only lately to notice was this: that he had always noticed relatively little of what was going on inside of, and among, the things he encountered; and this led him to recall noticing always what he had already possessed himself of: shining objects of memory. So that when, for example, he passed by something growing, something that had or had not bloomed yet, he would have had to wander back into the bright mountain meadow all ringed about with high pines and where all the names grew, to pluck a flower of designation and bear it back, through the shadowy woods, to the spot of attention. And it was because he could notice so little that he was able to call attention to things so startlingly sometimes. His mind was always wandering. He could point the way home.

(1986)

HARRY MATHEWS (1930–)

❧

Three Entries from *20 Lines a Day*

A man and a woman marry. For their first meal at home she bakes a ham, preparing it as she always does, at the start slicing off both its ends before setting it in the pan. The ham is delicious, her husband delighted. "Why do you make it that way," he later asks her, "slicing the ends off?" "I don't know *why*," she answers, "except that I learned to do that from my mother." Curious, the husband asks his mother-in-law at their next meeting, "Why do you slice both ends off the ham when you make it in the delicious way you taught your daughter?" "I don't know *why*," she answers. "I learned how to make it from my mother." The husband insists that he and his wife visit her grandmother, whom he again asks: "You bake ham in a wonderful way that has been adopted by your daughter and then by your granddaughter. Can you tell me why in this recipe one slices off the ends of the ham before cooking it?" "Don't know why *they* do it," the old lady replies, "but when I made it, the ham wouldn't fit in the pan."

This fable, illustrating our inevitable ignorance about why things happen the way they do, was told to us on the first day of the More Time Course, which included many other goodies: how to avoid fatigue by sleeping less, how to manage disagreeable emotions by scheduling them, how to replace paying bills by making contributions to institutions one admires (such as Con Ed, restaurants, taxicabs).

(New York, 4/20/83)

In bright late-winter sunlight, your mail sits on a neighbor's window-sill, leaning neatly stacked against the window. The child gets out of the car to fetch it. Back at the house, you take the envelopes and packages and open them eagerly, almost (but you are a grown-up and know better) feverishly. What will those sealed contents reveal? What changes small and great will they bring to your life? Questions both foolish and irresistible. As if something might change, as if the post-man (now a briskly efficient young woman) might deliver to you the message, the ultimate message that you've been waiting all your life for, that would make your life clear and complete. Sometimes the ultimate message is in fact received. It reads, more or less: "Your ligament issues from a spa that is given various narcissisms at various time-tables: lozenge, credulity, goggles. And not only your ligament (and that of others): the prodigy that generates mayday has the same orthography. You and the upkeep are one. Give up sugarbowls." At such moments you realize, and you remember, that such messages have never been lacking, and that they are all the same, and that the problem (if that is the word) doesn't involve receiving but decipher-ing what is received again and again, day after day, minute after minute.

The letter that made you happiest recently (someone planned to devote an issue of his magazine to your work) was opened without such expectation, without expectation of any kind. You found it deposited in your mailbox unusually early on a gray morning in Paris, where your important mail is rarely sent, on your way out to breakfast, still numb from sleep.

(Lans, 3/6/84)

If you decided to decode the "ultimate message" of two days ago, you might find the task less forbidding than it at first seemed. Encoding and decoding mean substitution: as a first step, replace all words in the message that strike you as obscure with their most likely dictionary definitions. The message then would read: "Your connecting bond issues from a mineral spring that has attributed to it various [forms of] excessive love of yourself, according to the listings of various arrivals and departures: pleasantly flavored medication; gullibility; protective tinted spectacles. And not only your connecting bond (and that of oth-ers): the fearful event that generates [your] signals of distress manifests the same method of representing sounds by literal symbols. You are one with the maintenance [of things] in proper operation, condi-tion, and repair. Give up your covered sweets." — You already have been provided with more accessible meanings. The very process of dis-covering and transcribing started possibilities of interpretation flashing in your imagination: the "mineral spring" seemed to appear for the exact purpose of reflecting Narcissus. . . . Much, if not all, of the message can be read as an injunction to give up pleasurable escapes (cough drops, dark glasses, sugar) and to accept the conditions of existence. Those conditions frighten you, but they also give you your life. That the conditions include a *mineral* spring and that you are connected to the "proper operation" of what is outside you imply a link with the inorganic world that remains hard to grasp. Furthermore the "method of representing sounds by literal symbols," common to what binds you to the world and to the frightening event, demands investigation.

(Lans, 3/8/84)

MARK STRAND (1934–)

~

In the Privacy of the Home

You want to get a good look at yourself. You stand before a mirror, you take off your jacket, unbutton your shirt, open your belt, unzip your fly. The outer clothing falls from you. You take off your shoes and socks, baring your feet. You remove your underwear. At a loss, you examine the mirror. There you are, you are not there.

(1964)

Success Story

Had I known at the outset the climb would be slow, difficult, at times even tedious, I would have chosen to walk the length of one of the local valleys, resigning myself to limited views, low thoughts, and a life that inspired none of the loftier disenchantments.

But how was I to know? The ground seemed level at first, and the walks were wide. Only gradually did I become aware of climbing; the going got rougher, I would be short of breath, pauses were frequent. Often I would have to retrace my steps until I found a more promising route.

I continued through all seasons and can recall how hopeless my venture seemed during those long winter nights and how, during the Spring when my determination thawed, I would have to imagine the Winter again, the cold, the discomfort.

If there were times I doubted arriving, I know now that my fears were groundless, for here I am, at the peak of my form, feeling the great blue waste of sky circle the the scaffold of my achievement. What more is there? I count myself among the blessed. My life is all downhill.

(1964)

From a Lost Diary

I had not begun the great journey I was to undertake. I did not feel like it. At breakfast, I thought of writing to Goethe, but of course did not. I had not met him yet, so could not pretend to be on good terms with him. Would I sit for Raeburn? I turned it over a few times and chose not to. Why should I commit my looks on a particular day to the casual glances of history? I stared a long time at the green fields to the west of the house, and watched with numb fascination the immobility of two spotted cows. Lunch was out of the question, and so was the letter to Wordsworth. I was sure he would not respond. Would I myself write a poem? I had never written one, but decided that nothing would be lost by postponing the experiment. There is so much not to do! Not to visit Blake or Crabb Robinson. Not to write Corot and tell him about the cows. Not to write Turner about my vision of the sun that like a red cry sank and smothered in rippling water until finally far away the water fell into the soundless chasms of an infinite night. What a relief! My mother, hunched over her needlework, urged me to write my sister to whom I had nothing to say. "In many instances it is better and kinder to write nothing than not to write," said she, quoting someone or other. A day so much like the others, why do anything about it? Why even write this down, were it not for my going on record as not having lived. After all, who can believe what is not written down? That I have withdrawn from the abuses of time means little or nothing. I am a place, a place where things come together, then fly apart. Look at the fields disappearing, look at the distant hills, look at the night, the velvety, fragrant night, which has already come, though the sun continues to stand at my door.

(1990)

Chekhov: A Sestina

Why him? He woke up and felt anxious. He was out of sorts, out of character. If only it would go away. Ivashin loved Nadya Vishnyevskaya and was afraid of his love. When the butler told him the old lady had just gone out, but that the young lady was at home, he fumbled in his fur coat and dresscoat pocket, found his card, and said: "Right." But it was not right. Driving from his house in the morning to pay a visit, he thought he was compelled to it by the conventions of society which weighed heavily upon him. But now it was clear that he went to pay calls only because somewhere far away in the depths of his soul, as under a veil, there lay hidden a hope that he would see Nadya, his secret love. And he suddenly felt pitiful, sad, and not a little anxious. In his soul, it seemed to him, it was snowing, and everything was fading away. He was afraid to love Nadya, because he thought he was too old for her, his appearance unattractive, and did not believe that a young woman like her could love a man for his mind or spiritual character. Everything was dim, sharing, he felt, the same blank character. Still, there would rise at times in him something like hope, a glimpse of happiness, of things turning out all right. Then, just as quickly, it would pass away. And he would wonder what had come over him. Why should he, a retired councillor of state, educated, liberal-minded, a well-traveled man; why should he, in other words, be so anxious? Were there not other women with whom he could fall in love? Surely, it was always possible to fall in love. It was possible, moreover, to fall in love without acting out of character. There was absolutely no need for him to be anxious. To be in love, to have a young pretty wife and children of his own, was not a crime or a deception, but his right. Clearly, there was something wrong with him. He wished he were far away ... But suddenly he hears from somewhere in the house the young officer's spurs jingle and then die away. That instant marked the death of his timid love. And in its vanishing, he felt the seeds of a different sort of melancholy take root within him. Whatever happened now, whatever desolation might be his, it would build character. Yes, he thought, so it is only right. Yes, all is finished, and I'm glad, very glad, yes, and I'm not let down, no, nor am I in any way anxious. No, certainly not anxious. What he had to do now was to get away. But how could he make it look right? How could he have thought he was in love? How out of character! How very unlike him!

(1990)

MICHAEL BENEDIKT (1935–)

The Doorway of Perception

If it was one thing he knew—even standing outside in the yard—it was that the universal problem had to be solved, the Doorway of Perception opened, behind which, despite the extraordinary demands he often made of himself, he still felt trapped in the vestibule of mimicry. So, he knocked on the door. But no one opened it. He tried the knob, but it seemed to be stuck. (He thought he heard a tumbler start to click inside the lock—but then it stopped). He bent down and attempted to pick the lock using the keys from his own apartment door—but of course, that produced absolutely no result whatsoever. Impatiently, he arose, walked back across the yard, and threw all his weight against the door from fifteen feet away! . . . but for some reason, that didn't work either. Again and again he tried to break through that damned door, running at it across the yard from still greater and greater distances, but time after time nothing happened—except that the last time he threw his weight against it, the entire building came crashing down around it! And still, the door stood. Slowly, he backed up a dozen yards to the furthermost limits of the yard, which was surrounded by a fence; and once again launched himself at the door—but this time he only succeeded in smashing his spinal column! Finally, from his brand new wheelchair, he tried nuclear dynamite. The earth fell down around the door; he realized that the sky was falling—he actually moved both Heaven and Earth! Just before they fell, he managed to peer at eye-level from his wheelchair through the keyhole. But all he saw back there was someone holding up a small hand mirror—the tiny, inexpensive kind they sell at dime stores; and, in the center of the mirror, directly opposite the keyhole and looking directly back at him, was an eye.

(1976)

❧

A Performance at Hog Theater

There was once a hog theater where hogs performed as men, had men been hogs.

One hog said, I will be a hog in a field which has found a mouse which is being eaten by the same hog which is in the field and which has found the mouse, which I am performing as my contribution to the performer's art.

Oh let's just be hogs, cried an old hog.

And so the hogs streamed out of the theater crying, only hogs, only hogs . . .

(1973)

The Pilot

Up in a dirty window in a dark room is a star which an old man can see. He looks at it. He can see it. It is the star of the room; an electrical freckle that has fallen out of his head and gotten stuck in the dirt on the window.

He thinks he can steer by that star. He thinks he can use the back of a chair as a ship's wheel to pilot this room through the night.

He says to himself, brave Captain, are you afraid?

Yes, I am afraid; I am not so brave.

Be brave, my Captain.

And all night the old man steers his room through the dark . . .

(1976)

The Taxi

One night in the dark I phone for a taxi. Immediately a taxi crashes through the wall; never mind that my room is on the third floor, or that the yellow driver is really a cluster of canaries arranged in the shape of a driver, who flutters apart, streaming from the windows of the taxi in yellow fountains . . .

Realizing that I am in the midst of something splendid I reach for the phone and cancel the taxi: All the canaries flow back into the taxi and assemble themselves into a cluster shaped like a man. The taxi backs through the wall, and the wall repairs . . .

But I cannot stop what is happening, I am already reaching for the phone to call a taxi, which is already beginning to crash through the wall with its yellow driver already beginning to flutter apart . . .

(1977)

The Rat's Tight Schedule

A man stumbled on some rat droppings.

Hey, who put those there? That's dangerous, he said.

His wife said, those are pieces of a rat.

Well, he's coming apart, he's all over the floor, said the husband.

He can't help it; you don't think he wants to drop pieces of himself all over the floor, do you? said the wife.

But I could have flipped and fallen through the floor, said the husband.

Well, he's been thinking of turning into a marsupial, so try to have a little patience; I'm sure if you were thinking of turning into a marsupial he'd be patient with you. But, on the other hand, don't embarrass him if he decides to remain placental, he's on a very tight schedule, said the wife.

A marsupial? A wonderful choice! cried the husband . . .

(1985)

The Canoeing Trip

I had planned a canoeing trip. But then, after some considerable thought, I thought I'd rather go canoeing on an ocean liner. They have more facilities than simple canoes.

But then I saw that an ocean liner would not fit the stream I had planned for my canoeing trip.

And so, after considerable thought, I decided not to think again, but simply to exist.
But even that becomes tiresome.
So I began to think again.

But then, after some considerable thought, I decided not to think again . . .

(1997)

The New Father

A young woman puts on her father's clothes and says to her mother, I'm your new husband.

Just you wait till your father gets home, scolds the mother.

He's already home, says the young woman.

Please don't do this to your father, he's worked so hard all his life, says the mother.

I know, says the young woman, he needs a rest.

When the father gets home he's dressed in his daughter's clothes. And as he steps into the house he calls, hi mom and dad, I'm home . . .

(2001)

∾

Five Poems
from *The Reproduction of Profiles*

You told me, if something is not used it is meaningless, and took my temperature which I had thought to save for a more difficult day. In the mirror, every night, the same face, a bit more threadbare, a dress worn too long. The moon was out in the cold, along with the restless, dissatisfied wind that seemed to change the location of the sycamores. I expected reproaches because I had mentioned the word love, but you only accused me of stealing your pencil, and sadness disappeared with sense. You made a ceremony out of holding your head in your hands because, you said, it could not be contained in itself.

In order to understand the nature of language you began to paint, thinking that the logic of reference would become evident once you could settle the quarrels of point, line, and color. I was distracted from sliding words along the scales of significance by smoke on my margin of breath. I waited for the flame, the passage from eye to world. At dawn, you crawled into bed, exhausted, warning me against drawing inferences across blind canvas. I ventured that a line might represent a tower that would reach the sky, or, on the other hand, rain falling. You replied that the world was already taking up too much space.

At first sight, it did not look like a picture of your body. Any more than the fog rolling in from the sea, covering and uncovering the surface of the river, seemed an extreme. I made excuses for your hesitation because I thought you wanted to contain everything, unimpaired by spelling errors. Then I saw you were trying to lean against the weight of missing words, a wall at the end of the world. But I knew, though it tired me to imagine even a fraction of the distance, that it continued at least as far as one can run from danger, where two women had been washed up on a delay. Neither words nor the rigor of sentences, you said, could stem the steady acceleration of the past.

As the streets were empty in the early morning, I had made the spaces between words broad enough for a smile which could reflect off the enamel tower clock. Being late is one of my essential properties. Unthinkable that I should not possess it, and not even on vacation do I deprive myself of its advantages. Nevertheless I cannot recall a time when I did not try to hide this by changing the shape of my mouth and appearing breathless. The sky was shading from hesitant to harsh, which was not bound to correspond to any one color or tableau vivant. The climate is rainy, no doubt about it, and ready to draw its curtain over my clauses and conjunctions. But what if I had made the spaces too wide to reach the next word and the silence.

The fog was not dense enough to hide what I didn't want to see, nor did analysis resolve our inner similarities. When you took the knife out of your pocket and stuck it into your upper arm you did not tell me that, if the laws of nature do not explain the world, they still continue its spine. There was no wind, the branches motionless around the bench, a dark scaffolding. A few drops of blood oozed from your wound. I began to suck it, thinking that, because language is part of the human organism, a life could end as an abrupt, violent sentence, or be drawn out with economy into fall and winter, no less complicated than a set of open parentheses from a wrong turn to the shock of understanding our own desires.

(1987)

CHARLES SIMIC (1938–)

❦

Three Poems
from *The World Doesn't End*

We were so poor I had to take the place of the bait in the mouse-trap. All alone in the cellar, I could hear them pacing upstairs, tossing and turning in their beds. "These are dark and evil days," the mouse told me as he nibbled my ear. Years passed. My mother wore a cat-fur collar which she stroked until its sparks lit up the cellar.

(1989)

"Everybody knows the story about me and Dr. Freud," says my grandfather.

"We were in love with the same pair of black shoes in the window of the same shoe store. The store, unfortunately, was always closed. There'd be a sign: DEATH IN THE FAMILY or BACK AFTER LUNCH, but no matter how long I waited, no one would come to open.

"Once I caught Dr. Freud there shamelessly admiring the shoes. We glared at each other before going our separate ways, never to meet again."

(1989)

It was the epoch of the masters of levitation. Some evenings we saw solitary men and women floating above the dark tree tops. Could they have been sleeping or thinking? They made no attempt to navigate. The wind nudged them ever so slightly. We were afraid to speak, to breathe. Even the nightbirds were quiet. Later, we'd mention the little book clasped in the hands of the young woman, and the way that old man lost his hat to the cypresses.

In the morning there were not even clouds in the sky. We saw a few crows preen themselves at the edge of the road; the shirts raise their empty sleeves on the blind woman's clothesline.

(1989)

The Magic Study of Happiness

In the smallest theater in the world the bread crumbs speak. It's a mystery play on the subject of a lost paradise. Once there was a kitchen with a table on which a few crumbs were left. Through the window you could see your young mother by the fence talking to a neighbor. She was cold and kept hugging her thin dress tighter and tighter. The clouds in the sky sailed on as she threw her head back to laugh.

Where the words can't go any further—there's the hard table. The crumbs are watching you as you in turn watch them. The unknown in you and the unknown in them attract each other. The two unknowns are like illicit lovers when they're exceedingly and unaccountably happy.

(1992)

Contributor's Note

I pleaded with my Death to at least allow me to nibble my pencil while he took bites of me. He kindly let me have a sheet of paper and an eraser too.

My lifelong subject, despite appearances to the contrary, was always an unknown woman who made me forget my name every time we bumped into each other on the street.

—Who am I, I asked my Death, but he just licked his fingers in reply.

The unknown woman wasn't any more forthcoming. She paid me no mind whatsoever, even though I was often sprawled before her on the sidewalk like an old dog overcome with memories of happier days.

Once at the bus stop, she asked me for the time in a voice that promised a life of bliss. I blurted out something about my Death, how he's even found me a publisher, but she was no longer listening.

It had started to rain. Everybody ran for cover. I did too. We watched her take off her high-heel shoes and pull down her panty hose. Then she marched through the puddles, head thrown back, arms spread wide as if she were about to fly.

I wanted to join her, but I hesitated, and then the torrential rain blurred the sight of her and made her vanish forever.

(1997)

MARGARET ATWOOD (1939–)

❦

Women's Novels

For Lenore

1. Men's novels are about men. Women's novels are about men too but from a different point of view. You can have a men's novel with no women in it except possibly the landlady or the horse, but you can't have a women's novel with no men in it. Sometimes men put women in men's novels but they leave out some of the parts: the heads, for instance, or the hands. Women's novels leave out parts of the men as well. Sometimes it's the stretch between the belly button and the knees, sometimes it's the sense of humor. It's hard to have a sense of humor in a cloak, in a high wind, on a moor.

   Women do not usually write novels of the type favored by men but men are known to write novels of the type favored by women. Some people find this odd.

2. I like to read novels in which the heroine has a costume rustling discreetly over her breasts, or discreet breasts rustling under her costume; in any case there must be a costume, some breasts, some rustling, and, over all, discretion. Discretion over all, like a fog, a miasma through which the outlines of things appear only vaguely. A glimpse of pink through the gloom, the sound of breathing, satin slithering to the floor, revealing what? Never mind, I say. Never never mind.

3. Men favor heroes who are tough and hard: tough with men, hard with women. Sometimes the hero goes soft on a woman but this is always a mistake. Women do not favor heroines who are tough and hard. Instead they have to be tough and soft. This leads to linguistic difficulties. Last time we looked, monosyllables were male, still dominant but sinking fast, wrapped in the octopoid arms of labial polysyllables, whispering to them with arachnoid grace: *darling, darling.*

4. Men's novels are about how to get power. Killing and so on, or winning and so on. So are women's novels, though the method is

different. In men's novels, getting the woman or women goes along with getting the power. It's a perk, not a means. In women's novels you get the power by getting the man. The man is the power. But sex won't do, he has to love you. What do you think all that kneeling's about, down among the crinolines, on the Persian carpet? Or at least say it. When all else is lacking, verbalization can be enough. *Love.* There, you can stand up now, it didn't kill you. Did it?

5. I no longer want to read about anything sad. Anything violent, anything disturbing, anything like that. No funerals at the end, though there can be some in the middle. If there must be deaths, let there be resurrections, or at least a Heaven so we know where we are. Depression and squalor are for those under twenty-five, they can take it, they even like it, they still have enough time left. But real life is bad for you, hold it in your hand long enough and you'll get pimples and become feeble-minded. You'll go blind.

   I want happiness, guaranteed, joy all round, covers with nurses on them or brides, intelligent girls but not too intelligent, with regular teeth and pluck and both breasts the same size and no excess facial hair, someone you can depend on to know where the bandages are and to turn the hero, that potential rake and killer, into a well-groomed country gentleman with clean fingernails and the right vocabulary. *Always,* he has to say, *Forever.* I no longer want to read books that don't end with the word *forever.* I want to be stroked between the eyes, one way only.

6. Some people think a woman's novel is anything without politics in it. Some think it's anything about relationships. Some think it's anything with a lot of operations in it, medical ones I mean. Some think it's anything that doesn't give you a broad panoramic view of our exciting times. Me, well, I just want something you can leave on the coffee table and not be too worried if the kids get into it. You think that's not a real consideration? You're wrong.

7. *She had the startled eyes of a wild bird.* This is the kind of sentence I go mad for. I would like to be able to write such sentences, without embarrassment. I would like to be able to read them without embarrassment. If I could only do these two simple things, I feel, I would be able to pass my allotted time on this earth like a pearl wrapped in velvet.

   She had the startled eyes of a wild bird. Ah, but which one? A screech owl, perhaps, or a cuckoo? It does make a difference. We do not need more literalists of the imagination. They cannot read *a body like a gazelle's* without thinking of intestinal parasites, zoos, and smells.

She had a feral gaze like that of an untamed animal, I read. Reluctantly I put down the book, thumb still inserted at the exciting moment. He's about to crush her in his arms, pressing his hot, devouring, hard, demanding mouth to hers as her breasts squish out the top of her dress, but I can't concentrate. Metaphor leads me by the nose, into the maze, and suddenly all Eden lies before me. Porcupines, weasels, warthogs, and skunks, their feral gazes malicious or bland or stolid or piggy and sly. Agony, to see the romantic *frisson* quivering just out of reach, a dark-winged butterfly stuck to an overripe peach, and not to be able to swallow, or wallow. *Which one?* I murmur to the unresponding air. *Which one?*

(1983)

In Love with Raymond Chandler

An affair with Raymond Chandler, what a joy! Not because of the mangled bodies and the marinated cops and hints of eccentric sex, but because of his interest in furniture. He knew that furniture could breathe, could feel, not as we do but in a way more muffled, like the word *upholstery,* with its overtones of mustiness and dust, its bouquet of sunlight on aging cloth or of scuffed leather on the backs and seats of sleazy office chairs. I think of his sofas, stuffed to roundness, satin-covered, pale blue like the eyes of his cold blond unbodied murderous women, beating very slowly, like the hearts of hibernating crocodiles; of his chaises longues, with their malicious pillows. He knew about front lawns too, and greenhouses, and the interiors of cars.

This is how our love affair would go. We would meet at a hotel, or a motel, whether expensive or cheap it wouldn't matter. We would enter the room, lock the door, and begin to explore the furniture, fingering the curtains, running our hands along the spurious gilt frames of the pictures, over the real marble or the chipped enamel of the luxurious or tacky washroom sink, inhaling the odor of the carpets, old cigarette smoke and spilled gin and fast meaningless sex or else the rich abstract scent of the oval transparent soaps imported from England, it wouldn't matter to us; what would matter would be our response to the furniture, and the furniture's response to us. Only after we had sniffed, fingered, rubbed, rolled on, and absorbed the furniture of the room would we fall into each other's arms, and onto the bed (king-size? peach-colored? creaky? narrow? four-posted? pioneer-quilted? lime-green chenille-covered?), ready at last to do the same things to each other.

(1992)

FRANK BIDART (1939–)

❦

Borges and I

We fill pre-existing forms and when we fill them we change them and are changed.

The desolating landscape in Borges' "Borges and I"—in which the voice of "I" tells us that its other self, Borges, is the self who makes literature, who in the process of making literature falsifies and exaggerates, while the self that is speaking to us now must go on living so that Borges may continue to fashion literature—is seductive and even oddly comforting, but, I think, false.

The voice of this "I" asserts a disparity between its essential self and its worldly second self, the self who seeks embodiment through making things, through work, who in making takes on something false, inessential, inauthentic.

The voice of this "I" tells us that Spinoza understood that everything wishes to continue in its own being, a stone wishes to be a stone eternally, that all "I" wishes is to remain unchanged, itself.

With its lonely emblematic title, "Borges and I" seems to be offered as a paradigm for the life of consciousness, the life of knowing and making, the life of the writer.

The notion that Frank has a self that has remained the same and that knows what it would be if its writing self did not exist—like all assertions about the systems that hold sway beneath the moon, the opposite of this seems to me to be true, as true.

When Borges' "I" confesses that Borges falsifies and exaggerates it seems to do so to cast aside falsity and exaggeration, to attain an entire candor unobtainable by Borges.

This "I" therefore allows us to enter an inaccessible magic space, a hitherto inarticulate space of intimacy and honesty earlier denied us, where voice, for the first time, has replaced silence.

—Sweet fiction, in which bravado and despair beckon from a cold panache, in which the protected essential self suffers flashes of its existence to be immortalized by a writing self that is incapable of performing its actions without mixing our essence with what is false.

Frank had the illusion, when he talked to himself in the cliches he used when he talked to himself, that when he made his poems he was changed in making them, that arriving at the order the poem suddenly arrived at out of the chaos of the materials the poem let enter itself out of the chaos of life, consciousness then, only then, could know itself, Sherlock Holmes was somebody or something before cracking its first case but not Sherlock Holmes, act is the cracked mirror not only of motive but self, *no other way,* tiny mirror that fails to focus in small the whole of the great room.

But Frank had the illusion that his poems also had cruelly replaced his past, that finally they were all he knew of it though he knew they were not, everything else was shards refusing to make a pattern and in any case he had written about his mother and father until the poems saw as much as he saw and saw more and he only saw what he saw in the act of making them.

He had never had a self that wished to continue in its own being, survival meant ceasing to be what its being was.

Frank had the illusion that though the universe of one of his poems seemed so close to what seemed his own universe at the second of writing it that he wasn't sure how they differed even though the paraphernalia often differed, after he had written it its universe was never exactly his universe, and so, soon, it disgusted him a little, the mirror was dirty and cracked.

Secretly he was glad it was dirty and cracked, because after he had made a big order, a book, only when he had come to despise it a little, only after he had at last given up the illusion that this was what was, only then could he write more.

He felt terror at the prospect of becoming again the person who could find or see or make no mirror, for even Olivier, trying to trap the beast who had killed his father, when he suavely told Frank as Frank listened to the phonograph long afternoons lying on the bed as a kid, when Olivier told him what art must be, even Olivier insisted that art is a mirror held up by an artist who himself needs to see something, held up before a nature that recoils before it.

We fill pre-existing forms and when we fill them we change them and are changed.

Everything in art is a formal question, so he tried to do it in prose with much blank white space.

(1997)

FANNY HOWE (1940–)

❧

Everything's a Fake

Coyote scruff in canyons off Mulholland Drive. Fragrance of sage and rosemary, now it's spring. At night the mockingbirds ring their warnings of cats coming across the neighborhoods. Like castanets in the palms of a dancer, the palm trees clack. The HOLLYWOOD sign has a white skin of fog across it where erotic canyons hump, moisten, slide, dry up, swell, and shift. They appear impatient—to make such powerful contact with pleasure that they will toss back the entire cover of earth. She walks for days around brown trails, threading sometimes under the low branches of bay and acacia. Bitter flowers will catch her eye: pink and thin honeysuckle, or mock orange. They coat the branches like lace in the back of a mystical store. Other deviant men and women live at the base of these canyons, closer to the city however. Her mouth is often dry, her chest tight, but she is filled to the brim with excess idolatry. It was like a flat mouse—the whole of Los Angeles she could hold in the circle formed by her thumb and forefinger. Tires were planted to stop the flow of mud at her feet. But she could see all the way to Long Beach through a tunnel made in her fist. Her quest for the perfect place was only a symptom of the same infection that was out there, a mild one, but a symptom nonetheless.

(1997)

Doubt

Virginia Woolf committed suicide in 1941 when the German bombing campaign against England was at its peak and when she was reading Freud whom she had staved off until then.

Edith Stein, recently and controversially beatified by the Pope, who had successfully worked to transform an existential vocabulary into a theological one, was taken to Auschwitz in August, 1942.

One year later Simone Weil died in a hospital in England—of illness and depression—determined to know what it is to know. She, as much as Woolf, sought salvation in a choice of words.

But multitudes succumb to the sorrow induced by an inexact vocabulary.

While a whole change in discourse is a sign of conversion, the alteration of a single word only signals a kind of doubt about the value of the surrounding words.
Poets tend to hover over words in this troubled state of mind. What holds them poised in this position is the occasional eruption of happiness.

While we would all like to know if the individual person is a phenomenon either culturally or spiritually conceived and why everyone doesn't kill everyone else, including themselves, since they can—poets act out the problem with their words.

Why not say "heart-sick" instead of "despairing"?
Why not say "despairing" instead of "depressed"?

Is there, perhaps, a quality in each person—hidden like a laugh inside a sob—that loves even more than it loves to live? If there is, can it be expressed in the form of the lyric line?

Dostoevsky defended his later religious belief, saying of his work, "Even in Europe there have never been atheistic expressions of such power. My hosannah has gone through a great furnace of doubt."

According to certain friends, Simone Weil would have given everything she wrote to be a poet. It was an ideal but she was wary of charm and the inauthentic. She saw herself as stuck in fact with a rational prose line for her surgery on modern thought. She might be the archetypal doubter but the language of the lyric was perhaps too uncertain.

As far as we know she wrote a play and some poems and one little prose poem called "Prelude."

Yet Weil could be called a poet, if Wittgenstein could, despite her own estimation of her writing, because of the longing for a transformative insight dominating her word choices.

In "Prelude" the narrator is an uprooted seeker who still hopes that a conversion will come to her from the outside. The desired teacher arrives bearing the best of everything, including delicious wine and bread, affection, tolerance, solidarity (people come and go) and authority. This is a man who even has faith and loves truth.

She is happy. Then suddenly, without any cause, he tells her it's over. She is out on the streets without direction, without memory. Indeed she is unable to remember even what he told her without his presence there to repeat it, this amnesia being the ultimate dereliction.

If memory fails, then the mind is air in a skull. This loss of memory forces her to abandon hope for either rescue or certainty.

And now is the moment where doubt—as an active function— emerges and magnifies the world. It eliminates memory. And it turns eyesight so far outwards, the vision expands. A person feels as if she is the figure inside a mirror, looking outwards for her moves. She is a forgery.

When all the structures granted by common agreement fall away and that "reliable chain of cause and effect" that Hannah Arendt talks about—breaks—then a person's inner logic also collapses. She moves and sees at the same time, which is terrifying.

Yet strangely it is in this moment that doubt shows itself to be the physical double to belief; it is the quality that nourishes willpower, and the one that is the invisible engine behind every step taken. Doubt is what allows a single gesture to have a heart.

In this prose poem Weil's narrator recovers her balance after a series of reactive revulsions to the surrounding culture by confessing to the most palpable human wish: that whoever he was, he loved her.

Hope seems to resist extermination as much as a roach does.

Hannah Arendt talks about the "abyss of nothingness that opens up before any deed that cannot be accounted for." Consciousness of this abyss is the source of belief for most converts. Weil's conviction that evil proves the existence of God is cut out of this consciousness.

Her Terrible Prayer—that she be reduced to a paralyzed nobody—desires an obedience to that moment where coming and going intersect before annihilation.

And her desire: "To be only an intermediary between the blank page and the poem" is a desire for a whole- heartedness that eliminates personality.

Virginia Woolf, a maestro of lyric resistance, was frightened by Freud's claustrophobic determinism since she had no ground of defense against it. The hideous vocabulary of mental science crushed her dazzling star-thoughts into powder and brought her latent despair into the open air. Born into a family devoted to skepticism and experiment, she had made a superhuman effort at creating a prose-world where doubt was a mesmerizing and glorious force.

Anyone who tries, as she did, out of a systematic training in secularism, to forge a rhetoric of belief is fighting against the odds. Disappointments are everywhere waiting to catch you, and an ironic realism is so convincing.

Simone Weil's family was skeptical too, secular and attentive to the development of the mind. Her older brother fed her early sense of inferiority with his condescending intellectual putdowns. Later, her notebooks chart a superhuman effort at conversion to a belief in affliction as a sign of God's presence.

Her prose itself is tense with effort. After all, to convert by choice (that is, without a blast of revelation or a personal disaster) requires that you shift the names for things, and force a new language out of your mind onto the page.

You have to make yourself believe. Is this possible? Can you turn "void" into "God" by switching the words over and over again? Any act of self-salvation is a problem because of death which always has the last laugh, and if there has been a dramatic and continual despair hanging over childhood, then it may even be impossible.

After all, can you call "doubt" "bewilderment" and suddenly be relieved?

Not if your mind has been fatally poisoned . . . But even then, it seems, the dream of having no doubt continues, finding its way into love and work where choices matter exactly as much as they don't matter—when history's things are working in your favor.

(2000)

TOM CLARK (1941–)

❧

Death, Revenge and the Profit Motive

Death is good, revenge is a waste of time, and who ever thought up the profit motive didn't understand either of those things, John said, tipping his head back to pour another drink into it. He was paying twelve hundred dollars a month to keep Mary in a glass and redwood shack with a hot tub in the hippest canyon in town, he said. And now she wouldn't even talk to him, and—he said—he was dying. "But only to get even!"

(1981)

Five Fondly Remembered Passages from My Childhood Reading

"When they had inched about as close as they dared, they crouched down, parted the tall grass and beheld an amazing spectacle. Thousands upon thousands of the tiny creatures had assembled around an old tree stump upon which their leader sat addressing his subjects. As it turned out, the King of the Mice was not a mouse at all, but a small boy!"

L.G. Stevens, *King of the Mice*

"I think it would be great if we got the wagon out of the garage and pulled it around the neighborhood and put things in it," said the Head-on-the-Right.

"I'm tired," said the Head-in-the-Middle.

"Isn't it supposed to get dark soon?" asked the Head-on-the-Left.

"We could collect different things and bring them home and keep them."

"You should have thought of that a little earlier."

"Does your mother know you're here?" asked the Head-on-the-Left.

"I haven't seen my mother for days," said the Head-in-the-Middle, and the heads on either side, eyebrows knitted, turned to look at him and wondered about the consequences of what he had just said.

Penelope Graves, *The Boy with Three Heads*

"Don't forget to take a cardigan," Mother called from the top of the stairs, "just in case you fall into a dark pit full of things with sharp teeth on your way home from the picture show."

Sigert Manes, *The Trouble with Mother*

"Tony, that house you've been pointing to isn't so far off in the distance, you know. It's really just a very small house a few feet in front of you."

"Gee, you're right, Paul. Hey, look, I can reach out and pick it up!"

"Sure, it fits right in your palm."

"Hey, lookit, there's a bunch of little people walking out the front door."

"Careful, some of them are starting to crawl up your arm!"

"Boy, this is really something!"

"One's under your sleeve!"

"Wow!"

R. Enright, *Fun with Perspective*

"Is that you playing the piano in there, Ellen?"

"No, it's Pinky. I told you she was the smartest kitten in the whole wide world!"

"Well, just don't ask me to pay for her lessons!" Mrs. Thompson joked as she entered the music room carrying a tray piled high with delicate china tea things.

Rebacca Wall, *Pinky's World Concert Tour*

(1999)

∾

A Story About the Body

The young composer, working that summer at an artist's colony, had watched her for a week. She was Japanese, a painter, almost sixty, and he thought he was in love with her. He loved her work, and her work was like the way she moved her body, used her hands, looked at him directly when she made amused and considered answers to his questions. One night, walking back from a concert, they came to her door and she turned to him and said, "I think you would like to have me. I would like that too, but I must tell you that I have had a double mastectomy," and when he didn't understand, "I've lost both my breasts." The radiance that he had carried around in his belly and chest cavity—like music—withered very quickly, and he made himself look at her when he said, "I'm sorry. I don't think I could." He walked back to his own cabin through the pines, and in the morning he found a small blue bowl on the porch outside his door. It looked to be full of rose petals, but he found when he picked it up that the rose petals were on top; the rest of the bowl—she must have swept them from the corners of her studio—was full of dead bees.

(1989)

In the Bahamas

The doctor looked at her stitches thoughtfully. A tall lean white man with an English manner. "Have you ever watched your mum sew?" he asked. "The fellow who did this hadn't. I like to take a tuck on the last stitch. That way the skin doesn't bunch up on the ends. Of course, you can't see the difference, but you can feel it." Later she asked him about all the one-armed and one-legged black men she kept seeing in the street. "Diabetic gangrene, mostly. There really isn't more of it here than in your country, but there's less prosthesis. It's expensive, of course. And stumps are rather less of a shock when you come right down to it. Well, as we say, there's nothing colorful about the Caribbean." He tapped each black thread into a silver basin as he plucked it out. "Have you ever been to Haiti? Now there is a truly appalling place."

(1989)

144

Tall Windows

All day you didn't cry or cry out and you felt like sleeping. The desire
to sleep was light bulbs dimming as a powerful appliance kicks on.
You recognized that. As in school it was explained to you that pus
was a brave army of white corpuscles hurling themselves at the viru-
lent invader and dying. Riding through the Netherlands on a train,
you noticed that even the junk was neatly stacked in the junkyards.
There were magpies in the fields beside the watery canals, neat little
houses, tall windows. In Leiden, on the street outside the university,
the house where Descartes lived was mirrored in the canal. There was
a pair of swans and a sense that, without haste or anxiety, all the peo-
ple on the street were going to arrive at their appointments punctu-
ally. Swans and mirrors. And Descartes. It was easy to see how this
European tranquillity would produce a poet like Mallarmé, a middle-
class art like symbolism. And you did not despise the collective
orderliness, the way the clerks in the stores were careful to put bills in
the cash register with the Queen's face facing upward. In the house
next to the house where Descartes lived, a Jewish professor died in
1937. His wife was a Dutch woman of strict Calvinist principles and
she was left with two sons. When the Nazis came in 1940, she went to
court and perjured herself by testifying that her children were con-
ceived during an illicit affair with a Gentile, and when she developed
tuberculosis in 1943, she traded passports with a Jewish friend, since
she was going to die anyway, and took her place on the train to the
camps. Her sons kissed her good-bye on the platform. Eyes open.
What kept you awake was a feeling that everything in the world has
its own size, that if you found its size among the swellings and
diminishings it would be calm and shine.

(1989)

LYN HEJINIAN (1941–)

❧

Three Sections from *My Life*

We have come a long way from what we actually felt

If it were writing we would have to explain. I say that as much to comfort myself as to state something I think to be true. Dashing up out of the dark basement, pursued by the humid fear. Similarly, due to some peculiar sentimentality, people always want the runt of the litter. She sat every afternoon in her chair waiting for her headache, exactly as one might sit on a bench awaiting a bus. In a book I read the sentence, "the water is as blue as ink," which made me regret that so few people use fountain pens. Never give the blindman money without taking one of his pencils. When I went to Christian Science Sunday school, the teacher asked me what I wanted to be when I grew up, and I answered that I wanted to be a writer or a doctor. The words of the last one to speak continued to hover in the air, and that was embarrassing. A name trimmed with colored ribbons. At the circus men were selling live chameleons which wore tiny collars and were attached to red and yellow ribbons that one could pin to one's dress or shirt as a living jewel. As for we who "love to be astonished," mother love. The game of solitaire, of patience, is disappointing when it "comes out" the first time. It is impossible to return to the state of mind in which these sentences originated. So I borrowed my father's typewriter. There was a garden, a hole in the fence, a grandfather who had no religion—one can run through the holes in memory, wearing a wet hat, onto the sidewalk covered with puddles, and there are fingers in them. Similarly, a beautiful concert or an unusual autumn sunset makes me feel restless if I'm by myself, wanting someone with whom to share it. At noon, under no one's new moon. I didn't want the kids over to play, messing with my stuff. We were coughing after a day by the sea. That was the gap between behavior and feeling. This was a year at the breaking point, turning over, given the swift combination. That summer when I was nine I trained myself to hold my breath and stubbornly swim the full length of the pool under water and back, until the returning end of the pool went black. In the telephone room one heard the disembodied voice over the receiver while staring into the row of empty coats and hats, and when we played hide and seek with the other cousins, on those occasions when my grandparents had all the family to dinner, only the oldest cousins dared hide among them. An other is a possibility, isn't it. I have been spoiled with privacy, permitted the luxury of solitude. A pause, a rose, something on paper. I didn't want a party for my tenth birthday, I wanted my mother, who was there, of course, at the party, but from whom I was separated by my friends and because she was busy with the cake and the balloons. She kept a diary but she never read it. Yet those who scorn friendship can, without illusion but not without some remorse, be the finest friends in the world. Now the shower curtain is sexy. The gap indicated that objects or events had been forgotten, that a place was being held for them, should they chance to reappear. The sound of the truck had frightened the towhees away. Like the "big, round O" taught by the traditional penmanship teachers (the Palmer method, it was called), there was a big round "A" and we were to pronounce it, in place of the nasty, narrow "A" in words like cat and Ann. The high curb turned on the curve. The windows on the northwestern wall looked out toward the clock on the so-called Campanile by which my father, far-sighted, kept time. What was the meaning hung from that depend. Apples have bellies. She was a skinny little girl and her bathing suit fit her so loosely that when she sat to play on the beach the sand fell into the crotch and filled it like a little pouch. The toll bridge takes its toll, the span its fog, its paint. Nevertheless fleas, and therefore powders. You are not different from your friend, but with your friend you are different from yourself, and recognizing that, I withdrew, wanting to protect my honesty, because I had defined integrity on two dimensions. I pushed my thumb to make a lever of the blunt spoon, he took up the palette knife and ships came out of the blue, I hit the space bar. Actually I don't remember whether my father went with Braque or was only invited to do so one fine day outside of Paris to paint a landscape in plain air. And finally, on a visit to the zoo, as we were passing by the enclosure where the silver foxes were kept, I saw a flock of sparrows pecking at the ground of the enclosure, and one of them, venturing too close to a fox which was crouching in the shadow of an artificial rock, was suddenly seized by the fox, who swallowed it in a moment.

I wrote my name in every one of his books

It was awhile before I understood what had come between the stars, to form the constellations. They were at a restaurant owned by Danes. Now that I was "old enough to make my own decisions," I dressed like everyone else. People must flatter their own eyes with their pathetic lives. The things I was saying followed logically the things that I had said before, yet they bore no relation to what I was thinking and feeling. There was once a crooked man, who rode a crooked mile—thereafter he wrote in a crooked style characteristic of 19th-century prose, a prose of science with cumulative sentences. The ideal was of American property and she had received it from a farmer. It includes buying thrillers and gunmen's coats. I was more terrified of the FBI agents than of the unspecified man who had kidnapped, murdered,and buried the girl in the other fifth grade in the hill behind school. A pause, a rose, something on paper. It was at about this time that my father provided me with every right phrase about the beauty and wonder of books. Colored cattle were grazing on a California hillside, so much of a single yellow that from this distance and at this hour it was impossible to see any gradation of light and shadow. Individuality is animated by its sense of the infinite. I play a sentimental role. The debater "makes his point," and in games, points tell the winner. These one suddenly finds childish, embarrassing, but not yet dull. Fallow power, bright red and yellow. We say thought wanders where it should sweep. As for we who "love to be astonished," she pretends she is a blacksmith. In the hot lot beside the tire dealer a crew of two eats lunch. There is always plenty to do until one is bored, and then the boredom itself generates the lack, generates its own necessary conditions. The supernatural makes it cry. Now she's a violinist. What is certain, at least, is that one must avoid dishonest work. I quote my mother's mother's mother's mother's mother: "I must every day correct some fault in my morality or talents and remember how short a time I have to live." You might say she created her reality simply because she "would not have it, any other way." It is hard to turn away from moving water. She suggested we take "a nice nap." Even when I was too old for the pony rides at the park, I loved the little creatures, and I watched my younger sister clinging to the saddle horn as the ponies plodded around the narrow circle, feeling superior, since on Saturdays I took riding lessons on real horses, and yet envious, too, since it was not Saturday and it was my sister and not I who was riding now. You are so generous, they told me, allowing everything its place, but what we wanted to hear was a story. A blare of sound, a roar of life, a vast array of human hives, reveling in education. What a situation. Whenever you've exhausted setting, topic, or tone, begin a new paragraph. The refrigerator makes a sound I can't spell. The finches have come at last to the feeder. The magician had come to entertain the children at the birthday party. It was called mush, and we ate it for breakfast in patterns, like pudding. We were like plump birds along the shore. Green night divining trees, scooped too. What memory is not a "gripping" thought. But it's a happy song. It took all day. He had stolen a tin of nuts and given them to me and now I had to return them to the store, like a thief returning to the shelf, but I managed to pull it off and put them back. The romance of the vanished. I had begun to learn, from the experience of passionate generosity, about love.

Yet we insist The windows were open and the morning air
that life is full was, by the smell of lilac and some darker
of happy chance flowering shrub, filled with the brown and
chirping trills of birds. As they are if you could have nothing but quiet and shouting. Arts, also, are links. I picture an idea at the moment I come to it, our collision. Once, for a time, anyone might have been luck's child. Even rain didn't spoil the barbecue, in the backyard behind a polished traffic, through a landscape, along a shore. Freedom then, liberation later. She came to babysit for us in those troubled years directly from the riots, and she said that she dreamed of the day when she would gun down everyone in the financial district. That single telephone is only one hair on the brontosaurus. The coffee drinkers answered ecstatically. If your dog stays out of the room, you get the fleas. In the lull, activity drops. I'm seldom in my dreams without my children. My daughter told me that at some time in school she had learned to think of a poet as a person seated on an iceberg and melting through it. It is a poetry of certainty. In the distance, down the street, the practicing soprano belts the breeze. As for we who "love to be astonished," money makes money, luck makes luck. Moves forward, drives on. Class background is not landscape—still here and there in 1969 I could feel the scope of collectivity. It was the present time for a little while, and not so new as we thought then, the present always after war. Ever since it has been hard

for me to share my time. The yellow of that sad room was again the yellow of naps, where she waited, restless, faithless, for more days. They say that the alternative for the bourgeoisie was gullibility. Call it water and dogs. Reason looks for two, then arranges it from there. But can one imagine a madman in love. Goodbye; enough that was good. There was a pause, a rose, something on paper. I may balk but I won't recede. Because desire is always embarrassing. At the beach, with a fresh flush. The child looks out. The berries are kept in the brambles, on wires on reserve for the birds. At a distance, the sun *is* small. There was no proper Christmas after he died. That triumphant blizzard had brought the city to its knees. I am a stranger to the little girl I was, and more—more strange. But many facts about a life should be left out, they are easily replaced. One sits in a cloven space. Patterns promote an outward likeness, between little white silences. The big trees catch all the moisture from what seems like a dry night. Reflections don't make shade, but shadows are, and do. In order to understand the nature of the collision, one must know something of the nature of the motions involved—that is, a history. He looked at me and smiled and did not look away, and thus a friendship became erotic. Luck was rid of its clover.

(1987)

JOE BRAINARD (1942–1994)

❧

Freud

From Freud we learn that when a wife smashes a vase to the floor it is really her husband's head that lies there broken into many pieces.

History

With history piling up so fast, almost every day is the anniversary of something awful.

(1974)

LOUIS JENKINS (1942–)

~

Football

I take the snap from center, fake to the right, fade back . . . I've got protection. I've got a receiver open downfield. . . . What the hell is this? This isn't a football, it's a shoe, a man's brown leather oxford. A cousin to a football maybe, the same skin, but not the same, a thing made for the earth, not the air. I realize that this is a world where anything is possible and I understand, also, that one often has to make do with what one has. I have eaten pancakes, for instance, with that clear corn syrup on them because there was no maple syrup and they weren't very good. Well, anyway, this is different. (My man downfield is waving his arms.) One has certain responsibilities, one has to make choices. This isn't right and I'm not going to throw it.

(1995)

Appointed Rounds

At first he refused to deliver junk mail because it was stupid, all those deodorant ads, money-making ideas and contests. Then he began to doubt the importance of the other mail he carried. He began to randomly select first class mail for non-delivery. After he had finished his mail route each day he would return home with his handful of letters and put them in the attic. He didn't open them and never even looked at them again. It was as if he were an agent of Fate, capricious and blind. In the several years before he was caught, friends vanished, marriages failed, business deals fell through. Toward the end he became more and more bold, deleting houses, then whole blocks from his route. He began to feel he'd been born in the wrong era. If only he could have been a Pony Express rider galloping into some prairie town with an empty bag, or the runner from Marathon collapsing in the streets of Athens, gasping, "No news."

(1995)

The Prose Poem

The prose poem is not a real poem, of course. One of the major differences is that the prose poet is simply too lazy or too stupid to break the poem into lines. But all writing, even the prose poem, involves a certain amount of skill, just the way throwing a wad of paper, say, into a wastebasket at a distance of twenty feet, requires a certain skill, a skill that, though it may improve hand-eye coordination, does not lead necessarily to an ability to play basketball. Still, it takes practice and thus gives one a way to pass the time, chucking one paper after another at the basket, while the teacher drones on about the poetry of Tennyson.

(2000)

∾

Light as Air

1

It's calm today. I sit outside, or inside by the window, and look out, and for a moment I realize my left hand is holding up my head. I see the light on everything, trees, hills, and clouds, and I do not see the trees, hills, and clouds. I see the light, and it plays over my mind that it is any day, not today, just day.

2

The wind is making the trees swoosh and the volume goes up and down. I have been sitting here for some time, at first looking out at the grass and trees and sky, and then, turning more and more into my mind and its noticing things, gradually looking at nothing of what was before my eyes. A great cutting slash arced across the last turn of the mental pathway I had wandered down and up, and was approaching me from the left. I cocked my head to that left. Slash, slash in the woods. My legs chilled. I will wait until I hear it once more, then I will get up and go inside.

Silence.

3

In times of trouble and despondency I turn to sportswear. I have just added to my wardrobe three pairs of pastel-colored shorts and four light-gray T-shirts and a yellow cotton pullover so elegant and offhand it must have been designed in France. I put on my new clothes, lace up my new white shoes, and see people. They say, "You look nice. Are those shorts new?"

"Yes, they are," I answer.

Then I go back home and sit on the porch under the sky in my new shorts.

I look at you sometimes when you're not aware of it. I look at you in those moments the way a stranger might so I can see you better than I usually do. And in fact you do always look fresh and new and similar to the person I think of as you. I love the way you look. And I feel happy just to be here looking at you, the way the dog sits at the feet of us, his great gods. I sit at the feet of the thing that is you. I look at your feet.

5

I take off my clothes and am in the air, me flowing through it and it flowing around me. I look to the right. The first cottages of the little village, the first houses of the town, the first buildings of the city: bones, flesh, and clothing. Air around it all. Air I cannot breathe, because I am also a structure I am moving past, a tomb, a monument, a big nothing.

He is a man of many vectors, that assemble and reassemble, the way music comes first from the air, then from a piece of wood grown in air. Then the air is in a museum in a country you are not permitted to enter at this time because your vectors are not in order. You must go home and reassemble your rods and cones: night is falling, the soft gray mist of his breath.

7

I dreamed I had become a tall hamburger piloting a plane going down in a remote jungle waving up at me with inexpensive green cardboard natives ecstatic at the arrival, at last, of their messiah. A radiant hamburger bun top opened above me as I floated softly into their gyrating angular green midst.

I come to a mental clearing where I can speak only from the heart. Free of the baggage of who I happen to be, and of all the porters who must carry the baggage, and the exorbitant taxi ride into a fuller version of the same small personality, I take, for what seems to be the first time in a long time, a breath that goes deeper than the bottom of the lungs, and in the pause that comes at the end of that breath there appears a little mirror, light fog on it clearing quickly.

9

The palm of my hand is in Sunday, groggy, sabbatical. The rest of me is in Wednesday, up there and to the left, in the sky. I see you need a light, though you have nothing to smoke. You left your smoking utensils in Thursday. Let me recall my hand and fetch them for you. There, now you are creating puffs. But they do not dissipate. They form shadow copies of my hand that is moving toward your face.

10

It dawns on me that I'm repeating myself. Another day and there I am, calm outside in the air with my hand returning along its vectors. In this mental clearing the photons are jumping all around the savages. Suddenly the witch doctor brings his face to mine and shouts, "Mgwabi! Mgwabi!" pointing to my photons. I reach up and take the light from his face and fold it with the fingers on my hands and it dawns on me that I'm repeating myself.

11

At the end of the light I raise my voice from down there to up here and you are not here. I could shout until the words change colors and it would make no difference. Your vectors are heading out away from the voice of my hand and toward what it is pointing to, that bright cloud over there, the one with the burning edges, handsome and lighter than air at last.

12

A cold streak runs through the sky now the color of wet cement that forms the body of the man whose brain is at a height of more miles than can be found on earth. This emotional absolute zero is like a spine conducting thick fog and thin rain through him, and when the sun's vectors approach his surface they turn and move parallel to it. Who is this big cement man? And how do I know whether or not he is the same who came this morning and threw on the power that sent the electricity branching through my heart?

13

It's dark today. I sit inside, my right hand touching my head. I look at the floor, the fabrics, the smoke from my mouth. It's as if there isn't any light, as if part of things being here is what light they have inseparable from themselves, not visible. The table doesn't stand for anything, although it remembers the tree. The table isn't immortal, though it hums a tune of going on forever. The table is in Friday, with me, both of us here in this dark, miserable day, and I have the feeling I'm smiling, though I'm not.

(1988)

Album

The mental pictures I have of my parents and grandparents and my childhood are beginning to break up into small fragments and get blown away from me into empty space, and the same wind is sucking me toward it ever so gently, so gently as not even to raise a hair on my head (though the truth is that there are very few of them to be raised). I'm starting to take the idea of death as the end of life somewhat harder than before. I used to wonder why people seemed to think that life is tragic or sad. Wasn't it also comic and funny? And beyond all that, wasn't it amazing and marvelous? Yes, but only if you have it. And I am starting not to have it. The pictures are disintegrating, as if their molecules were saying, "I've had enough," ready to go somewhere else and form a new configuration. They betray us, those molecules, we who have loved them. They treat us like dirt.

(2001)

MICHAEL PALMER (1943–)

～

A word is coming up on the screen, give me a moment. In the meantime let me tell you a little something about myself. I was born in Passaic in a small box flying over Dresden one night, lovely figurines. Things mushroomed after that. My cat has twelve toes, like poets in Boston. Upon the microwave she sits, hairless. The children they say, you are no father but a frame, waiting for a painting. Like, who dreamed you up? Like, gag me with a spoon. Snow falls — winter. Things are aglow. One hobby is Southeast Asia, nature another. As a child I slept beneath the bed, fists balled. A face appeared at the window, then another, the same face. We skated and dropped, covering our heads as instructed. Then the music began again, its certainty intact. The true dancers floated past. They are alive to this day, as disappearing ink. After the storm we measured the shore. I grew to four feet then three. I drove a nail through the page and awoke smiling. That was my first smile. In a haze we awaited the next. You said, "Interior colors." You said, "Antinucleons." You said, "Do not steal my words for your work." Snow falls — winter. She hands out photographs of the Union dead. Things are aglow. I traded a name for what followed it. This was useless. The palace of our house has its columns, its palms. A skull in a handcart. I removed a tongue and an arm, but this was useless. On Tuesday Freud told me, "I believe in beards and women with long hair. Do not fall in love." Is there discourse in the tropics? Does the central motif stand out clearly enough? In this name no letters repeat, so it cannot be fixed. Because it's evening I remember memory now. Your English I do not speak. A word is coming up on the screen.

(1988)

JAMES TATE (1943–)

❧

The Second Greatest Story Ever Told

Billy tried several times to wave his hand through some solid object, certain it would give, would prove to be no more than a flimsy projection. And when he lost in this game of confidence, he laughed uproariously, as though to say: I knew it!

He was well into his fourth quart of vodka. He had been drinking for three days. There was definitely something peaceful about it. Clean, neat, clear. The ice-machine couldn't keep up. To hell with it.

He had stopped staggering and was no longer tired. He felt as though he were watching himself on the tube, the skeleton of the story shown through like a timeless Late Movie. The humanity of it overwhelmed him! How he wished to throw his lot in with the pack, a headlong sacrifice! He had thought until now that he was somehow on a stalk, he was the favored jester's tool, comic and frightening, but still the only one of its kind.

He could still call Roberta; she had given him a second chance before. She seemed to see beyond his fluctuations, his flips and twitches. She knew him before he was born. She had been there all along.

Of course the call wouldn't do much good if she knew he was drunk. But he wasn't, not now. Now he saw how they served interlocking fates. She would come back, as always. She would forgive him. They could make it work. They had always said that.

Billy balanced himself against the wall and the table as he made his way toward the kitchen phone. He grabbed for the phone. He lunged and stabbed at it. It was empty air in his hand.

"Not this time, Billy," her voice said.

Billy stared at the evasive phone. His legs crumbled beneath him until he lay like an unpropped dummy against the counter. There's got to be more than this, he slobbered. Now he was drooling all over himself, imitating a bum he had once stumbled over in the Bowery. And then he laughed, remembering the sign the bum had tied around his neck: *The Second Greatest Story Ever Told,* and in pencil below: 5¢. The bum's face was pocked with repulsive sores, mange or leprosy.

Now Roberta's face swam up through the bum's. Billy crawled toward the twin image which shimmered before him 'twixt its double-identity like some cheap modern religious relic. "Come back!" he cried. "I need you!"

(1974)

Same Tits

It was one of those days. I was walking down the St. and this poster glassed in a theater billboard caught my eye. A really gorgeous set of tits. It was noon, hot as hell outside. So I said what the hell, paid my $2.50 and went in. Got a seat all by myself right in the middle. The curtain opens: there's the same poster by itself in the middle of the stage. I sat there sweating. Finally decided to get the hell out of there. It was still noon, hot as hell outside.

(1976)

The List of Famous Hats

Napoleon's hat is an obvious choice I guess to list as a famous hat, but that's not the hat I have in mind. That was his hat for show. I am thinking of his private bathing cap, which in all honesty wasn't much different than the one any jerk might buy at a corner drugstore now, except for two minor eccentricities. The first one isn't even funny: Simply it was a white rubber bathing cap, but too small. Napoleon led such a hectic life ever since his childhood, even farther back than that, that he never had a chance to buy a new bathing cap and still as a grown-up—well, he didn't really grow that much, but his head did: He was a pinhead at birth, and he used, until his death really, the same little tiny bathing cap that he was born in, and this meant that later it was very painful to him and gave him many headaches, as if he needed more. So, he had to vaseline his skull like crazy to even get the thing on. The second eccentricity was that it was a *tricorn* bathing cap. Scholars like to make a lot out of this, and it would be easy to do. My theory is simple-minded to be sure: that beneath his public head there was another head and it was a pyramid or something.

(1986)

Distance from Loved Ones

After her husband died, Zita decided to get the face-lift she had always wanted. Half-way through the operation her blood pressure started to drop, and they had to stop. When Zita tried to fasten her seat-belt for her sad drive home, she threw-out her shoulder. Back at the hospital the doctor examined her and found cancer run rampant throughout her shoulder and arm and elsewhere. Radiation followed. And, now, Zita just sits there in her beauty parlor, bald, crying and crying.

My mother tells me all this on the phone, and I say: Mother, who is Zita?

And my mother says, I am Zita. All my life I have been Zita, bald and crying. And you, my son, who should have known me best, thought I was nothing but your mother.

But, Mother, I say, I am dying . . .

(1989)

Rapture

"If you sit here a long time and are real quiet, you just might get to see one of those blue antelope," I said to Cora. "I'd do anything to see a blue antelope," she said. "I'd take off all my clothes and lie completely still in the grass all day." "That's a good idea," I said, "taking off the clothes, I mean, it's more natural." I'd met Cora in the library the night before and had told her about the blue antelope, so we'd made a date to try and see them. We lay naked next to one another for hours. It is a beautiful, sunny day with a breeze that tickled. Finally, Cora whispered into my ear, "My god, I see them. They're so delicate, so graceful. They're like angels, cornflower angels." I looked at Cora. She was disappearing. She was becoming one of them.

(2000)

Bernie at the Pay Phone

I came out of the post office and there was Bernie Stapleton talking on a pay phone. Bernie had been hiding from me for seven years. I had loaned him a thousand dollars for an emergency and I never heard from him again. He wasn't sure if I had recognized him, so he turned his back to me and hung his head down. Bernie didn't know what it was to earn a living. He just moved from one scam to another, narrowly evading the law. But I had always had a soft spot in my heart for Bernie. I waited at a certain distance for him to get off the phone. I knew he was sweating blood. "Bernie," I said, "where have you been? I've missed you." He was massively uncomfortable. "I've been away. I've been running an investment firm in the Bahamas. Yeah, I've missed you too. How've you been?" "Well, to tell you the truth, I'm kind of down on my luck," I said, which was a lie. "Maybe I could help you out, Simon. If you could come up with, say, a couple hundred bucks, I could turn it into something substantial real fast," he said. Bernie never changed. Everything around us was changing so fast I couldn't keep up, and there was Bernie at the pay phone making nickel and dime deals the way he's always done. "I think I could come up with that much," I said. "Then meet me here tomorrow at three. A little favor for an old friend, that's the least I can do." Bernie was standing tall now. He really believed he was an investment banker in the Bahamas, and not some scuzzy little rat holed up in Shutesbury without a pot to piss in. I admired that to no end. "Thanks, Bernie, I'll see you tomorrow," I said.

(2001)

Triptych

MORNING

6:30	(2)	Sunrise
	(4)	Knowledge
	(5)	Comparative Geography
	(13)	Images and Things
	(71)	Listen and Learn
7:00	(2)	News
	(4)	News
	(5)	WIDE WORLD
	(8)	Public Affairs
7:30	(4)	Young Africans
	(9)	Elsie Aquacade
	(10)	The Young and the Restless
	(13)	Religious Humoresque
	(71)	Espionage
8:00	(2)	Asian Dimension
	(5)	To Be Announced
	(6)	Vanishing Point. A Sentinel in Swamplight; snow falling on black mud.
	(10)	WEATHER. Flood footage, birds hop from branch to branch as the water rises higher and higher.
8:30	(8)	PERIPLUM

	(9)	Mr. Itchy Starlight
	(11)	DUENDE. He drives into a tree, he listens to the apples bounce off the hood of his car.
8:45	(9)	WEATHER. Thunderclaps, the clouds stampede.
	(10)	SUBMISSION
9:00	(2)	Bugs Bunny
	(7)	Snorkeling with Captain Bravo
	(8)	TALES. "Why all this fear and trembling?" said the Wizard to the Shrew. "Is life all you know?"
9:30	(80)	Violence in Blue
	(4)	Lisping Marauder
	(71)	El Reporter
10:00	(7)	SERMON. What part of paradise is made of memory.
	(9)	SCIENCE. A hammock rope is tied around a tree; as the trunk grows the bark swallows the rope and leaves an interesting scar.

10:30 (13) MODERN EXPLORATION. The space a seemingly mindless, rush hour crowd leaves around a raving idiot.

(71) BLINDSPOT

11:00 (2) FANFARE. Blood on a concrete piano.

(4) LOVELORN. Figure on a mountaintop digging up seashells.

(5) Dragonquest

(7) Elizabethan and Nova Scotian Music (with Charles North).

11:30 (9) FEATURE. Telling fortunes by burning seaweed.

(13) MUTINY. Fog drifts up to the house and crashes through the windows. Elephants bark in the distance.

(71) FUTURAMA

AFTERNOON

12:00 (4) News

(7) News and weather. The wind hunting silence.

(8) INQUISITION

12:30 (2) A CHILLING TALE.

A man with long blonde hair hands a threatening note to a teller with long blonde hair.

(13) MODERN EXPLORATION. A deer trying to climb a ladder.

(71) NECROPOLIS

(6) INTERLUDE. Poisoned rats rot in the walls. You vacuum large black flies off the screens.

1:00 (5) WHITE STRAWBERRIES

(7) SNORT. No war buff, me.

(8) Damaged Perspective

(9) APPLIANCES AT AN EXPOSITION

(10) Smut

1:30 (6) TIME SPAN. ". . . and the spiders were singing in the wells."

(71) SCIENCE. An examination into the earwax of various races. Curious results.

(80) WEATHER. Bleak snowlight, black helicopters to the rescue.

1:45 (4) Dream Overload

(5) A Stack of Bibles

2:00 (2) VIGIL. 8 people on a train platform

reading little books.

(4) DISCOVERY. My elbow, the left one, the first time I've noticed it in years. Highlights: scars from unremembered wounds, new hair.

(5) Polyphemus

(13) LA HISTORIA. The men in Columbus' crew are alotted over two liters of red wine per diem.

2:30 (6) Mostly Prose. A bug flies through my eye. The crowd cheers.

(8) CHERISHED FORMS

3:00 (7) Conquistador

(13) MODERN EXPLORATION. Spaces in the air where the wind waits disguised as silence.

4:00 (4) JUMPING JESUS

(5) Split Second

4:30 (6) VANISHING POINT. And I sink through the chilly rain and leafless trees, past the colorful clothes left out on the line.

(8) SPORTS AND WEATHER. Click.

clunk. people bowling in the fog.

5:00 (2) HOMILY. A long lost color returns to earth in a fleet of clouds, ending millennia of heretofore inexplicable melancholia.

(9) BITCH ON WHEELS

6:00 (2) Hitleresque

(13) ARCHAEOLOGY. Pillars strewn wowiezowie across the sea floor of a sunken palladium.

(71) RALPH WONDERFUL

(80) Bucharest

7:00 (2) News

(4) Cow with a hair-lip: Moof.

(7) NEWS AND WEATHER. Intermittent gales which drown the crickets, hundreds of acorns hit the roof and roll down the shingles.

EVENING

7:30 (13) Brahms. Piano Concerto 2 in B flat major.

(45) Pythagoras

8:00 (2) UPDATE. The magicians explain

why they failed.

(9) SOUVENIR.
A pubic hair, a per-
fect 6, on a bar of
soap.

9:00 (7) ART which was not
interested in motion
or time.

(9) HOUR OF BLISS

(11) STRANGE
ENCOUNTER.
"Neither darkness
nor light," said the
Swamp Angel,
"Neither darkness
nor light can fill
my eyes."

10:00 (2) CUISINE. Does
torn bread really
taste better than
sliced bread?

(8) Black Dimes.

10:30 (7) MY BLOOD RAN
COLD

(9) The Young Elpenor.
Besotted, he falls
off roof, breaks
neck, dies. The
sea-dark wine.

(11) KARMA. The live
leafless branches
and the dead tree
against the sky, all
grappling with the
wind.

(71) TIME AND TOL-
ERANCE. An
invisible nude enters
the elevator. She's
chewing gum.

11:00 (2) Moon out of focus

(5) INTERMISSION.
She leaves the table,
her elbows are
wet.

(6) Cloud Armada

(8) Hours bubbling
in the everlasting
wake of paradise.

(11) CANYON.
Another herd face-
less and innumer-
able rushes by
without showing
Biff and Sally the
way out.

11:30 (5) WAVES wearing
warbonnets charge
a pair of plump
identical twins.

(6) FIFI FLEES—
FOUL PLAY
FEARED.

(8) TYPICAL
BAUDELAIRE:
"... no point is
sharper than that
of the infinite."

12:00 (2) LUMINARY.
In 1903, he turned
his attention to the
east ...

(9) WATERLOO.
Napoleon loses
because severe
case of hemorrhoids
prevents him from
concentrating on
the course of the
battle.

(11) FINISHING
    TOUCHES. A
    cloud floats up to

the moon and stops.
Jolting finale
avoided.

(1982)

Acknowledgments

The author wishes to express his profound gratitude to the following publications in which some of these works previously appeared: *Architectural Digest:* "This Lime-tree Bower My Prison"; *Teen Life:* "On the Death of Chatterton"; *Cosmopolitan:* "Constancy to an Ideal Object"; *Bon Appétit:* "Drinking versus Thinking", "The Eagle and the Tortoise"; *La Cucina Italiana:* "Fire, Famine and Slaughter"; *House Beautiful:* "Kublai Khan", "This Lime-tree Bower My Prison"; *Better Homes and Gardens:* "This Lime-tree Bower My Prison", "Reflections on Having Left a Place of Retirement", "Fears in Solitude", "Dejection: an Ode"; *Modern Bride:* "The Rime of the Ancient Mariner"; *American Bride:* "A Lover's Complaint to His Mistress Who Deserted Him in Quest of a More Wealthy Husband in the East Indies"; *Mechanics Illustrated:* "Work Without Hope"; *Popular Mechanics:* "Work Without Hope"; *Interiors:* "Kublai Khan"; *Sports Illustrated:* "Dejection: an Ode"; *Hustler:* "Christabel."

(1999)

JOHN GODFREY (1945–)

⁓

So Let's Look At It Another Way

Any woman who can give birth to God deserves, I think, a pretty lively dole, provided by God, however, not by me. I've got my own eggs to hatch, and my own coat to button in the particulate wind. Gather around me, streetcorners, and I will give you the avenue of your dreams! I will give three sharp coughs while your fingertips read that spot inside my hip, my pelvis tone, my sixth-story bone. I'll be here when the whole *world* shakes, I'll be compatible to cheapness and to achievement. I'll have ambitions on my mind and panties on my floor. I'll have tons of red paint on my black-paint door. And you know what else? I'll call it "killer monkey doing all this stuff too close to prayer."

So let's look at it another way. It's 9 a.m. and I'm walking west from my door. The only person on the shadowed side of the street, and the shadow is cool, is a thin girl with long wavy hair, hiding her face, which she holds down. White girl slinking where to the east? All night long turned to misery crystals by the Hopperesque walls. I beg your pardon, lady, on behalf of your trade. I see on you the marks your monkeys made.

Invisible monkeys blow into the naked eye, and dust big as rocks. October is taking place so beautifully, and when I sleep pain touches my hair. That's why I always seem to be running past parked cars, and past you whom I love. In some crazy way I am running for your pleasure, out of all the pleasures I could imagine.

(1984)

170

BERNADETTE MAYER (1945–)

ᕲ

Visions or Desolation

Come on, there's always the chance kids will do this, fight uncon-
trollably crazy screaming like howling buddhas and tearing each
other's never cut before hair out, the bigger ones hitting the smaller
ones on the heads with metal tops like latent homo- and heterosexu-
als with fierce exclamatory natures. Our plan is to just do everything
ourselves without any babysitters for the next two weeks and then the
classes are over, then we'll go to New York for a while again, the mid-
wife said I had a neat uterus and she could feel whole arms and legs of
the baby, I was waking and talking to a woman on the phone the other
day about a playgroup and she kept using the word "shoot," kept say-
ing, "Shoot I would do anything" and "Shoot I understand what you
mean, yes shoot," then we'll come back here and spend January get-
ting ready to have the baby, then the baby will be born at the end of
that month, I can't find Dr. Spock can you? but before that we have to
gather together all the things we need for the birth and for the baby,
cotton balls and undershirts and roasted towels and a bureau for the
baby's clothes and Marie needs a new coat, and we have to do some
laundry sometime, when she plays outside now and squats to dig in
the dirt the skin of her back is exposed to the air, and they both need
new tights, there isn't any snow on the ground yet, it's easy to rely on
the beat Poets when you're teaching, any more abstract stuff often
turns the students off, they find Frank O'Hara much too difficult, I
also want alot of red velvet material and a big red rug to induce feel-
ings that can go past the moon, it's full again today, those regressive
souls in my classes keep talking about how LSD makes deformed
babies, these matches are called Rosebud because they have red tips of
fire, so many times when you're pregnant people can't help but tell
you all the worst stories they ever heard, I miss the part of Main Street
in Lenox right in front of the bank where the crosswalk led across to
the entrance to the library and the buses and cars came circling
around the obelisk, Henniker's equivalent of an obelisk is a kind of
former fountain on a triangular island at the foot of which is always
lying an old apple core and a discarded ribbon, when I look up I see
a portrait of a man holding a glove, if Russell doesn't see us at all

171

tomorrow perhaps he'll think we're not there, I have only twenty minutes left if I'm going to get any sleep, what can I give you, is writing this offering? Lying in bed is a turmoil, anything can enter in, early tomorrow a woman will come with some children, she will be able to explain things to me about this town, she teaches cross-country skiing, now why don't I do something like that instead of wondering only about babies, poetry, the city, the country and the wisdom I was trying to talk to you about, yet I must've sounded a little corrupt when I said that. I do wonder also about you and your way of slumping in a chair which confounds your other way of looking like a jogger in pajamas, I shouldn't mention pajamas or everyone will make fun of me, I'm sort of looking forward to this January of heavy snows and waiting, bitter cold and never parting again for a while. I don't like teaching, it distracts us, it's like everything else everybody says is healthy, skiing jogging and sitting up straight and being independent, eating seaweed and living in the country, the protean brain, or the other way around: Montherlant is nothing if not protean. A peninsula is a body of land almost completely surrounded by water. Some old people live on one can of soup a day. A little peach in the orchard grew, a little peach of emerald hue. . . . I was reading this novel about a man who burned his girlfriend's house down and then later was almost completely the cause of her father's death and they try to make a case for this rogue being rather an expression of the girl's own destructive instincts so the book winds up without a sense of humor (ENDLESS LOVE) and so am I, it's better to go back to NOTES FROM THE UNDERGROUND for that. More subtle like the weather's blatancy (does that mean wind?). But I'm sure you never asked me for my opinions, you asked me for something of beauty, like the idea of the constructing of a house, something less than esoteric, something formal that also has a use, a wedding song or a description of some semiprecious stones. How am I supposed to fit into this life where children eat so much expensive fruit and leave their trucks in the sand to be run over by the diaper man, will the fleshy inflorescence of a collection of color photographs still look like a pineapple or pine cone or a small bomb that looks like one of those? You and I like having each other to ourselves, I compare the two hands of the two yous but I still can't tell if the hurt one is swollen, why do we have so many injuries lately, is it wrong to walk into a door or let windows slam on your hands, to be slightly stabbed by the midwife to determine the iron content. . . . Something shifts and as Wittgenstein would say, and anybody else not normal, to take some pleasure in being obsessively careful, to quietly comb out the baby's hair and take one's time, to decorate the children with ribbons and whisper to them, to prepare special foods, secret inducements, to linger conversing about the dreams in bed, to encourage the counting of peanuts, these are the methods of the usual, inducements to the ordinary, to pass the time, to adduce pleasure, to encounter danger, to see silver spots before the eyes without fear, the safest form within which to take risks, the advertisement of the day's misery if I can still look up and see the man with the glove and a chance image of the accumulation of objects, the storehouse of pictures which will not work out in memory, there's only one time when you can't be doing this or that kind of work and have something like a drink make it easier than it is, and that's when you're giving birth to a baby but there's nothing new about that. I wish I could try it as a man for once and be the one watching nervously instead of the inhabitant of this always female body, always momentarily fertile and prone to that if I can use that word, it's worse than taking LSD, not over till it's over, hoping the baby will be born before another child wakes up, warning people that your screams are not real screams like in a movie or book, expressions of the forward movement of time or movements of the forward expression of time like words, in that case scream is to lean forward and make the time pass faster, hours by clocks in what they still call labor, different from plain work, working in contractions of the muscles of the . . . and so on, you know all about it I'm sure, lucidly there's space in between during which you feel like yourself again and that is like the book, then when the baby is finally born you don't know for a moment if you're thinking of yourself or the other, there's no reason why the words other and mother ought like an otter to rhyme, they didn't in Middle English, but then you wouldn't want to know the derivations for mother, the lees or dregs, I won't go into that, which is why it's difficult to remember to immediately hold the baby, you don't know the baby is different from you, especially if someone else is there. I had a baby once drawn out by forceps from my unwitting unconscious body and when I woke up I said, what was it. It's worth the tedious trip of consciousness with all the unnecessary pains to thus conquer nature with memory's astuteness, it's like the perception of color in after images. There is an end to the sensation, so of this letter.

(1992)

ALICE NOTLEY (1945–)

Untitled

the purple menstrual blood on the toilet paper, with small clots is the horse's. the horse in blinders goes. silver spine behind a shape. in a long blue dress in the cave, I asked the golden light to make me warm but it did not. there were other secretions on the toilet paper, sticky familiar substances. I can't identify which would signify grief if I were meaning the realm of the cries of the throat of the city pigeon hated. she wrote all over my door, I said I have to live here you know. there are blunt boxlike black shapes ahead. every one of them means its silence as the light breathes and grows in the cool cabriolet pulled by a horse unseen. then we were aboard a ship, and the horse swam alongside, I was taking the most elementary course afraid I wouldn't pass the test, because the diction of the essays must be elegant, the drawings exquisitely textured, how can there be a test going on? I call the predator to my shoulder, I remember to walk. I'm leaving the cafe before the reading, which they the young can give. I'll go wherever I want. the blood on my thighs.

you will will you. the feelings are a puddle of purple for wisdom blood, and the other secretions are objective as well but still unnamed by society: the last of the idea of a nature. you can grieve for the loss of identity, if you want to. the parts have not been fitting. that's why "I" arrived. "I" will neither take the course nor bother about the blood any more. "I" is the horse, "I" is I, am in my metallics, as the box was similar metal-encased I, casting off, the images are meaningless, but there. I stopped reflecting the stain grew and the purple saturated the sheet. the one who tells us about the horse is pale and pure. the menses of a horse in the room of painful emissions, of a house. in a house. this horse. and trees bend down in the whole world denied, grief only encounters ashtrays as if I were smoking, put it out. I'm free because there's much less to matter to, I am freer, I'm the overseer of the body.

my hair is a mess, uncombed, pinned back and up, all brown. I'm wearing a denim skirt, and denim jacket. I help the young man with spiky hair position himself behind the microphone, then I leave the room, a cafe where a poetry reading will take place. to the side are two other young poets with spiky hair, sitting in highchairs. I leave to the cave as always because alone I is free, the long blue dress is to see that blue is its choice of image but the meaning was forgotten. I has been selected because I couldn't simplify my direction. I knows everything next. I in blue, I with owl, I into light, I fly up or down. I the horse and I bleeds, that is just bleeding. I is secreting emotional and intellectual matter, soft and dark, I doesn't I don't need it any more.

(2002)

Seurat

It is a Sunday afternoon on the Grand Canal. We are watching the sailboats trying to sail along without wind. Small rowboats are making their incisions on the water, only to have the wounds seal up again soon after they pass. In the background, smoke from the factories and smoke from the steamboats merge into tiny clouds above us, then disappears. Our mothers and fathers walk arm in arm along the shore clutching tightly their umbrellas and canes. We are sitting on a blanket in the foreground, but even if someone were to take a photograph, only our closest relatives would recognize us: we seem to be burying our heads between our knees.

I remember thinking you were one of the most delicate women I had ever seen. Your bones seemed small and fragile as a rabbit's. Even so, beads of perspiration begin to form on your wrist and forehead— if we were to live long enough we'd have been amazed at how many clothes we forced ourselves to wear. At this time I had never seen you without your petticoats, and if I ever gave thought to such a possibility I'd chastise myself for not offering you sufficient respect.

The sun is very hot. Why is it no one complains of the heat in France? There are women doing their needlework, men reading, a man in a bowler hat smoking a pipe. The noise of the children is absorbed by the trees. The air is full of idleness, there is the faint aroma of lilies coming from somewhere. We discuss what we want for ourselves, abstractly, it seems only right on a day like this. I have ambitions to be a painter, and you want a small family and a cottage in the country. We make everything sound so simple because we believe everything is still possible. The small tragedies of our parents have not yet made an impression on us. We should be grateful, but we're too awkward to think hard about very much.

I throw a scaling rock into the water; I have strong arms and before the rock sinks it seems to have nearly reached the other side.

When we get up we have a sense of our own importance. We could not know, taking a step back, looking at the total picture, that we would occupy such a small corner of the canvas, and that even then we are no more than tiny clusters of dots, carefully placed together without touching.

(1975)

❧

Stereo

Marriage marriage is like you say everything everything in stereo stereo fall fall on the bed bed at dawn dawn because you work work all night. Night is an apartment. Meant to be marriage. Marriage is an apartment & meant people people come in in because when when you marry marry chances are there will be edibles edibles to eat at tables tables in the house. House will be the apartment which is night night. There there will be a bed bed & an extra bed bed a clean sheet sheet sheet or two two for guests guests one extra towel. Extra towel. How will you be welcomed? There will be drinks drinks galore galore brought by armies of guests guests casks casks of liquors liquors and brandies brandies elixirs sweet & bitter bitter bottle of Merlot Merlot Bustelo coffee. Will you have some when I offer. When you are married married there will be handsome gifts for the kitchen kitchen sometimes two of every thing. Everything is brand brand new new. Espresso coffee cups, a Finnish plate, a clock, a doormat, pieces of Art. And books of astonishing Medical Science with pictures. Even richer lexicons. When you are married married there will be more sheets sheets & towels towels arriving arriving & often often a pet pet or two two. You definitely need a telephone when you are married. Two two lines lines. You need need separate separate electronicmail electronicmail accounts accounts. When you are married married you will have sets sets of things things, of more sheets and towels matching, you will have duplicates of things, you will have just one tablecloth. When you are married married you will be responsible when neighbors neighbors greet you. You will smile smile in unison unison or you might say he is fine, she is fine, o she is just down with a cold, o he is consoling a weary traveler just now, arrived from across the Plains. She my husband is due home soon, he my wife is busy at the moment, my husband he is very very busy busy at the moment moment this very moment. Meant good-bye, good-bye. When you are married married sex sex will happen happen without delay delay. You will have a mailbox mailbox and a doorbell doorbell. Bell bell ring ring it rings rings again a double time. You do not have to answer. That's sure for when you are married people people understand understand you do not not have to answer answer a doorbell doorbell because sex sex may happen happen without delay delay. You will hear everything twice, through your ears and the ears of the other. Her or him as a case case maybe be. He & he & her & her as a case case may be may be. When you are married married you can play play with names names and rename yourself if you like. You can add a name, have a double name with a hyphen if you like. You can open joint accounts when you are married. Marriage is no guarantee against depression. A shun is no guarantee against anything. Marriage is no guarantee against resolution. Revolution is a tricky word word. Here, you hear here? Marriage is sweeter sweeter than you think. Think.

(2000)

~

Shoot the Horse

They wanted my brother-in-law to shoot the horse. They said, "The horse must die." My brother-in-law liked horses and sure didn't want to shoot one. But what could he do? The people who said "The horse must die" were rich and powerful. They owned many things—the horse for one. What they said went. If they said to you "Go fuck yourself," you did. If they said "Beat it," you beat it. If they said "Eat shit," you had to eat shit. You had to do what they told you. They said to him, "The horse must die. Shoot the horse." So my brother-in-law got his gun.

Once I was in the woods with my brother-in-law. It was in the middle of winter and we both wore snow-shoes. We came to a stream deep in the woods and he told me that he had to go check something and that I should wait for him. I said okay. He left and I waited about an hour and a half for him to come back. I was afraid to move since I figured that I'd get lost. I was sure that I would be attacked by bats, snakes, bears, whatever might live in the woods. But finally he came back before anything had a chance to attack me. Another time he gave me a rifle to carry in case we might meet up with any bobcats. There was a bounty on bobcats at that time which meant that if you shot one, you could collect some money.

But he sure didn't want to shoot the horse. He just had to shoot it because they told him to. So he got his gun and walked over to the stable. An Oriental gentleman took care of the horse. My brother-in-law walked right up to the Oriental gentleman and said, "I come to shoot this horse." The Oriental gentleman asked, "Why?" My brother-in-law said, "Because they told me to." So the Oriental gentleman brought the horse out of the stable for my brother-in-law to shoot.

It was a real nice day, the day my brother-in-law shot the horse. The sun was shining and the green mountains looked very pretty. The horse was quite handsome and popular. The Oriental gentleman started to cry. The horse looked at my brother-in-law. But my brother-in-law looked right back at him. He said to the horse, "I come to shoot you dead," and he lifted his gun, took aim, and shot the horse in the neck.

But the horse took off, heading for the woods. Blood was spouting from his neck. My brother-in-law took off after him. Soon they were in the woods and the blood from the horse's neck was gushing out all over the trees. My brother-in-law shot the horse in the ass and the horse started to bleed from the ass too. But he kept running with my brother-in-law chasing him. My brother-in-law kept after him, but he was getting tired. He didn't know how the horse could have so much blood inside him. He got very angry at the horse. He yelled to the horse, "I'll kill you, you sorry son of a bitch" and "I'll blow your stupid fucking head off, you sorry son of a bitch." The ordeal was very frustrating for my brother-in-law.

My brother-in-law was covered with horse blood. He had been chasing the horse for about twenty minutes, but the horse kept going. It seemed like there was rich red horse blood splattered all over the woods. My brother-in-law knew that he wouldn't be able to chase the horse much longer. The horse wasn't going too fast, but he just never stopped long enough for my brother-in-law to get a good shot off into his brain.

Finally, my brother-in-law collapsed and the horse kept going. He lay on the ground for a minute, soaked with warm horse blood, and when he looked up again, there was no sign of the horse, except for the trail of horse blood. My brother-in-law got up and said, "You fucking sorry son of a bitch." What would he tell the people who had said to him "The horse must die"?

My brother-in-law staggered back to the stable where he had first shot the horse in the neck. The Oriental gentleman was there and was still crying. When he saw how my brother-in-law was drenched in blood, he became terribly frightened.

My brother-in-law was so angry and frustrated that he shot the Oriental gentleman in the face. As he shot him, he said, "You sorry son of a bitch." The Oriental gentleman's hands flung up to his face when he got shot, but there was nothing there but bloody mush and he was dead already anyway.

The people who told him to "shoot the horse" were very understanding when my brother-in-law explained what had happened. "Those things happen," they said.

(1975)

B.J. ATWOOD-FUKUDA (1946–)

∾

The Wreck of the *Platonic*

The guy at the next table reminded her of her first serious boyfriend, but even as the word *serious* surfaced to the chattery part of her brain that was already watching someone hear her tell the story long since gone barnacle-encrusted as myth, already hearing her own voice run it out like Morse code on the quiet of a moonless, star-splattered sky, she realized as if pronouncing it for the very first time what a euphemism *serious* was, I mean it might have served some purpose in the early sixties when anyone would have understood that it meant the first boy she'd *fucked*, not loved, since in those days girls rarely fucked their first loves, assuming that girls back then loved for the first time at thirteen or fourteen the way they do now only more intensely, if anything, since girls back then not only didn't assume that the relationship, which they didn't call it, if any, would be consummated but, if they'd been raised in those days of the double standard to be, well, *nice*, they were mostly scared silly of the very idea notwithstanding the depth of their craving, the intensity of their fascination with the throbbing flesh for which it, mere 'very idea' in the starch voices of a million middle-class white moms, was but a limp stand-in, a shriveled shill, a most unreasonable, wimpy facsimile thereof. So they built the ship *Platonic* to warn us not to screw; what it had to do with Plato, we didn't have a clue. Poor Plato, alas, lamented the incapacity of chairs to approach the ideal of chairness; no chair, however hard it might try, could ever achieve in his eyes the beauty of that naked, unmediated state. Poor Plato, obsessed with chairs. No wonder she and her girlfriends had wondered why abstinence was called Platonic or, more precisely, why it meant not-fucking, since if they'd run into the word at all it would have been somebody's uncle in AA, and who ever talked about that back then; and finally, when they got to philosophy in school, how the hell Platonic got conjured from Plato, a man who had once lived and breathed and jerked himself off, they supposed, against the backs of chairs in various states of imperfection—rocky, rickety, rocking—the doctor in the deep blue sea only knew. Poor Plato, lured off his true and proper course, fetched up on a floating slagheap of sophistry, hoisted on a pinnacle of pieties arch and brittle as ice. O they built the ship *Platonic* to warn us not to screw, and they thought we'd get on board and enjoy the frigid view. Were they wrong. Young girls and boys saw right through their parents' ploys, husbands and wives had to reassess their lives. Was it sad? no doubt, o so sad, she thought as she eyed the guy at the next table over and watched that clone of her first serious boyfriend lean back in his chair so it squealed and moaned under his weight, so its legs thrust up to reveal at once the fragility and force of the attachment, the dazzling impermanence of the greater whole—a form which surpassed, in its corporeal perfection, any ideal to which it might have sought or been forbidden to aspire. O spire, o pinnacle of pieties erupting on the sweet breath of night, plunging into the dark, fragrant, teeming, blooming sea. How they lied, yee-hah! how we laughed and cried, how they sighed when that great ship went down.

(1999)

ANDREI CODRESCU (1946–)

༄

De Natura Rerum

I sell myths not poems. With each poem goes a little myth. This myth is not in the poem. It's in my mind. And when the editors of magazines ask me for poems I make them pay for my work by passing along these little myths which I make up. These myths appear at the end of the magazine under the heading ABOUT CONTRIBUTORS or above my poems in italics. Very soon there are as many myths as there are poems and ultimately this is good because each poem does, this way, bring another poet into the world. With this secret method of defying birth controls I populate the world with poets.

(1973)

Secret Training

The busdriver of the Mission bus at 1 A.M. is a statistician of chance, he computes his run of luck by mentally guessing how many people will get on his bus at each stop. Every time he guesses wrong he chalks it up to the ODDS column; when he guesses right he puts it in EVENS. This way he learns the ratio of occurrence of luck in his guesses and cunningly uses his knowledge to win his way through Las Vegas and Monte Carlo to owning a giant fleet of taxicabs in which he introduces a strange sort of meter that charges passengers not according to miles travelled but to random guesses based on the character, wealth and astrological signs of the clientele; these meters are so accurately timed to the owner's ratio of luck that soon he is rich enough to own an airline but this airline is soon outlawed and the owner put in jail because half the planes crash for inexplicable reasons through sudden streaks of disorder in his relations to chance.

(1973)

Power

Power is an inferiority complex wound up like a clock by an inability to relax. At the height of my power I have to be taken to a power source in the woods where I am recharged. This power source is not actually in the woods: it's in my mother. It hums quietly in her heart like an atomic plant and the place to plug in is her eyes.

(1973)

❦

Bases

Birds in flight switch places above and below a hypothetical bar—
like a visual trill—though imitation in vulgar.

The idea that each individual is a unique strain: weight and counter-
weight in the organization of memory. So many forms representing,
presumably, a few wishes.

Chew the fat in order to spill the milk, in other words, from which the
selfsame woman emerges.

What the cool tomato cubes forming a rosette around this central
olive have to do with love and happiness.

Thrilled to elaborate some striking variant of what we imagine to be
a general, if fabricated, condition.

Two men on the street wax their teal-green, 50's Mercury.

She thinks the two are lovers, but you say you disagree. Now she's
angry either because you mimic, or because you merely mimic, igno-
rance of such things.

She uses intercourse to symbolize persuasion.

Old people never appear to have reserved judgment in the manner of
a poised beauty.

She dreamed the ill were allowed to wander at ease through the
reconstructed, but vacant, Indian village.

Her eyes scanning the near range with a feeble sense of their being like
children sledding, though never having done that adds a campiness to
the "Whoo-ee" of "I see."

You're not crying because you can't find the thing you made, but because she won't help. She won't because she's comfortable, reading—but not really because now you've stuck your head behind her shoulder sobbing and pretending to gasp. She goes away to pick up your clothes, but also to see if she can find the thing you want. You tell her it looks like a crab. While she's gone you find it underneath her chair. You insist, bitterly, that you knew where it was all along; you were just testing her ability to see. It's like keeping her eye on a bouncing dot. She says either you're lying now or you were lying before when you were sobbing for it and needed her help. Really she thinks you were lying both times, all along, but not exactly.

Now the news is of polls which measure our reactions to duplicity.

She puts her tongue to the small hole, imitating accuracy.

(1988)

Middle Men

The story is told from the view-point of two young technicians, one fat and one thin, who must give their superior a moment by moment account of their attempts to monitor the subject. Suspense occurs, occasionally, when they must tell the superior that they're having trouble keeping the listening devices within range. We sympathize with the hunted subject, but also with the clearly competent, frequently exasperated technicians, whose situation is, after all, much more like our own.

(1999)

Imaginary Places

Reading, we are allowed to follow someone else's train of thought as it starts off for an imaginary place. This train has been produced for us—or rather materialized and extended until it is almost nothing like the ephemeral realizations with which we're familiar. To see words pulled one by one into existence is to intrude on a privacy of sorts. But we *are* familiar with the contract between spectator and performer. Now the text isn't a train but an actress/model who takes off her school uniform piece by piece alone with the camera man. She's a good girl playing at being bad, all the time knowing better. She invites us to join her in that knowledge. But this is getting us nowhere.

(2002)

MICHAEL BURKARD (1947–)

∾

A Conversation About Memory

"Today I was hungry and I wanted to ask how I appeared to someone else." The moon also starves in the illusion of the raft. "The trees are like old doors" but are they: for the cold horse the hair is with fire and, because the detail of the moon is blood, neither retrieves the flowers you remember from the coast, because that is easy. Can we agree shame is the lifting of the main purpose, I mean taking it out as if you were driving only to see the lights drift, as if you were alone: you do not even want to stop for the mines and yes, all that past is now conclusive as the darkness dripping with grass, because the house is too heavy, an escape, and you can only relax in the window. "Another person is breaking into the water" and if you could accompany them you could feel bad, an instrument for black stars. This is the third time you have tried to speak to you. In three coats, moving up the street to three houses, "the always burnt figure of the branches" ascending only as air, in the air of being farther from you than ever before: keeping parts of the road lit, interminable "parts" because there is no returning to their location. Someone *has* drowned, and if the hands are a poor construction it is the sea then, and the stars, interminable as parts, even, and yet a strange kind of wreckage. You have summarized this before, you thought the nets had repeated two distances. Each repeated the other. Kneel near a fire: "The hands release whatever they've been holding." Enough, yet this is not the way night begins. Yet night dedicates this, as your death, as your going simply into another field.

(1977)

◦∿◦

The Thirteenth Woman

In a town of twelve women there was a thirteenth. No one admitted she lived there, no mail came for her, no one spoke of her, no one asked after her, no one sold bread to her, no one bought anything from her, no one returned her glance, no one knocked on her door; the rain did not fall on her, the sun never shone on her, the day never dawned on her, the night never fell for her; for her the weeks did not pass, the years did not roll by; her house was unnumbered, her garden untended, her path not trod upon, her bed not slept in, her food not eaten, her clothes not worn; and yet in spite of all this she continued to live in the town without resenting what it did to her.

(1976)

In the Garment District

A man has been making deliveries in the garment district for years now: every morning he takes the same garments on a moving rack through the streets to a shop and every evening takes them back again to the warehouse. This happens because there is a dispute between the shop and the warehouse which cannot be settled: the shop denies it ever ordered the clothes, which are badly made and of cheap material and by now years out of style; while the warehouse will not take responsibility because the clothes are paid for and of no use to the wholesalers. To the man all this is nothing. They are not his clothes, he gets paid for this work, and anyway he intends to leave the company soon, though the right moment has not yet come.

(1992)

Agreement

First she walked out, and then while she was out he walked out. No, before she walked out, he walked out on her, not long after he came home, because of something she said. He did not say how long he would be gone or where he was going, because he was angry. He did not say anything except "That's it." Then, while he was out, she walked out on him and went down the road with the children. Then, while she was out, he came back, and when she did not return and it grew dark, he went out looking for her. She returned without seeing him, and after she had been back some time, she walked out again with the children to find him. Later, he said she had walked out on him, and she agreed that she had walked out on him, but said she had only walked out on him after he walked out on her. Then he agreed that he had walked out on her, but only after she said something she should not have said. He said she should agree that she should not have said what she said and that she had caused the evening's harm. She agreed that she should not have said what she said, but then went on to say that the trouble between them had started before, and if she agreed she had caused the evening's harm, he should agree he had caused what started the trouble before. But he would not agree to that, not yet anyway.

(1997)

AARON FOGEL (1947–)

❧

The Chessboard Is on Fire

1

The ant stood up on two legs looks like a chesspiece maybe a bishop.

These wooden rings of different radii, stacked concentrically—make a chesspiece, which one not clear, because it's on fire, unidentifiable, unmistakable. But you don't know what we mean, we're all gangsters without a gang, fantoccini.

The stained and clear glass windows alternate. A demographic priest, full of impatient proverbs, speaks under a baldachin of twisted trees—of life—is it?

2

"... if those shmigglaroonies that live their shithead lives in bilkoland had only once said to me, look here, shmiggle ... then I'd have what to go on, to begin the negotiations ..." "Shokh mat!'"

"That pligl calls everybody he knows a shmiggle." That's Italian. "Shah mat!"

("Lift up your Hefty bag and look in it midsummer when the larvae swarm and tell me if in that douchebag you don't see the provost's and the censor's scared imaginations: crowded dreams numerousness without numinousness imaginary gluts of people overpopulation smirks on shifting faces street, tunnel, wall, orange fire escape, street, crossings, tracks, another tunnel, swarming over the leftover rightover cartons and the rest to get out")

3

In a sandbank in the parish of Uig near peat moss and shipwreck they found chesspieces, figurines, robust, humorous. The bishops hold crozier hooks to their cheeks; some bless; some read books; the knights grim, compact; the queens palm their faces, pin-eyed, aghast; the kings lean forward over their swords. Scored shapes, cornery ovals with flat bases, serve as pawns. Our pieces are more abstract.

Rings above rings! Closed horseshoes, thrown simply, by a kilned ghost, across the yard, the ceramist.

4

This hominid ant on two legs looks like a chesspiece: he holds a bishopric or a rookery.

He's got a diagonal strategy — pawns massacred — massacres pawned. All activities, no actions, half ground, Brueghel's picture, the census at Bethlehem, activities, local accountability; and slightly past that to a freer infinite, the other census, with no need for the one infinite birth to offset particular births: so in the sheen of bad demography, a poetic sheen that offsets particular shinings, the poetries become self-appointed local juntas, amphitheaters of northern dream violence, drama exiled south to machiavellian theaters.

Hey, lettuce head, you're the only narrator left. Think your way from the migrant workers' hands to the neoconservatives' tables, dialogue's got all the vowels starting with i, pretty green, but hey see here they in this mercurial estuary the fish dying the they in an alchemy of quicksilver freedoms.

5

University warden or lieutenant or whatever plant who grows in linoleum and reads verse; complacent easy demographer "population explosion" p's of rigged terror baby "booms"; collectivity-designer; exponential resistance polyrhythms logistics; percussion apocussion; eyes closed he listens to the late Autumn holocaust poem, savoring the December cadences (what polysemy!) nugae marketed, streaks of quotational blood. Just like that, yes just. Translation-worship. Frieda used to say over and over: "I did not do my work." An autistic child. A diagnosis of agnosia.

"Yiddish — well. We believe in communication."

6

An ant stands up on two legs — looks around defiantly like a chesspiece.

The new moon's dark bundling says: you didn't do your job your job is to migrate.

The most important migration's perhaps from perhaps to maybe and if you ask us whether we've made it the answer's maybe.

Exempt and stet! Right in the halfmoon's face: you have no right to question us you have aphasia.

The father feared unemployment; his courage was broken. A cold Memorial day. Winter dovetails with summer.

Blacklists: long Washington wall. A fear of migration. To read Yiddish well!

7

The sun slid forced to behind the checkered clouds on the reflective umbrella over the chessmaster's head (he made his living in a dirty yellow straw hat playing in public seldom interrogated by the sergeants). He played there in University Square under a striped umbrella in the checkering rain. It was still raining. He was still winning. Someone was reading a poem by Auden there, every long line of it like the technical name of a newly instituted disease, but though the square was vibrant in the chickenshit rain that caulked the bricks with light and the hominid ants upstanding like chesspieces slid quietly toward a decent autism in old auditoriums in still worse places there was unlikely and banal torture, activity furious at not being action. Omnia migrant, one ant said. Apocussion.

8

But prose is Moses. — "We'd made a mistake and had been making it for millennia, not nihilism it was messianism and had been treeing us for god doesn't know how long and the truth is if it weren't for Moses' migratory nonmessianic ideas he had nothing to do with a messiah or for that matter if it weren't for his brother's nonmessianic staff stiff negotiatory rhetoric and empty apostrophes and empty dialogues there'd be no movement away from the slave civilization. Neither the symbols nor the negotiations saved us. Rescued not saved. He died there: migratory nonmessiah. To remain slaves we invented the idea of a messiah. The mistake: there are no translations; no messiahs, symbols of negotiation; only the empty negotiations themselves. So then we were looking out the windows of the rainrunneled shmigglaroonie cars ourselves and saw the migrant children in the fields lifting heavily as if they were trying to hoist up their parents' toys."

Now we know what you mean (of coerce, of coerce).

9

Judah and dialogue!

(Cupid's darts and the black map arrows of migration. "Let the trapped wizards who yawn in their music boxes stay there if they want to in the pawn shops." "All the board!" the three-year-old shouts joyously over his electric trains. "All the board!")

The chessboard is on fire. The flat, even squares of handcrafted wood burn evenly. No children in no fields. Rails. In the game, the king is never actually taken off, but if the board burns, the king also burns. The bishop becomes himself for the first time. The train: the terrain. You grasped it from the start (they told me about it when I was too young) so don't pretend now that this is some obscure language when all of them are private, exclusionary genocidal dialects. You are a wonderful translator. You catch the defensive truth of the original. In the well of Yiddish. Now you buried yourselves in translations instead of dialogue because it was safer to audit elsewhere than to listen to your own people, though dialogue is the wrong term for something else.

Over the mercurial estuary a kind of nonmessianic sunlight. It's not a story. The story of the stories isn't a store.

(1990)

YUSEF KOMUNYAKAA (1947–)

～

Nude Interrogation

Did you kill anyone over there? Angelica shifts her gaze from the Janis Joplin poster to the Jimi Hendrix, lifting the pale muslin blouse over her head. The blacklight deepens the blues when the needle drops into the first groove of "All Along the Watchtower." I don't want to look at the floor. *Did you kill anyone? Did you dig a hole, crawl inside, and wait for your target?* Her miniskirt drops into a rainbow at her feet. Sandalwood incense hangs a slow comet of perfume over the room. I shake my head. She unhooks her bra and flings it against a bookcase made of plywood and cinderblocks. *Did you use an M-16, a hand-grenade, a bayonet, or your own two strong hands, both thumbs pressed against that little bird in the throat?* She stands with her left thumb hooked into the elastic of her sky-blue panties. When she flicks off the blacklight, snowy hills rush up to the windows. *Did you kill anyone over there? Are you right-handed or left-handed? Did you drop your gun afterwards? Did you kneel beside the corpse and turn it over?* She's nude against the falling snow. *Yes.* The record spins like a bull's-eye on the far wall of Xanadu. *Yes,* I say. *I was scared of the silence. The night was too big. And afterwards, I couldn't stop looking up at the sky.*

(1998)

197

The Hanoi Market

It smells of sea and earth, of things dying and newly born. Duck eggs, pig feet, mandarin oranges. Wooden bins and metal boxes of nails, screws, ratchets, balled copper wire, brass fittings, jet and helicopter gadgets, lug wrenches, bolts of silk, see-through paper, bamboo calligraphy pens, and curios hammered out of artillery shells.

Faces painted on coconuts. Polished to a knife-edge or sealed in layers of dust and grease, cogs and flywheels await secret missions. Aphrodisiacs for dream merchants. A silent storm moves through this place. Someone's worked sweat into the sweet loaves of bread lined up like coffins on a stone slab.

She tosses her blonde hair back and smiles down at everyone. Is it the squid and shrimp we ate at lunch, am I seeing things? An adjacent stall blooms with peacock feathers. The T-shirt waves like a pennant as a sluggish fan slices the humidity.

I remember her white dress billowing up in a blast of warm air from a steel grate in New York City, reminding me of Miss Firecracker flapping like a flag from an APC antenna. Did we kill each other for this?

I stop at a table of figurines. What was meant to tear off a leg or arm twenty years ago, now is a child's toy I can't stop touching.

Maybe Marilyn thought she'd erase herself from our minds, but she's here when the fan flutters the T-shirt silkscreened with her face. The artist used five shades of red to get her smile right.

A door left ajar by a wedge of sunlight. Below the T-shirt, at the end of two rows of wooden bins, a chicken is tied directly across from a caged snake. Bright skin—deadly bite. I move from the chicken to the snake, caught in their hypnotic plea.

(1998)

A Summer Night in Hanoi

When the moviehouse lights click off and images flicker-dance against the white walls, I hear Billie's whispered lament. *Ho Chi Minh: The Man* rolls across the skin of five lynched black men, branding them with ideographic characters.

This scene printed on his eyelids is the one I was born with. My face is up there among the poplar leaves veined into stained glass. I'm not myself here, craving a mask of silk elusive as his four aliases.

He retouches photographs, paints antiques, gardens, cooks pastries, and loves and hates everything French. On his way to Chung-king to talk with Chiang K'ai-shek about fighting the Japanese, as day runs into night, he's arrested and jailed for fourteen months. Sitting here in the prison of my skin, I feel his words grow through my fingertips till I see his southern skies and old friends where mountains are clouds. As he tosses kernels of corn to carp, they mouth silent O's through the water.

Each face hangs like swollen breadfruit, clinging to jade leaves. How many eyes are on me, clustered in the hum of this dark theatre? The film flashes like heat lightning across a southern night, and the bloated orbs break open. Golden carp collage the five faces. The earth swings on a bellrope, limp as a body bag tied to a limb, and the moon over-flows with blood.

(1998)

MAUREEN SEATON (1947–)

❧

Toy Car

Slippery as the word *deserve*. How the Catholic never gets washed out of you, the temple crushed completely. Once my husband brought home a little car. It fit beside the sleds and carriages like a toy for some-one bigger than a toddler, smaller than a rock star. My husband deserved it, he said, and who was I to doubt him knowing as I did how his mother lifted him into her lap and pressed against his small back, the names of her troubles seared in his skin like Latin in the mind of a ten-year-old. *Introibo ad altare Dei.* I will go in to the altar of God. *Ad Deum qui laetificat juventutem meam.* To God who is the joy of my youth. I couldn't help the way I felt about toy cars and Bangladesh. The Jesuit in my book bag wrote on the board a thousand times: It's harder for a rich man, etc. . . . The Sister of Sorrow in my lunch box crossed herself and thrust her hands up her cavernous sleeves. I had great ideas, my essays on the poor rivaled Merton and Marx. I was tortured by the hair shirt of my nondesires, I was living on the mountain and I couldn't get down. I lay beside my husband at night and thought: Who is this man who deserves such a tiny auto-mobile that costs more to fix than food for a family of six in the South Bronx for a whole year? I thought: I am too tired to deserve anything and look, how shameless my rich husband, how wild his hair blows on the winds of Westchester in his toy car with the luscious leather seats big enough for him and someone else.

(1996)

Lateral Time

I'd never held the ashes of a dead man but I'd always wanted to know a famous artist, so I reached out my left hand and she spilled him into my palm. He was flame-white, his flesh dust, he was tiny

200

bones you could play with—they could be doll parts—peaceful in my hand like light. I kept my hand open in case he needed air and I knew it was not the essence of him but nevertheless I whispered: Don't worry, you're safe with me. I whispered: I love your paintings. This happened on the Upper West Side in '89 as the light changed over the Hudson, and that light was in the apartment sliding on floor and walls as we passed a dead man's bones between us, weeping.

Once I spent the winter in Manhattan with a woman whose desires were so unlike mine the air in the kitchen was sweetly skewed. She told me: *Pleasure,* and I bent at the refrigerator choosing the precise onion. I told her: *Juice,* and she stood at the stove removing lemon seeds from basmati. We were perfect as thumbs, we were starved and greedy as shorebirds, dipping down, grabbing our food, devouring it.

Now I've begun to write "NO!" on my body parts, small cross-stitched reminders to throw me back and hook another. Tattoo on my right breast, sticker on my colon, scribble of bright blue between my ovaries, hollowed now of eggs but still handy to balance me out. The day I decide to go I'll erase the words from my body then disintegrate quickly like any dying fool, you'll see me rising from the shore—equal time lateral time—don't hurry into anything but love.

The man who lives in 4D sleeps above me every night in the same rectangle of space, one floor up, beside the door, our double beds appearing to the gods like open-face sandwiches with two chubby figures shifting and rolling in dreams or trooping to the bathroom. Sometimes I watch Tai Chi on cable at 6 A.M. because the man upstairs has jumped so hard from his bed, and sometimes I sleep right through til 9 or 10, his footfalls barely piercing dawn.

(2001)

LESLIE SCALAPINO (1948–)

∾

That They Were at the Beach

A Sequence

She heard the sounds of a couple having intercourse and then getting up they went into the shower so that she caught a sight of them naked before hearing the water running. The parts of their bodies which had been covered by clothes were those of leopards. During puberty her own organs and skin were not like this though when she first had intercourse with a man he removed his clothes and his organ and flesh were also a leopard's. She already felt pleasure in sexual activity and her body not resembling these adults made her come easily which also occurred when she had intercourse with another man a few months later.

———

When sexual unions occurred between a brother and sister they weren't savages or primitive. She had that feeling about having intercourse with men whose organs were those of leopards and hers were not. Walking somewhere after one of these episodes she was excited by it though she might not have made this comparison if she'd actually had a brother. At least the woman she had seen in the shower had a leopard's parts. In these episodes when she'd had intercourse with a man he didn't remark about her not being like that. And if women had these characteristics which she didn't it made her come more easily with him.

———

She overheard another couple together and happened to see them as she had the couple in the shower. The nude part of the woman was like herself and the man had the leopard's parts so that she had the same reaction and came easily with someone, as she had with a sense of other women having a leopard's traits and herself isolated. The man with whom she had intercourse did not say anything that showed he had seen a difference in her and that made her react physically. Yet other women seemed to have a leopard's characteristics except for this one she'd seen.

Again it seemed that a man with whom she had intercourse was her brother and was ardent with her—but this would not have occurred to her had she really had a brother. Yet her feeling about him was also related to her seeing a woman who was pregnant and was the only one to be so. The woman not receiving attention or remarks on the pregnancy excited her; and went together with her sense of herself coming easily and yet not being pregnant until quite awhile after this time.

————

She also felt that she came easily feeling herself isolated when she was pregnant since she had the sense of other women having leopards' organs. They had previously had children. She was the only one who was pregnant and again she saw a couple together, the man with leopard's parts and the woman not having these characteristics.

Again she could come since her body was different from the adult who had some parts that were leopards', and having the sense of the women having had children earlier than her and their not having younger children now.

————

Her liking the other women to have had children when she was pregnant had to do with having them there and herself isolated—and yet people not saying much about or responding to the pregnancy. She thought of the man coming as when she caught a sight of the couple together—being able to come with someone a different time because she had a sense of a woman she'd seen having had her children earlier. There being a difference of age, even ten years, between a child she'd have and those the other women had had.

————

She happened to see some men who were undressed, as if they were boys—one of them had the features and organ of a leopard and the others did not. The difference in this case gave her the sense of them being boys, all of them rather than those who didn't have leopards' characteristics and this made her come easily with someone.

It was not a feeling of their being a younger age, since the men were her own age, and she found the men who lacked the leopard features to be as attractive as the one who had those features. She had the feeling of them as adults and her the same age as them, yet had the other feeling as well in order for her to come then.

She saw a couple who were entwined together and her feeling about them came from the earlier episode of seeing the men who were nude and having the sense of them being adolescent boys. Really she'd had the sense of the men she'd seen as being adults and herself the same age as them. The couple she watched were also around the same age as herself—the man being aware of someone else's presence after a time and coming. The woman pleased then though she had not come.

She had intercourse with the man who had the features and organs of a leopard and whom she had first seen with the group of men who lacked these characteristics. The other men were attractive as he was. Yet having the sense of the difference between him and the others, she found it pleasant for him to come and for her not to come that time. The same thing occurred on another occasion with him.

She compared the man to plants, to the plants having a nervous aspect and being motionless. The man coming when he had the sense of being delayed in leaving—as if being slowed down had made him come and was exciting, and it was during the afternoon with people walking around. He was late and had to go somewhere, and came, with a feeling of delay and retarding—rather than out of nervousness.

(1985)

TOM WHALEN (1948–)

~

Why I Hate the Prose Poem

An angry man came into the kitchen where his wife was busying herself about supper and exploded.

My mother told me this story every day of her life, until one day she exploded.

But it is not a story, she always pointed out. It's a prose poem.

One day I saw a man feeding a hot dog to his dog. The hot dog looked like a stick of dynamite.

Often simply the sight of a prose poem makes me sick.

I am unmarried and live alone in a small house.

In my spare time, I am cultivating a night garden.

(2000)

AGHA SHAHID ALI (1949–2001)

∾

Return to Harmony 3

Two summers? Epochs, then, of ice.

But the air is the same muslin, beaten by the sky on Nanga Parbat, then pressed on the rocks of the nearer peaks.

I run down the ramp.

On the tarmac, I eavesdrop on Operation Tiger: Troops will burn down the garden and let the haven remain.

This is home—the haven a cage surrounded by ash—the fate of Paradise.

Through streets strewn with broken bricks and interrupted by paramilitaries, Irfan drives me straight to the Harmonies ("3" for my father—the youngest brother!), three houses built in a pastoral, that walled acreage of Harmonies where no one but my mother was poor.

A bunker has put the house under a spell. Shadowed eyes watch me open the gate, like a trespasser.

Has the gardener fled?

The Annexe of the Harmonies is locked—my grandmother's cottage—where her sons offered themselves to her as bouquets of mirrors. There was nothing else to reflect.

Under the windows the roses have choked in their beds. Was the gardener killed?

And the postman?

In the drawer of the cedar stand peeling in the verandah, a pile of damp letters—one to my father to attend a meeting the previous autumn, another an invitation to a wedding.

My first key opens the door. I break into quiet. The lights work.

The Koran still protects the house, lying strangely wrapped in a *jamawar* shawl where my mother had left it on the walnut table by the fireplace. Above, *If God is with you, Victory is near!*—the framed calligraphy ruthless behind cobwebs.

I pick up the dead phone, its number exiled from its instrument, a refugee among forlorn numbers in some angry office on Exchange Road.

But the receiver has caught a transmission: Rafi's song from a film about war: *Slowly, I so slowly, kept on walking, / and then was severed forever from her.* THIS IS ALL INDIA RADIO, AMRITSAR. I hang up.

Upstairs, the window too is a mirror; if I jump through it I will fall into my arms.

The mountains return my stare, untouched by blood.

On my shelf, by Ritsos and Rilke and Cavafy and Lorca and Iqbal and Amichai and Paz, my parents are beautiful in their wedding brocades, so startlingly young!

And there in black and white my mother, eighteen years old, a year before she came a bride to these Harmonies, so unforgivenly poor and so unforgivingly beautiful that the house begins to shake in my arms, and when the unarmed world is still again, with pity, it is the house that is holding me in its arms and the cry coming faded from its empty rooms is my cry.

(1997)

☙

inside gertrude stein

Right now as I am talking to you and as you are being talked to, without letup, it is becoming clear that gertrude stein has hijacked me and that this feeling that you are having now as you read this, that this is what it feels like to be inside gertrude stein. This is what it feels like to be a huge typewriter in a dress. Yes, I feel we have gotten inside gertrude stein, and of course it is dark inside the enormous gertrude, it is like being locked up in a refrigerator lit only by a smiling rind of cheese. Being inside gertrude is like being inside a monument made of a cloud which is always moving across the sky which is also always moving. Gertrude is a huge galleon of cloud anchored to the ground by one small tether, yes, I see it down there, do you see that tiny snail glued to the tackboard of the landscape¿ That is alice. So, I am inside gertrude; we belong to each other, she and I, and it is so wonderful because I have always been a thin woman inside of whom a big woman is screaming to get out, and she's out now and if a river could type this is how it would sound, pure and complicated and enormous. Now we are lilting across the countryside, and we are talking, and if the wind could type it would sound like this, ongoing and repetitious, abstracting and stylizing everything, like our famous haircut painted by Picasso. Because when you are inside our haircut you understand that all the flotsam and jetsam of hairdo have been cleared away (like the forests from the New World) so that the skull can show through grinning and feasting on the alarm it has created. I am now, alarmingly, inside gertrude's head and I am thinking that I may only be a thought she has had when she imagined that she and alice were dead and gone and someone had to carry on the work of being gertrude stein, and so I am receiving, from beyond the grave, radioactive isotopes of her genius saying, take up my work, become gertrude stein.

Because someone must be gertrude stein, someone must save us from the literalists and realists, and narratives of the beginning and end, someone must be a river that can type. And why not I¿ Gertrude is insisting on the fact that while I am a subgenius, weighing one hundred five pounds, and living in a small town with an enormous furry male husband who is always in his Cadillac Eldorado driving off to sell something to people who do not deserve the bad luck of this merchandise in their lives—that these facts would not be a problem for gertrude stein. Gertrude and I feel that, for instance, in *Patriarchal Poetry* when (like an avalanche that can type) she is burying the patriarchy, still there persists a sense of condescending affection. So, while I'm a thin, heterosexual subgenius, nevertheless gertrude has chosen me as her tool, just as she chose the patriarchy as a tool for ending the patriarchy. And because I have become her tool, now, in a sense, gertrude is inside me. It's tough. Having gertrude inside me is like having swallowed an ocean liner that can type, and, while I feel like a very small coat closet with a bear in it, gertrude and I feel that I must tell you that gertrude does not care. She is using me to get her message across, to say, I am lost, I am beset by literalists and narratives of the beginning and middle and end, help me. And so, yes, I say, yes, I am here, gertrude, because we feel, gertrude and I, that there is real urgency in our voice (like a sob that can type) and that things are very bad for her because she is lost, beset by the literalists and realists, her own enormousness crushing her, and we must find her and take her into ourselves, even though I am the least likely of saviors and have been chosen perhaps as a last resort, yes, definitely, gertrude is saying to me, you are the least likely of saviors, you are my last choice and my last resort.

(1999)

The Person

for Lyn Hejinian

Increasingly, then, the person becomes a way of doing something, never explicitly experienced as such, because it is the world that is felt, its mute pressure filling out the corners, as of a rhyme. The room gathers each sitter in. The light changes, imperceptibly, always. One, the inevitable protagonist of a paragraph built on second thought, would like nothing better than to sum up and in the application describe that process by which so much detail has been set aside, so as to be clear of it, to stand in the pale light unframed by the body of years spent in collation. The assembly of days, none identical to the last, has taken up much time. So many sources, however, have informed the final mix, that it bears an irreducible mark, one not possible to describe in so many words. The person looks around and sees the same things. It is necessary to change without touching them.

Here a street or a sky or a bridge become emblems in an elaborate game whose rules the person is only beginning to understand, although an avid player since early childhood. Perhaps it is the availability of such images that prevents one from recognizing their true meaning until much later, when one has withdrawn or been withdrawn from them, through an illness or brush with death, but one has not had time for such things, or been spared them by luck. Mostly it is the call of others that diverts the attention.

If a child or a woman or a man or an old man or a young woman or a person of questionable age approaches you, what do you think? Many wish to first get out of the way. Others jump at what may seem like the main chance. The one particular person I have come to consider has thought rather to be of assistance, to the extent possible, in relation to this, that and the other thing, however. In this way, this person has become an extraordinary resource for a good number of people. What remains to be seen is a person, walking over a bridge.

What is of more interest, however, from the point of view of a junk-yard of mangled signs heaped up in silent protest against a century devoted to the material possession of form, is when a person eludes any simple formulation relative to that interest.

The person is, as cliché-ridden isomorph, a creature of habit. One has certain convictions, obsessions, eccentricities, stylistic features, indications that set one, by prescription, apart. All this is begging the question, a delay tactic, for what most impresses its mark on the spirit, an insistence lived, a laugh in the face of horror, marks its presence without recourse to definition. It is the world that is felt, but it is a made place, and within it they make it who alter its composition simply by living and doing as they will and can do.

(1998)

CHARLES BERNSTEIN (1950–)

Comraderie turns to rivalry when 12 medical students learn that only seven of them will be admitted to the hospital.

A CIA agent is ordered to feign a breakdown to trap a spy at a mental hospital.

A field study of Zululand's mosquitoes and velvet monkeys reveals them to be carriers of viral diseases that cause high fever and bone-wracking pain.

Defeat comes to the Nazi conquerer: Film footage highlights the February bombing of Dresden; the advance over the Rhine, through the Ruhr and into the heart of Germany; and, from the east, the Russian encirclement of Berlin.

A brilliant doctor's erratic behavior causes concern at the hospital.

On-the-street subjects render fragmented versions; a two-way mirror provides some unexpected "reflections"; a pair of outdoor phone-booths and two muddled conversations befuddle a man.

A backstage view is interwoven with a tragic story.

A detective is captured by a mobster who plans to hook him on heroin and then deny him a fix until he reveals the whereabouts of the jealous hood's former girlfriend.

A retarded young man witnesses a murder but is not articulate enough to tell his story to the police.

A husband is betrayed in medieval Japan where adultery is punishable by death.

Julie grows attached to an abandoned baby.

A grim smuggling operation and a dead hippie lead to intrigue in Malta.

Boxed candy includes frog-filled chocolates.

A girl finds herself between the worlds of the living and dead.

Henrietta Hippo believes she can predict the future by reading the letters in her alphabet soup.

A man withers away after being exposed to a strange mist.

Conspiracy of silence hampers look into fatal beating of teenage thug.

Bachelors are all agape over a new girl in town.

Rob sees red when Laura goes blond.

"Genocide." Graphic film footage depicts Hitler's persecution and extermination of the Jewish population in Germany and in the occupied countries.

A mental patient returns home to a cold mother and a domineering husband.

A freewheeling narcotics agent works with a junkie's vengeful widow to track down a shadowy syndicate boss.

Everyone chips in to help Henrietta Hippo bake enough pies for the country fair.

It's the dog pound for Roger when Jeannie turns him into a poodle.

Nellie has the most lines in the school play, but the player to get the most out of the project is a girl who uses the play to bring her reclusive widowed mother back into society.

A hot-shot flier thinks he can wage a one-man war in Korea.

A woman tries to keep her individuality after marriage.

Bilko feverishly schemes for a way to escape the summer's heat.

Lucy makes an impression on her first day at her new job when she breaks the water cooler and floods the office.

Midget creatures emerge from the center of the earth.

An emotionally unstable woman unconsciously blots out all memory of seeing her date murdered by her closest friend.

The corrosiveness of envy and jealousy is demonstrated.

A blind girl is terrorized by persons unknown at a country estate.

Strange signals from a nearby island.

A young woman's horror of leprosy plagues her.

(1983)

ANNE CARSON (1950–)

∾

On Waterproofing

Franz Kafka was Jewish. He had a sister, Ottla, Jewish. Ottla married a jurist, Josef David, not Jewish. When the Nuremberg Laws were introduced to Bohemia-Moravia in 1942, quiet Ottla suggested to Josef David that they divorce. He at first refused. She spoke about sleep shapes and property and their two daughters and a rational approach. She did not mention, because she did not yet know the word, Auschwitz, where she would die in October 1943. After putting the apartment in order she packed a rucksack and was given a good shoeshine by Josef David. He applied a coat of grease. Now they are waterproof, he said.

(1992)

On Orchids

We live by tunneling for we are people buried alive. To me, the tunnels you make will seem strangely aimless, uprooted orchids. But the fragrance is undying. A Little Boy has run away from Amherst a few Days ago, writes Emily Dickinson in a letter of 1883, and when asked where he was going, he replied, Vermont or Asia.

(1992)

On Hedonism

Beauty makes me hopeless. I don't care why anymore I just want to get away. When I look at the city of Paris I long to wrap my legs around it. When I watch you dancing there is a heartless immensity like a sailor in a dead-calm sea. Desires as round as peaches bloom in me all night, I no longer gather what falls.

(1992)

On Shelter

You can write on a wall with a fish heart, it's because of the phosphorus. They eat it. There are shacks like that down along the river. I am writing this to be as wrong as possible to you. Replace the door when you leave, it says. Now you tell me how wrong that is, how long it glows. Tell me.

(1992)

CAROLYN FORCHÉ (1950–)

∽

The Colonel

What you have heard is true. I was in his house. His wife carried a tray of coffee and sugar. His daughter filed her nails, his son went out for the night. There were daily papers, pet dogs, a pistol on the cushion beside him. The moon swung bare on its black cord over the house. On the television was a cop show. It was in English. Broken bottles were embedded in the walls around the house to scoop the kneecaps from a man's legs or cut his hands to lace. On the windows there were gratings like those in liquor stores. We had dinner, rack of lamb, good wine, a gold bell was on the table for calling the maid. The maid brought green mangoes, salt, a type of bread. I was asked how I enjoyed the country. There was a brief commercial in Spanish. His wife took everything away. There was some talk of how difficult it had become to govern. The parrot said hello on the terrace. The colonel told it to shut up, and pushed himself from the table. My friend said to me with his eyes: say nothing. The colonel returned with a sack used to bring groceries home. He spilled many human ears on the table. They were like dried peach halves. There is no other way to say this. He took one of them in his hands, shook it in our faces, dropped it into a water glass. It came alive there. I am tired of fooling around he said. As for the rights of anyone, tell your people they can go fuck themselves. He swept the ears to the floor with his arm and held the last of his wine in the air. Something for your poetry, no? he said. Some of the ears on the floor caught this scrap of his voice. Some of the ears on the floor were pressed to the ground.

(May 1978)

JAMES RICHARDSON (1950–)

Vectors: Thirty-six Aphorisms and Ten-Second Essays

1.

The road reaches every place, the short cut only one.

2.

Those who demand consideration for their sacrifices were making investments, not sacrifices.

3.

Despair says, *I cannot lift that weight.* Happiness says, *I do not have to.*

4.

Pessimists live in fear of their hope, optimists in fear of their fear.

5.

What you give to a thief is stolen.

6.

You've never said anything as stupid as what people thought you said.

7.

Who gives his heart away too easily must have a heart under his heart.

8.

I am saving good deeds to buy a great sin.

9.

If the couple could see themselves twenty years later, they might not recognize their love, but they would recognize their argument.

10.

Disillusionment is also an illusion.

11.

Our lives get complicated because complexity is so much simpler than simplicity.

12.

The wound hurts less than your desire to wound me

13.

The best way to know your faults is to notice which ones you accuse others of.

14.

No matter how much time I save, I have only now.

15.

Water deepens where it has to wait

16.

Ah, what can fill the heart? But then, what *can't*?

17.

Opacity gives way. Transparency is the mystery.

18.

Shadows are harshest when there is only one lamp.

19.

All stones are broken stones.

20.

To paranoids and the elect, everything makes sense.

21.

The first abuse of power is not realizing that you have it.

22.

Each lock makes two prisons.

23.

It's amazing that I sit at my job all day, and no one sees me clearly enough to say, "What is that boy doing behind a desk?"

24.

There are silences harder to take back than words.

25.

It's easy to renounce the world till you see who picks up what you renounced.

26.

Writer: how books read each other.

27.

Of all the ways to avoid living, perfect discipline is the most admired.

28.

Happiness is not the only happiness.

29.

If you want to know how they could forget you, wait till you forget them.

30.

I'm hugely overpaid. Except compared to the people I work with.

31.

Who breaks the thread, the one who pulls, the one who holds on?

32.

All work is the avoidance of harder work.

33.

You who have proved how much like me you are: how could I trust you?

34.

Desire, make me poor again.

35.

Experience tends to immunize against experience, which is why the most experienced are not the wisest.

36.

All things in moderation, wisdom says. And says last *Do not be too wise.*

(2001)

JOHN YAU (1950–)

∾

Predella

A blue woolen glove folded over like an old one dollar bill someone keeps hidden in their wallet just in case, a crumpled galosh, a rubber boot half-submerged in slush (remnants of a scene of unimagined violence?)

A convoy of hats dispersed into the evening. The night was pulling its shade over the dirty window of the city. Half a face pushes out of the darkness, a boxing glove, and veers off down the narrowing corridor. An intersection of voices—how not to be snagged there the way a nylon stocking catches on a heel; a tear in the veneer. She thought about how she wiggled into her bra the way she settled in to a role; by moving around until she was comfortable. On the radio a song celebrating the joys of love in sincere doggerel.

mounds of snow, complete with plateaus, threatening boulders, cliff faces, and the danger of avalanches

Gray sky and gray underwear; everything was taking on the color of the city. As he bent down to pick up his crumpled dungarees from the floor, he was reminded of Claude Rains in *The Invisible Man;* the insane laughter echoing on the train platform; he had heard it again; the hatchet-faced man next to him in the diner reading the newspaper (he was, for some reason, wearing tan driving gloves); the story of a woman who killed and fed the family dog to her whining daughter and alcoholic husband. The headline was in bold type: MOM SERVES PUP STEW TO STEWED POP.

furrows of snow; perfectly preserved tire tracks. It was as if a city had started growing in a farmer's field where he had, just the morning before, been plowing. Everyone teetered; some fell; a new kind of gravity; life on the moon—

Mrs. Garland was as thin as the blue and green handkerchief she often twisted between her hands while talking, continuing the story she had been telling for thirty-five years, or ever since her husband did not return home one evening. Her best friend, Mrs. Central, was also thin, though in her case it was a matter of bones more than flesh. Her skin did not have that quality of moonlight shining through paper windows; an image Mrs. Central often used to express her humble origins because, as she noted; "Since the Japanese live in paper houses—they must be extremely poor, though certainly neat and well mannered, as everyone knows."

so much so the days would have to begin elsewhere.

(1980)

Summer Rental

Mrs. Trashbag was unable to come to any reasonable appraisal of what was standing in front of her temporary desk, just that the old man's upswept hair bore a striking resemblance to the sleeves of his pleated, plaid coat. Who, her numbered underlings in the storeroom were whispering, could have possibly had the urge to rip all the plastic flowers out of their imported sleeping jackets? Was it the same culprit that last weekend stole a dozen infected parrots from the east wing of the castle's library? These are the questions haunting the pockmarked halls of the old tavern down by the harbor. Later, morning's leftover light is marked "dismal" and sent to the laboratory, where a team of agents carefully sifts through the spokes and glare.

The crew has gathered near where the evening's shadows thicken their fur in anticipation of the coming weather. Everyone else in the parking lot knows the movie is just an excuse to tell a bad story in livid colors. A woman caresses the knotholes of her wooden leg. Petey tries swallowing a woolen scarf. Meanwhile, the actors and actresses trying out for the lead roles believe they will be able to revive the remainders of their careers. Next to the parking lot, in a government funded home for semi-retired adolescents, the newly appointed director wonders who has been pissing in the umbrella stand. His secretary secretly covets contact with grated substances. In the cellar, a spotted paw defiles a garment made of coal.

Thick with snakes and headbands, a stricken aroma undulates through a broken window. Once you are apprehended, you are returned to your room, and left with a plate of hot wax. This is what we in the institution fondly refer to as "living beyond your beans."

A cow imitates a car and crashes into a telephone pole. Grackles shriek and wolves whimper, but Byron Trashbag continues dozing, the brute hours of enforced labor wriggling through his muscles. He had had the worms before, but not like this. It is the month when penalties must be paid and extra facial hair removed from offending surfaces, the month when last year's prisoners are lowered into the lower bunkers, and music hour consists of the same insurgent anthem played backwards.

The ambitious assistant director heard himself announce to the seagulls still glued to the eaves of the burning roof: Once you've mutilated the night in your sleep, there is no turning back.

(2000)

❧

Pretty Happy!

I have no siblings who've killed themselves, a few breakdowns here and there, my son sometimes talking back to me, but, in general, I'm pretty happy. And if the basement leaks, and fuses fart out when the coffee machine comes on, and if the pastor beats us up with the same old parables, and raccoons overturn the garbage cans and ham it up at 2 o'clock in the morning while some punk is cutting the wires on my car stereo, I can still say, I'm pretty happy.

Pretty happy! Pretty happy! I whisper to my wife at midnight, waking to another night noise, reaching for the baseball bat I keep hidden under our bed.

(1997)

Tex-Mex

"Everything in this world passes, but love will last forever." If this is true, then where is my Gigi this morning? I am naked, half-embalmed, like a worm at the bottom of a brown bottle, a certain Black-eyed Susan curled around my leg, only the sound of my palomino weeping in the prairie grass. My battery is dead, my cactus has growing pains . . . We were searching for the Old Dutchman's mine, our guide Buck a consummate rough rider in every kind of saddle. Joe the Bad and Jim the Ugly brought up the rear. "Call me Blue or Coyote," I drawled, which made Gigi laugh. Or was it my Styrofoam pith helmet with the smiley-face decal on front? "We'll be breaking virgin territory," Buck grunted, but all I saw was a huge pyramid of cast-off microwave ovens. The day wore on, the sun dragging it westward like a withered foot. We shot a few elk and wild pigs, milked some rattlesnakes. At the hoedown at Apache Jack's, we shared campfire stories. "I had a cheesy childhood," I began, "one with many holes in it, and a heavy

Thing, a Thing like the last tree left standing so you can build a house around it." "When you're done, Stretch," Buck said, opening a large, brown bottle of mescal, "can you pass the beans?" What do I remember? The raw outline of a covered wagon branded on Buck's forearm, his red hair bristling like porcupine quills, and then bushwhacked I was by a certain Black-eyed Susan, whose snoring now seems as cruel as hunger—the price to pay for going home with the wrong Gigi.

(1998)

MAXINE CHERNOFF (1952–)

His Pastime

A man held his breath. Unlike other men, who momentarily hold their breath, then gasp like small bags bursting, this man continued for days. He stopped working and gave up all nourishment. His face turned blue as a police uniform, then black. Even his shadow held its breath, motionless on the floor. A newspaper heard of this man, perched on his breath like a flagpole. They sent a reporter to cover the story. The man holding his breath served the reporter cookies and tea. In response to the reporter's first question, the man politely exhaled. His breath, like a funnel, upturned all the things in the room. Unimpressed, the reporter lifted himself from under his chair and cracked teacup. The next day, on his way to work, the man who had held his breath read an editorial decrying swindlers, fanatics, and thrill-seekers.

(1979)

Vanity, Wisconsin

Firemen wax their mustaches at an alarm; walls with mirrors are habitually saved. At the grocery women in line polish their shopping carts. Children too will learn that one buys meat the color of one's hair, vegetables to complement the eyes. There is no crime in Vanity, Wisconsin. Shoplifters are too proud to admit a need. Punishment, the dismemberment of a favorite snapshot, has never been practiced in modern times. The old are of no use, and once a year at their "debut," they're asked to join their reflections in Lake Lablanc. Cheerfully they dive in, vanity teaching them not to float. A visitor is not embarrassed to sparkle here or stand on his hotel balcony, taking pictures of his pictures.

(1979)

The Inner Life

for Tymoteusz Karpowicz

After they decreed the end of lovemaking, we thought only of sleeping. Under our covers, each separate as a masthead at sea, we practiced dreaming. For it was the source of our only comfort, our only ties with emotions hazy as deceased uncles. Now we dreamed desperately. Those who couldn't remember their dreams became insurance risks, showing up frequently in the papers as suicides or crime statistics. We were advised to look for mates who appeared to be affluent dreamers: heavy eyelids, an avid indifference to appearance, lights out early, very early in bedroom windows. You may be surprised we took mates at all, but we still grew lonely and wanted something to touch, even if it vanished when we opened our eyes. Those who excelled at dreaming were chosen to represent us. The forty hour week was replaced by the forty hour sleep. It was through our "sleep experience" that we earned advancement at work. New television series featured dream phantoms to replace late night horror shows, falling dreams instead of daily soap operas, and flying dreams for children. Who succumbed to the old feeling of helplessness when the paraphernalia for heroism was stored in every brain? Soon even our buildings were designed to resemble pillows and our young ones judged intelligent not by how soon they spoke the hackneyed "Mama" but by how accomplished they were at sleeping. Intelligence tests were given to determine what they could sleep through and our prodigies withstood avalanches easily as the cracking of porcelain thimbles. As with all major changes in civilization, the historians were at first puzzled. Many had retired to rest homes where they dreamed the rebuilding of the Roman Empire, the finding of a lost continent, the absence of Hitler. We had lost all sense of nationalism and all instinct for aggression. *One man, one pillow* became the slogan and even the most impoverished seemed satisfied. Some awake even part of the day suspected that the government had foreseen the outcome. Certain extremists refused to dream, claiming their unconscious was a tool in a scheme more diabolical than

Manifest Destiny. But from the solid white building that stood impalpable as a dream image of a building, we heard no denial of the charges, just the assured snoring of men in serious pajamas.

(1979)

RITA DOVE (1952–)

Kentucky, 1833

It is Sunday, day of roughhousing. We are let out in the woods. The young boys wrestle and butt their heads together like sheep—a circle forms; claps and shouts fill the air. The women, brown and glossy, gather round the banjo player, or simply lie in the sun, legs and aprons folded. The weather's an odd monkey—any other day he's on our backs, his cotton eye everywhere; today the light sifts down like the finest cornmeal, coating our hands and arms with a dust. God's dust, old woman Acker says. She's the only one who could read to us from the Bible, before Massa forbade it. On Sundays, something hangs in the air, a hallelujah, a skitter of brass, but we can't call it by name and it disappears.

Then Massa and his gentlemen friends come to bet on the boys. They guffaw and shout, taking sides, red-faced on the edge of the boxing ring. There is more kicking, butting, and scuffling—the winner gets a dram of whiskey if he can drink it all in one swig without choking.

Jason is bucking and prancing about—Massa said his name reminded him of some sailor, a hero who crossed an ocean, looking for a golden cotton field. Jason thinks he's been born to great things—a suit with gold threads, vest and all. Now the winner is sprawled out under a tree and the sun, that weary tambourine, hesitates at the rim of the sky's green light. It's a crazy feeling that carries through the night; as if the sky were an omen we could not understand, the book that, if we could read, would change our lives.

(1980)

CARLA HARRYMAN (1952–)

∾

Magic (or Rousseau)

In order to play, one needs magic and Rousseau and must remember play. Sometimes magic is the obscurest impostor in play. An obscure rationalization imposes the word magic on Rousseau.

Now remember play has nothing to do with that Rousseauian freedom found in refusal.

Refusal more than anything else ends play.

And so we might play a game called the conjuring of Rousseau. It might go like this, let's pretend that Jean-Jacques Rousseau is the pawn in our game. On one side of the board is society. On the other side of the board is solitude. We can each pick a goal. One of us tries to force Rousseau into society, the other tries to land him in solitude. Whoever gets the pawn to the goal wins. Let's say Rousseau is walking along a Boulevard in silent reverie. The board, by the way, is made up of parks and boulevards, so when Rousseau "advances" he is always being advanced by way of a park or boulevard. Sometimes a player will draw a card that says, "What do you want, Jean-Jacques Rousseau?" If the spinner lands on *I would like to go home,* then the pawn is returned to the beginning and Rousseau sets out again from the starting spot. If the spinner lands on *I would like to tell the truth,* the player gets to spin again until he gets something he likes; since truth is bound to both solitude and society, this move becomes a matter of preference. In the center of the board is a personage with great powers: she is a witch. If Jean-Jacques lands on her spot it is because she has called him up. She calls him up, because his travels fascinate her. Now, this is extremely problematic. If Rousseau realizes that she has called him up, then he sees himself as a ghost. The player has a choice at this point, to get out of or stay in the ghost game. If it is decided to stay in the ghost game, Rousseau is provided with a series of options that he never recognized when he was alive. He can, for instance, opt to infiltrate society without being noticed. He can observe those who outlived him. He could, if he were on the ladder to revenge, scare them to death. They could become equals in death. Or he could live with the witch, who loves to make good on her resources. This he admires enor-

232

mously; although, she does not quite consider him her equal. With her, his solitude is indeed complete, since no one in the game believes in her existence.

(1995)

Matter

Love was alone with love. And there was nothing I could do about it. Love was alone with love. Why make another move? Why move? It's your turn over there, someone said, and I thought I'm going to open my legs and see what happens. Hurry up, lay down your cards. The cards were in my hand. I put down the card to see what would happen while I opened my legs. You open now, I said. And love responded quickly. You are a good player. Have you been playing long? I learned from an expert, said love. Is the expert still living. Yes, she is. A she, I said. Love was impatient and wanted to know if I had another move. I closed my legs up to see if that counted. Look at your hand, said love trying to be patient. And you, I said, prefer these cards over other forms of excitement. If you can't play, you'll never meet the expert, love replied. I didn't really care, but my body was standing on end at the thought of fucking. When I saw that I and my body were not the same, I knew what card to play and played it as soon as my turn came without second-guessing my opponent's position in the game.

(1995)

༄

Epistle

When the thief does come in the night, it is mid-afternoon on a sunny day, with everybody at work. Although we are unprepared, the house is ready. The door waits to be smashed open, the drawers to be pulled and left gaping. The things—whatever things he chooses—wait to be taken. They are always ready to be released from our care, from their obligations to us. The thing with sentimental value especially waits with a saintly indifference.

And the things are transfigured, given new meaning, as if they joined orders, took vows. When we meet them again, if we do, in the monastery of the pawnshop, they have earned a new humility, and we must try to persuade them back to their old life. Or we might glimpse at the symphony concert the stolen watch, like a golden snowflake, strapped to a young woman's wrist.

The thief is a communicant in a country that worships in secret, on the run. He improvises the elements of his ritual at every ceremony. In this one a gold watch with clasp and a cunning shell to cover its face. In that one an oblong case that may contain a violin or high powered rifle. In this one a collection of objects—an answering machine, a camera, a pair of binoculars, a laptop computer. In another, moving service, a .38 caliber revolver. In every period of worship these things take on the numinosity of faith, each with its inherent worth abruptly revealed.

Theologians spring up among our friends. Our visitor, they say, had been watching us, studying us, there was some plan. We join them in speculating on the location of our possessions, the new plane they occupy, and their miraculous return.

The man spraying to check for fingerprints says this scrotebag will not be back. He finds nothing and crowns each empty place with a halo of soot. His severity and solemnity are like John Knox's, if he smoked after the service and complained bitterly about sin moving into the better neighborhoods, because of the mayor's new policies. Knox fuming, after his fulminations in the pulpit. Knox driving off in a crime scene van.

We attached ourselves to things, and now we feel like amputees. The wrist of the watch, severed. The fingers snapped from the neck of the violin. The eye of the camcorder plucked out. Where the laptop sat, a lapse.

We try to feel lucky in our violation. He could have burned down the house. He could have kidnapped the children. We could have surprised him and driven after him and been shot dead through the windshield. He didn't take the wedding album. He didn't take the TV. Here, safe in its drawer, he didn't take this. There, in plain sight on the desk, he didn't take that.

Now we see others as thieves or not as thieves. Anyone we pass is a felon or an upstanding citizen. We listen to the gospel of electronic security. Listen and believe. It is religious, but not a religion that brings joy or consolation. We enter the feast days of anxiety, the high holidays of suspicion.

This letter goes out with a list of things encoded that we still possess.

(2001)

MARY RUEFLE (1952–)

༄

Monument

A small war had ended. Like all wars, it was terrible. Things which had stood in existence were now vanished. I had come back because I had survived and survivors come back, there is nothing else left for them to do. I had been on long travels connected to the war, and I had been to the centerpiece of the war, that acre of conflagration. And now I was sitting on a park bench, watching ducks land and take off from a pond. They too had survived, though I had no way of knowing if they were the same ducks from before the war or if they were the off-spring of ducks who had died in the war. It was a warm day in the capital and people were walking without coats, dazed by the warmth, which was not the heat of war, which had engulfed them, but the warmth of expansion, in which would grow the idea of a memorial to the war, which had ended, and of which I was a veteran architect. I knew I would be called upon for my ideas in regards to this memorial and I had entered the park aimlessly, trying to escape my ideas, as I had been to the centerpiece, that acre of conflagration, and from there the only skill that returned was escapement, any others died with those who possessed them. I was dining with friends that evening, for the restaurants and theatres and shops had reopened, the capital was like a great tablecloth being shaken in midair so that life could be smoothed and reset and go on, and I had in my mind a longing to eat, and to afterwards order my favorite dessert, cherries jubilee, which would be made to flame and set in the center of the table, and I had in my mind the idea of submitting to the committee a drawing of an enormous plate of cherries, perpetually burning, to be set in the center of the park, as a memorial to the war, that acre of conflagration. And perhaps also in my mind was the hope that such a ridiculous idea would of course be ignored and as a result I would be left in peace, the one thing I desired, even beyond cherries. And I could see the committee, after abandoning my idea, remaining in their seats fighting over the designs of others, far into the after-hours of the work day, their struggles never seeming to end, and then I wanted to submit an idea of themselves as a memorial for the war, the conference table on an

236

island in the middle of the pond, though at least some of them would have to be willing to die in the enactment. And then I saw on the ground an unnamed insect in its solitary existence, making its laborious way through tough blades of grass that threatened its route, and using a stick that lay nearby I drew a circle around the animal—if you can call him that—and at once what had been but a moment of middling drama became a theatre of conflict, for as the insect continued to fumble lopsided in circles it seemed to me that his efforts had increased, not only by my interest in them, but by the addition of a perimeter which he now seemed intent on escaping. I looked up then, and what happened next I cannot describe without a considerable loss of words: I saw a drinking fountain. It had not suddenly appeared, it must have always been there, it must have been there as I walked past it and sat down on the bench, it must have been there yesterday, and during the war, and in the afternoons before the war. It was a plain gunmetal drinking fountain, of the old sort, a basin on a pedestal, and it stood there, an ordinary object that had become an unspeakable gift, a wonder of civilization, and I had an overwhelming desire to see if it worked, I stood up then and approached it timidly, as I would a woman, I bent low and put my hand on its handle and my mouth hovered over its spigot—I wanted to kiss it, I was going to kiss it—and I remembered with a horrible shock that in rising from the bench I had stepped on and killed the insect, I could hear again its death under my left foot, though this did not deter me from finishing my kiss, and as the water came forth with a low bubbling at first and finally an arch that reached my mouth, I began to devise a secret route out of the park that would keep me occupied for some time, when I looked up, holding the miraculous water in my mouth, and saw the ducks in mid-flight, their wings shedding water drops which returned to the pond, and remembered in amazement that I could swallow, and I did, then a bit of arcane knowledge returned to me from an idle moment of reading spent years ago, before the war: that a speculum is not only an instrument regarded by most with horror, as well as an ancient mirror, and a medieval compendium of all knowledge, but a patch of color on the lower wing segments of most ducks and some other birds. Thus I was able, in serenest peace, to make my way back to my garret and design the memorial which was not elected and never built, but remained for me an end to the war that had ended.

(2001)

237

∾

Because the ones I work for do not love me, because I have said too much and I haven't been sure of what is right and I've hated the people I've trusted, because I work in an office and we are lost and when I come home I say their lives are theirs and they don't know what they apologize for and none of it mended, because I let them beat me and I remember something of mine which not everyone has, and because I lie to keep my self and my hands my voice on the phone what I swallow what hurts me, because I hurt them—

I give them the hours I spend away from them and carry them, even in my sleep, at least as the nag of a misplaced shoe, for years after I have quit and gone on to another job where I hesitate in telling and I remember and I resent having had to spend more time with them than with the ones I love.

(1989)

Life is boundless. Matter is without edge. We grow always outward from ancient explosions and the heavenly bodies distance themselves from each other, then steady, balanced with various pulls. There is a new place.

Like a cartoon, like a promise that we, too, could buy new cars and eat anything, Armstrong bounced his puffy life onto the powder of the moon. We were all watching, tired of the delays.

If there is too much to keep track of, or if it is simply discouraging or overwhelming to live in the world, there is a hideout which can look something like the Sea of Tranquillity. There is aimlessness like dust in a light shaft. There are alternatives now: vacant expanses, time's measure lost, the emptiness that turns us inside and prods us empty and stupid like that funny flag he kept trying to straighten—taffeta-stiff and unruly. And then it stood out flat.

Disappointed in the dead moon, we could believe the myth of abandon, the giant step of surrender. We tired young, each begging, "Take me, weightlessness, where it is quiet, dark-sky'd and clean."

(1989)

FRAN CARLEN (1954–)

∾

Anna Karenina

1

All night everything was ending. Happiness defected to another family. "And how was your day," she would ask him. "Stupidly perfect. More like a gesture than a day," Karenin complained. The declension of bright start-overs divisible by a televised parade of swan-girls. "The more we want swift return, simulated union, apparel . . ." He began talking at length about resurrection. "Another drawn-out expository with pointed indifference," she sighed. Her phlegmatic eyewear and his long-suffering cravat were at cross-purposes. It would be interesting to see where he stood when the universe broke in two.

2

"I think . . ." "Prunes, don't get started on that again." He felt he was above brand-name bifurcation. Fixatives like fidelity and flight spelled fiction in her book. Anna paused to sense the tremor of the planet, wobbling in its lopsided orbit. Or the pull of an older world with more accessories.

3

Death came like a door suddenly blown open by the wind. Then came the stationing of strangers taking Polaroids. All at once she was a widow. She put on a disc. Schwanengesang always took away the bottom. Her problem was how to undo the domino of numbers. And redemption, threadcount, smog and plate tectonics all tossed together. Distilling dirt from money had driven some people mad (it was one of the paradoxes of modernism).

4

"Grizzled cult! Esthetes! Back away from the door!" The lamb showed up with pince-nez and a supercilious grin. He said his name was Andrey Bely, and he bore a striking resemblance to Andrey Bely.

"Where are your works on paper?" he demanded.

Movers took away the divan. "When she doesn't sing, she counts. When she stops counting, she sings. When she's not singing, she's counting. When she's not counting or singing, she cries," the factotum explained to the lamb.

"Tu es vraiment dégueulasse."

Animal cruelty. Movie lies. Levin missing. The blank noise of lack.

"An excursion to the seashore could alter everything."

"Ah, peregrination . . . is just so sweet you want to disappear," Bely brayed leaving.

5

Her fertility was mental. After all who can fault the wind? Well, everyone. It wasn't like her to ask why. She was going to die. She put on another disc. An oblong monologue about herself or transport. Dwelling on events that may never have happened. In her mind's eye: Alma Ata. And dread of slipping through the tissue of the ridiculous. Listening to the adagio she felt as lonely as the moon, and fell asleep with her hands in her pockets.

6

In the Bildungsroman, the hero never reads the gazette but deliberates his own demise or mankind's. She read *The Lives of the Saints*. At a moment's notice she could give up whom she desired. The paste of her saintly pallor. She ambled along yawning like a dog.

Would he call on her again, the lamby? She guessed nyet with certitude. He was the type who liked to stay up late and make senseless rhymes. That morning he offered her fish in a bucket if she could fetch him water without the bucket.

8

She spilled two glasses of tea but still had the keys to the dacha. At least the confiture and poésie were still intact. She had wanted him to stay all day, in the bathroom. She should have lacquered herself, put butter in the butter dish. "There goes the muse, the sepulchre, the tidy sacrifice, witless but uplifting reason," she thought as the door blew open.

"Cuttlefish! Why pay a fine for sugar! What are you, period. Nice and crisp, mind you!" Palimpsest, his calling card. "Anna?" Or was it palindrome?

"While you were away, I dreamt I was throwing everyone and breaking them, just like a child."

"Angels are allowed to watch but they can't get involved."

". . . trying to break the sound habit of reasoning."

"Yet since Vronsky you keep changing the subject back to yourself."

". . . to show up as myself in mimesis."

"Just imagine a devouring dragon in a crinoline. Medusa with more élan."

"That's your remedy for glossolalia?"

"Do you have any Pop-tarts?"

"I have some lamb-chops."

"Register your anguish as it breaks your heart and makes you want to die.

Sign here."

This devochka must lie. "Diaries take up space," she thought.

"Everything is born in ether," she tried.

"It's Folsom for you this time, baby," he replied.

Your basic enfant térrible. Behold, what, gone. "Goodnight, sweet pike, goodnight, goodnight . . ." Her toy-boat voice bobbed up and down over the surface of the song.

9

Or danger hanging voluptuously in mid-air, ebbing and flowing of faces, bedlam of incandescent limbs, vehicles, ragged archetypes, handy alchemical settings, lingual bridges to concomitant connectors, any system would do, certain death: sleeplessness.

10

Layered innuendo and memory. Checklist of her shortcomings. The poseurs were dropping like flies. The others were just lucky at cards. The next card she turned would bring her closer to death. There was the anesthesia plus the shiny lubricants they use for electroshock. Women from another continuum stood at the foot of her sledge. "Snap out of it, Anna."

(to be concluded)

(2000)

243

Anal Nap

Am an ass. Max calls, wants jam—fast. Can't. Sax's flat. Talks and rants. Max grabs dark Anna at bar, lass drank a malt, Max grappa. Play blackjack—what a lark. Anna asks Fat Sal, and Sal has smack. Anna bags a gram. Chants, Shall waltz! Falls alas daft Pallas. Bad crash—wan gal, Max brash, whacks Anna, what crap.

Catch a tram. Pass Schrafft's. Grab BLT and Franz Kafka at St. Mark's. Hank stands at bar and drags a fag. As a prank Jack'll smash Cal's watch. Cal slams Jack's glass at wall. Glass shards catch Nan. Nan bawls. Brat! All damp and sad. Back at B's pad, B barfs all day, shat. Saw B scratch wall and scrawl tract: Last Law. What a mad bard. Shan't last.

At park, Bach's rap, rap Bach. Car alarm. Van stalls and cabs and fast cars stand. Sat and had a nap. Want a warm black shawl, cash, mass, a dark psalm. Want calm.

(2000)

~

An Anointing

Boys have to slash their fingers to become brothers. Girls trade their Kotex, me and Molly do in the mall's public facility.

Me and Molly never remember each other's birthdays. On purpose. We don't like scores of any kind. We don't wear watches or weigh ourselves.

Me and Molly have tasted beer. We drank our shampoo. We went to the doctor together and lifted our specimen cups in a toast. We didn't drink that stuff. We just gargled.

When me and Molly get the urge, we are careful to put it back exactly as we found it. It looks untouched.

Between the two of us, me and Molly have 20/20 vision.

Me and Molly are in eighth grade for good. We like it there. We adore the view. We looked both ways and decided not to cross the street. Others who'd been to the other side didn't return. It was a trap.

Me and Molly don't double date. We don't multiply anything. We don't know our multiplication tables from a coffee table. We'll never be decent waitresses, indecent ones maybe.

Me and Molly do not believe in going ape or going bananas or going Dutch. We go as who we are. We go as what we are.

Me and Molly have wiped each other's asses with ferns. Made emergency tampons of our fingers. Me and Molly make do with what we have.

Me and Molly are in love with wiping the blackboard with each other's hair. The chalk gives me and Molly an idea of what old age is like; it is dusty and makes us sneeze. We are allergic to it.

Me and Molly, that's M and M, melt in your mouth.

What are we doing in your mouth? Me and Molly bet you'll never guess. Not in a million years. We plan to be around that long. Together that long. Even if we must freeze the moment and treat the photograph like the real thing.

Me and Molly don't care what people think. We're just glad that they do.

Me and Molly lick the dew off the morning grasses but taste no honey till we lick each other's tongues.

We wear full maternity sails. We boat upon my broken water. The katabatic action begins, Molly down my canal binnacle first, her water breaking in me like an anointing.

(1992)

Cold Calls

1. The spatial/temporal lacuna insures the possibility of temporary disruption—or permanent abortion—of service, insures only the probability of successful enunciation, its own passing over. Cf. Paul Laurence Dunbar as an example of such disruption, failure, breakdown: "My voice falls dead a foot from mine old lips/And but its ghost doth reach that vessel/passing, passing."[1]

2. God don't play that, so radio ratio—slippage: ebonics to tinkling the ivories, Eagle Nebula <M16, ice cream cones crowned with cherries, in short, EGGS, EGGS, EGGS ... "In contrast, stars forming in more isolated circumstances presumably can continue to gather materials from surrounding gas clouds until their mature stellar dynamics halt the growth."[2]

3. Foreign respondent—"How White American"—Amy Biehl—" 'Sister' "—chased across a street—"Died in a Township"—after her car was stopped—"one settler"—by a crowd of youths—"one bullet"—tripped—"I am not able to properly articulate any political ideology or motivation for my conduct"—fell—"South Africa is free today because of the bloodshed."[3]

4. Essay in a bottle cast out to sea, or placed in a jar on a hill in Tennessee, Penelope, weaving and unweaving, Scheherazade's thousand-plus deferments, time-lapsed Grecian Urn, bulk mailings, extensions of credit lines, free-market economies: manifold apocrypha: hope a project beyond approximate futures, Godot in which the thrown, not yet thrown back, esse.

5. In the salad bowl of the museum, the Blonde Negress, a vigilant anachronism, deserts her post and joins her fellow patrons, a line refraining (in) the head she calls her body: "Lo, I am black but I am comely too." Among the periods, she attempts rememory: Is "but" conjunctive? Disjunctive? Her?[4]

6. Not *de gustibus* but homegoing, via Heaven's Gate (< Hale-Bopp) — or another via: "Wherefore do we pray/Is not the God of the fathers dead?"[5] Or yet still a third via: "teeth or trees or lemons piled on a step."[6] Or yet still: two men sitting at a bar. One turns to the other: "Aren't you *the* Artie Shaw?" The other retorts: "No, I'm the other one."[7] Despite the end of identical actions at a distance (< Schrodinger's equation), pursuit converts us: ancestors of our hope, the via, the nectar.

7. from someone who, no longer there, abandoned handset swinging back and forth, fruit laced with strange, charm, top, and bottom—not vocabularized but ventriloquized—in an upright glass coffin rhyming with the "rough-hewn tribute in wood" to an anonymous African American rider, not "divinity alive in stone" aka "William Tecumseh Sherman at Fifth Ave. and 60th. Street in Birmingham, Ala." An anti-Trojan, virus astride.[8]

8. Inaudible howl, "foo seee like lee,"[9] the diving chrysalis[10]—hell with a little heaven in it[11]—and should it surface, should it find its way back home, should its first night back on earth not be its last

9. Ambivalence of double cadence: an extra nail, or the anvil then the claw

10. "Neither there nor there/Almost here/a little nearer to the stars/strangers to the left and right/pages turned, still to be turned,/still there, never to be mine/and here comes a smile/which never arrives—/'Can I get you some-thing?'/'Food/For future years.' "[12]

11. "All this in the hands of children, eyes already set/on a land we never can visit—it isn't there yet—"[13]

12. The "apron of leaves," the pieces of silver—what human, having embodied God as shame and guilt, would not be disappointed that only the same could disembody him?[14]

13. The New Grammar: Neo-Babel: "Trucks, limousines and pickups . . . smashed to pieces." Crashing into a skyscraper, a Boeing jet "disgorged its sinful passengers," "bodies spilling across the road into 'The Peaceful View' cemetery"—paradigm of grammar and Babel—from which their spirits "floated upwards towards a glowing image of Jesus high in the clouds."[15]

Endnotes

1. Paul Laurence Dunbar, "Ships that Pass in the Night," *The Complete Poems of Paul Laurence Dunbar* (Hakim's Publications, 210 South 52nd Street, Philadelphia, PA 19139), p. 64.
2. *The New York Times*, 11/3/95 and 11/30/95, Science Sections.
3. *The New York Times*, 8/27/93 and 7/9/97.
4. Lewis Alexander, "The Dark Brother," *Caroling Dusk*, edited and with a foreword by Countee Cullen (Citadel Press, 1993; orig. Harpers & Brothers, 1927), p. 124.
5. W. E. B. DuBois, "A Litany of Atlanta," *Caroling Dusk*, p. 27.
6. Amiri Baraka, "Black Art," *Transbluesency: Selected Poems 1961–1995*, edited by Paul Vangelisti (Marsilio Publishers, New York: 1995), p. 142.
7. *The New York Times*, 8/19/94.
8. Claude McKay, "Russian Cathedral," *Caroling Dusk*, p. 88; Judith Shea's "The Other Monument," as reported in *The New York Times*, 8/24/95.
9. Julia Tavalaro and Richard Tayson, *Look Up for Yes* (Kodansha International, 1997), p. 12.
10. Jean Dominique Bauby, *The Diving Bell and the Butterfly*, translated by Jeremy Leggatt (Alfred A. Knopf, 1997).
11. George MacDonald: "There is no heaven with a little hell in it." Circa 1886.
12. William Wordsworth, "Tintern Abbey," in *English Romantic Writers*, edited by David Perkins (Harcourt Brace Jovanovich, Inc. 1967), p. 209.
13. Miller Williams, "Of History and Hope," *The Ways We Touch* (University of Illinois Press, 1997).
14. Elaine Scarry, *The Body in Pain* (Oxford University Press, 1985), p. 360, footnote 23.
15. "The Coming Rapture," painting by an unknown artist, in Jeremy Marre and Hannah Charlton, *Beats of the Heart: Popular Music of the World* (Pantheon Books, 1985), p. 57.

(2000)

HARRYETTE MULLEN (?–)

∽

Variation on a Theme Park

My Mickey Mouse ears are nothing like sonar. Colorado is far less
rusty than Walt's lyric riddles. If sorrow is wintergreen, well then Walt's
breakdancers are dunderheads. If hoecakes are Wonder Bras, blond
Wonder Bras grow on Walt's hornytoad. I have seen roadkill damaged,
riddled and wintergreen, but no such roadkill see I in Walt's checkbook.
And in some purchases there is more deliberation than in the bargains
that my Mickey Mouse redeems. I love to herd Walt's sheep, yet well I
know that muskrats have a far more platonic sonogram. I grant I never
saw a googolplex groan. My Mickey Mouse, when Walt waddles, trips
on garbanzos. And yet, by halogen-light, I think my loneliness as reck-
less as any souvenir bought with free coupons.

(2002)

The Anthropic Principle

The pope of cosmology addresses a convention. When he talks the whole atmosphere changes. He speaks through a computer. When he asks can you hear me, the whole audience says yes. It's a science locked up in a philosophical debate. There are a few different theories. There could be many different realities. You might say ours exists because we do. You could take a few pounds of matter, heat it to an ungodly temperature, or the universe was a freak accident. There may be a limit to our arrogance, but one day the laws of physics will read like a detailed instruction manual. A plane that took off from its hub in my hometown just crashed in the President's hometown. The news anchor says the pilot is among the dead. I was hoping for news of the President's foreign affair with a diplomat's wife. I felt a mystical connection to the number of confirmed dead whose names were not released. Like the time I was three handshakes from the President. Like when I thought I heard that humanitarians dropped a smart blond on the Chinese embassy. Like when the cable was severed and chairs fell from the sky because the pilot flew with rusty maps. What sane pilot would land in that severe rain with hard hail and gale-force wind. With no signal of distress. With no foghorns to warn the civilians, the pilot lost our moral compass in the bloody quagmire of collateral damage. One theory says it's just a freak accident locked up in a philosophical debate. It's like playing poker and all the cards are wild. Like the arcane analysis of a black box full of insinuations of error.

(2002)

Sleeping with the Dictionary

I beg to dicker with my silver-tongued companion, whose lips are ready to read my shining gloss. A versatile partner, conversant and well-versed in the verbal art, the dictionary is not averse to the solitary habits of the curiously wide-awake reader. In the dark night's insomnia, the book is a stimulating sedative, awakening my tired imagination to the hypnagogic trance of language. Retiring to the canopy of the bedroom, turning on the bedside light, taking the big dictionary to bed, clutching the unabridged bulk, heavy with the weight of all the meanings between these covers, smoothing the thin sheets, thick with accented syllables—all are exercises in the conscious regimen of dreamers, who toss words on their tongues while turning illuminated pages. To go through all these motions and procedures, groping in the dark for an alluring word, is the poet's nocturnal mission. Aroused by myriad possibilities, we try out the most perverse positions in the practice of our nightly act, the penetration of the denotative body of the work. Any exit from the logic of language might be an entry in a symptomatic dictionary. The alphabetical order of this ample block of knowledge might render a dense lexicon of lucid hallucinations. Beside the bed, a pad lies open to record the meandering of migratory words. In the rapid eye movement of the poet's night vision, this dictum can be decoded, like the secret acrostic of a lover's name.

(2002)

SUSAN WHEELER (1955–)

❧

Invective: You Should Know

One

Now you are in a lather over their taking the Scrabble pieces and using them for decoration. Refresh yourself, bone up on organizational skills, *a three-ring binder and this new version of Whist will fit you out like new.* For they are beginning to talk when you bend to tie your shoe. They say, *the 'x' goes perfectly in this xylophone.* Before the Roman with the brogue begins his hatcheting, you will have draped yourself as a workhorse courtesan with plenty of extra letters to spare. You will have blanks for everyone, on demand. They will know *just how invaluable you are: their burgeoning pockets will attest to it.* So now, wipe the spittle from your rouged chin. The players are waiting for you.

Two

I knew my hand was not a valued commodity since I could not bring a powerful or even compelling family to it. It started with your dad's sweater, *that wonderful Italian cut,* watching you carried away by the romance of your dancer dad. Well it wasn't just *your* romance, everyone it seemed had a way of embellishing a family or in-laws—except perhaps for the thoroughly jaundiced, like mom, who didn't like anyone but the chirpy and anxious "helpers." It started when you held out the sweater and said, *Here it's my father's, it's a wonderful Italian cut, you can borrow this.* Suddenly all the Vegas motifs to the apartment lent you, the bearer, a tragic kind of 20th century captive of sleaze giant kind of thing, dangling the Italian cut sweater from your outstretched arm.

Three

In the meeting room your chaps, Festus, seemed out of place. How sunnily you seem to find the filetab that attaches to each article in seven. There was some talk among us studio sausages that you had run aground on the Foreign Correspondence project and canned the rest, and that is why you hum to yourself at table. Yesterday I saw your wife picking peaches into your rival's basket—she had the softest smile, like strawberries, hellbent on your ruin.

Four

I hadn't forgotten the favor you had done me in the barn catercorner to the milkpond those some ten years ago, and when that peacenik spoke ill of you I rose to your defense. I told him about your cock, dear heart, about the wiggle in its walk and the soft cradle you made of the down for my head. If I mentioned the leg you ran off with, my only steed, if I happened to say that the books you were selling could not substitute, if I said that your fingers were as fast and my fall as great as Lucifer's, that you and I are much alike, that His Will it was and His Will is cruel, if the peacenik then stared with incredulity, well you will have heard it all before, no, my precious one?

(1997)

APRIL BERNARD (1956–)

❧

Exegesis

The careful toe-step of the tabby out on errands. She provides the condition of containment tossed off, unperformed, gratuitous and therefore possible. So with every line scratch out an old date, ink full in the interstices, and do not reread. Her eyes do not flicker to see who seized the trophy woodrat and waved it on parade.

Once the battle is ended and the armies marched off, on whatever barrow or horse or big-wheeled wagon; and grass hints through charred ground; there I lie, not dead, curled in the netted hay roots of the new field. I am listening to grasshoppers remember themselves, and to the erratic looped notes of the towhee: a cascade cut short, begun again, cut short, has she forgotten, no, not this try, each note clear flashed as the yellow-green lights of the maple tree leaves that surround her, spiraling up and over and back in a helix of sound.

There is the possibility of a cabin, already I can hear the whipsaw gnash pine, the shavings release their resin that is song.

If it took an immolation to bare the ground, that is what it took.

So housed about by doubt, beams spiring, most sagrada of cities sky-lit in the tooth of this time, reaches.

(1993)

AMY GERSTLER (1956–)

❧

Dear Boy George

Only three things on earth seem useful or soothing to me. One:
wearing stolen clothes. Two: photos of exquisitely dressed redheads.
Three: your voice on the radio. Those songs fall smack-dab into my
range! Not to embarrass you with my raw American awe, or let you
think I'm the kinda girl who bends over for any guy who plucks his
eyebrows and can make tight braids—but you're the plump bisexual
cherub of the eighties: clusters of Rubens' painted angels, plus a dol-
lop of the Pillsbury dough boy, all rolled into one! We could go
skating, or just lie around my house eating pineapple. I could pierce
your ears: I know how to freeze the lobes with ice so it doesn't hurt.
When I misunderstand your lyrics, they get even better. I thought the
line I'M YOUR LOVER, NOT YOUR RIVAL, WAS I'M ANOTHER, NOT THE
BIBLE, or PRIME YOUR MOTHER, NOT A LIBEL, or UNDERCOVER BOUGHT
ARRIVAL. Great, huh? See, we're of like minds. I almost died when I
read in the *Times* how you saved that girl from drowning . . . dived
down and pulled the blubbering sissy up. I'd give anything to be the
limp, dripping form you stumbled from the lake with, draped over
your pale, motherly arms, in a grateful faint, as your mascara ran and
ran.

(1986)

Bitter Angel

You appear in a tinny, nickel-and-dime light. The light of turned milk and gloved insults. It could be a gray light you're bathed in; at any rate, it isn't quite white. It's possible you show up coated with a finite layer of the dust that rubs off moths' wings onto kids' grubby fingers. Or you arrive cloaked in a toothache's smoldering glow. Or you stand wrapped like a maypole in rumpled streamers of light torn from threadbare bedsheets. Your gaze flickers like a silent film. You make me lose track. Which dim, deluded light did I last see you in? The light of extinction, most likely, where there are no more primitive tribesmen who worship clumps of human hair. No more roads that turn into snakes, or ribbons. There's no nightlife or lion's share, none of the black-and-red roulette wheels of methedrine that would-be seers like me dream of. You alone exist: eyes like locomotives. A terrible succession of images buffets you: human faces pile up in your sight, like heaps of some flunky's smudged, undone paperwork.

(1990)

The Bear-Boy of Lithuania

Girls, take my advice, marry an animal. A wooly one is most consoling. Find a fur man, born midwinter. Reared in the mountains. Fond of boxing. Make sure he has black rubbery lips, and a sticky sweet mouth. A winter sleeper. Pick one who likes to tussle, who clowns around the kitchen, juggles hot baked potatoes, gnaws playfully on a corner of your apron. Not one mocked by his lumbering instincts, or who's forever wrestling with himself, tainted with shame, itchy with chagrin, but a good-tempered beast who plunges in greedily, grinning and roaring. His backslapping manner makes him popular with the neighbors, till he digs up and eats their Dutch tulip bulbs. Then you see just how stuffy human beings can be. On Sundays his buddies come over to play watermelon football. When they finally get tired, they collapse on heaps of dried grass and leaves, scratching themselves elaborately, while I hand out big hunks of honeycomb. They've no problem swallowing dead bees stuck in the honey.

A bear-boy likes to stretch out on the floor and be roughly brushed with a broom. Never tease him about his small tail, which is much like a chipmunk's. If you do, he'll withdraw to the hollow of some tree, as my husband has done whenever offended since he first left the broad-leafed woodlands to live in this city, which is so difficult for him. Let him be happy in his own way: filling the bathtub with huckleberries, or packing dark, earthwormy dirt under the sofa. Don't mention the clawmarks on the refrigerator. (You know he can't retract them.) Nothing pleases him more than a violent change in climate, especially if it snows while he's asleep and he wakes to find the landscape blanketed. Then his teeth chatter with delight. He stamps and paws the air for joy. Exuberance is a bear's inheritance. He likes northern light. Excuse me, please. His bellow summons me. Let me start again. True, his speech is shaggy music. But by such gruff instruction, I come to know love. It's difficult to hear the story of his forest years with dry eyes. He always snuffs damply at my hand before kissing it. My fingers tingle at the thought of that sensitive, mobile nose. You've no *idea* how long his tongue is. At night, I get into bed, pajama pockets full of walnuts. He rides me around the garden in the wheelbarrow now that I'm getting heavy with his cubs. I hope our sons will be much like their father, but not suffer so much discomfort wearing shoes.

(2000)

DIONISIO D. MARTÍNEZ (1956–)

❧

Avant-Dernières Pensées

IDYLLE

In today's mail I found the chain letter you've been sending for years. I know your handwriting, your desperation, the peculiar way in which you fold the paper. This plea, you tell me, has been around the world three, maybe four times. This plea is sacred. This plea is our last hope for anything. In theory, intimidation can penetrate anything. We all break sooner or later. The letters are carefully packed with case histories that go off like timed explosives. I can see you waiting for each one to go off, wondering if the one you designed for me will do the trick. One summer, you say, a Portuguese fisherman received this letter and burned it. He spent the rest of his life trying to read the ashes.

AUBADE

I thought it over. This letter is not sacred. It promises nothing. It is a plea for anything, which is like saying a plea for nothing. There was a faint barking as I walked toward the window. It was the sound dogs make when a stranger approaches. I began to doubt my own presence in the house, my hands opening the window to more barking. You must copy the entire letter, you said. The copies you make, the warning continued, must be indistinguishable from the source. I made the copies. I slept with the words beside me. This morning I thought it over. I tore the letter, replaced it with a blank sheet, folded the sheet in that peculiar way I learned from you.

MÉDITATION

On the coast of Portugal they began a tradition, you say. With the letters still inside the sealed envelopes, the wives of fishermen burn the mail they receive. This way, you tell me, superstition is impossible. But isn't this a superstition of sorts? It's really a mockery of belief, you say. I sometimes wonder how we've managed to correspond this long through chain letters. I wonder how we've been able to sustain this dialogue between two anonymous voices. I think of the widows along the Portuguese coast, their chain mail used as fuel for their stoves. I think of them selling rotten cod fish wrapped in anonymous letters that have circled the world three, maybe four times. I am spending the night in Viana do Castelo. I will send this postcard unsigned.

(1994)

CATHERINE BOWMAN (1957–)

❧

No Sorry

Do you have any scissors I could borrow? *No, I'm sorry I don't.* What about a knife? You got any knives? A good paring knife would do or a simple butcher knife or maybe a cleaver? *No, sorry all I have is this old bread knife my grandfather used to butter his bread with every morning.* Well then, how about a hand drill or hammer, a bike chain, or some barbed wire? You got any rusty razor-edged barbed wire? You got a chain saw? *No, sorry I don't.* Well then maybe you might have some sticks? *I'm sorry, I don't have any sticks.* How about some stones? *No, I don't have any sticks or stones.* Well how about a stone tied to a stick? *You mean a club?* Yeah, a club. You got a club? *No, sorry, I don't have any clubs.* What about some fighting picks, war axes, military forks, or tomahawks? *No, sorry, I don't have any kind of war fork, axe, or tomahawk.* What about a morning star? *A morning star?* Yeah, you know, those spiked ball and chains they sell for riot control. *No, nothing like that. Sorry.* Now, I know you said you don't have a knife except for that dull old thing your grandfather used to butter his bread with every morning and he passed down to you but I thought maybe you just might have an Australian dagger with a quartz blade and a wood handle, or a bone dagger, or a Bowie, you know it doesn't hurt to ask? Or perhaps one of those lethal multi-purpose stilettos? *No, sorry.* Or maybe you have a simple blow pipe? Or a complex airgun? *No, I don't have a simple blow pipe or a complex airgun.* Well then maybe you have a jungle carbine, a Colt, a revolver, a Ruger, an axis bolt-action repeating rifle with telescopic sight for sniping, a sawed-off shotgun? Or better yet, a gas-operated self-loading fully automatic assault weapon? *No, sorry I don't.* How about a hand grenade? *No.* How about a tank? *No.* Shrapnel? *No.* Napalm? *No.* Napalm 2. *No, sorry I don't.* Let me ask you this. Do you have any intercontinental ballistic missiles? Or submarine-launched cruise missiles? Or multiple independently targeted reentry missiles? Or terminally guided anti-tank shells or projectiles? Let me ask you this. Do you have any fission bombs or hydrogen bombs? Do you have any thermonuclear warheads? Got any electronic measures or electronic counter-measures or electronic counter-counter-measures? Got any biological weapons or germ warfare, preferably in aerosol form? Got any enhanced tactical neutron lasers emitting massive doses of whole-body gamma radiation? Wait a minute. Got any plutonium? Got any chemical agents, nerve agents, blister agents, you know, like mustard gas, any choking agents or incapacitating agents or toxin agents? *Well I'm not sure. What do they look like?* Liquid vapor powder colorless gas. Invisible. *I'm not sure. What do they smell like?* They smell like fruit, garlic, fish or soap, new-mown hay, apple blossoms, or like those little green peppers that your grandfather probably would tend to in his garden every morning after he buttered his bread with that old bread knife that he passed down to you.

(1997)

Of Flesh and Spirit

I was a virgin till I was 23. Then I always had more than one lover at the same time all secret.

In China, people are given the death sentence for watching a porno video while they can get free condoms and pills at any department store provided and mandated by law.

When my mother handed me my first bra which she made for me, I screamed and ran out the door in shame. She cut the bra into pieces because it was too small for her own use.

For 800 years, women's bound feet were the most beautiful and erotic objects for Chinese men. Tits and buns were nothing compared to a pair of three-inch "golden lotuses." They must be crazy or their noses must have had problems. My grandma's feet, wrapped day and night with layers of bandages, smelled like rotten fish.

The asshole in Chinese: the eye of the fart.

A 25-year-old single woman in China worries her parents. A 28-year-old single woman worries her friends and colleagues. A 30-year-old single woman worries her bosses. A 35-year-old single woman is pitied and treated as a sexual pervert.

The most powerful curse: fuck your mother, fuck your grandmother, fuck your great grandmother of eighteen generations.

One day, my father asked my mother if our young rooster was mature enough to jump, meaning to "mate." I cut in before my mother answered: "Yes, I saw him jump onto the roof of the chicken shed." I was ten years old.

Women call menstruation "the old ghost," the science book calls it "the moon period," and the refined people say "the moonlight is flooding the ditch."

My first lover vowed to marry me in America after he had my virginity. He had two kids, and an uneducated wife, and dared not ask for a divorce from the police. He took me to see his American Chinese cousin who was staying in the Beijing Hotel and tried to persuade his cousin to sponsor him to come to America. But his cousin sponsored me instead. That's how I am here and why he went back to his wife and is probably still cursing me.

Chinese peasants call their wives: that one in my house; Chinese intellectuals call their wives and concubines: the doll in a golden house; in the socialist system, husbands and wives call each other "my lover."

The story my grandma never tired of telling was about a man who was punished for his greed and had to walk around with a penis hanging on his forehead.

We don't say "fall in love," but "talk love."

When I left home, my father told me: never talk love before you are 25 years old. I didn't listen. Well, my first lover was a married coward. My first marriage lasted a week. My husband slept with me once, and I never saw him again.

(1993)

∾

Notes on the Orgasm

The orgasm is your invisible counterpart. She goes out in the world, wreaking havoc.

The orgasm knows all things are animate. The houses groan with grief and passion. Sometimes a mirror bursts from a wall and shatters, no longer content with mere images.

The orgasm tells you to be careful or, in the language of orgasms, to have fears. Orgasms thrive on danger.

The orgasm says we are all parts of herself. We are but launching pads for her spiritual development. After she is done with us, she will be ready for fucking angels.

The orgasm encourages us to let our minds wander. Usually this is good advice, but sometimes she gets lost in thought.

When the orgasm tells you that you are a mere object of her scientific research and the only real man on earth, the orgasm is slowly dissecting your body.

The orgasm will peel you like an orange. You may feel exposed, raw, even wounded. The orgasm wants you to live life without the rind.

The orgasm thinks people are like dresses. You don't just buy the first one off the rack. You try them on for size.

The orgasm tells you many stories. Some she will never finish. She cannot help herself. She always lies. Such beautiful lies. You want them all. Why would you need truth when you can have an orgasm?

Every now and then a casualty occurs. An orgasm accidentally injures or murders a man. She is startled by the moans escaping from his lips at this moment, so much like those of pleasure. She wonders if human pain is a kind of celebration.

Sometimes the orgasm falls in love with you. She cannot tear herself from your pungent flesh. For days you walk around, gasping for air. You are in a state of constant excitement. One day the orgasm abandons you. The entire world is reduced to a memory, a mere elegy to an orgasm.

In a single sitting a hungry orgasm can consume a man, socks and all. Women take more time.

Many dislike the speed of orgasm, the way she comes and goes and takes all she can get. The orgasm cannot help herself. She has no tomorrow.

According to the orgasm, there is no difference between real and imaginary events. Everything is a secret message only she can decipher.

Often the orgasm tells you a story about you. About you and about the secret powers lying dormant within you. She waits for you on street corners and follows you down dark alleys, whispering your name, softly, her hands passing continually over your hair, caressing your bare shoulders. At night you sleep fitfully and dream of her. You are unable to tell whether you are a dream of the orgasm, or if the orgasm is a dream of you.

The orgasm is very happy to be an orgasm. Sometimes she wonders what it would be like to be a man, sort of like the small boy who fills a Mason jar with spiders,wondering what it's like to be a fly.

(1993)

271

Always Have a Joyful Mind

How did I ever stand it? Those little sayings. Platitudes. The kind you always delivered, as if they were vitamins or the elixir of life. Take: *Beautiful thoughts make a beautiful day.* Or: *Always have a joyful mind.* As if I could live like an ant in honey. As if my mind could stay in one place forever, a tiny lit room, a strip of beach — sun-drenched skies. As if there were no one else, no strangers sleeping in your room. As if my lips were made of rose petals, and the sound of my thoughts were Pachelbel's canon, playing on repeat. As if sadness did not cling to my skin like a fine yellow dust. As if, just once, if only for a moment, that tiny thread connecting me to this earth, to the wine in my teacup, to the phone that stops answering me, to the street below where I see you walking though the winter snow, the rainy sidewalks, the sunlit cabs — could be cut as easily as *snip, snip*

and I would ascend like Mohammed's horse, like the rider of Mohammed's horse, or the angel of the rider of Mohammed's horse, or the halo of the angel of Mohammed's horse, a bright ring of light glimpsed for a moment by you, my dearest —

yes, you. But I wouldn't notice. I'd be too far above you. I and my ever-joyful mind.

(2001)

MICHAEL FRIEDMAN (1960–)

༄

Lecture

The telltale tapping one hears deep in the forest is the woodpecker at work. Timber. Thus, the instability of the text is the necessary underpinning of one's approach to the tree, leaves always in flux or falling, just as, for example, you are not the person you were when you first got here and fell into the abyss of my obsession. I called and you weren't home, so I called someone else instead. She was home. I would propose, then, a discourse that foregrounds and valorizes this instability.

(2000)

Death

Rupert Brooke and his ladyfriend stroll along the Cam. Before long he has gone up in a puff of smoke with "the flower of England's youth"—not a loser, surely, but beautiful, certainly, when I see him beneath the light blue rotunda of Pierson College library at midnight, fall, 1982, on the frontispiece of a first edition of his poems. High cheekbones, blonde hair, a side-part. Rimbaud was a beautiful loser. As we drove up Old Snakey, I realized you were my true love, like the Mysterious Island one has always imagined but never believed in, until waking on its shores. Later I stood alone on the turnpike, programming the possible routes to Beale Street via the Peabody Hotel. As darkness fell the band began to play, couples made their way to the roof.

(2000)

State

Several Frenchmen meet in the city square. Their conversation is lively and wide-ranging. At dusk, Diderot, Rousseau and Condorcet go their separate ways. A couple of days later I dropped by The Gauntlet in West Hollywood, where Bob worked. As I looked around, photos of something Bob called a "Prince Albert" caught my attention. He spent a few minutes explaining how it works and how much he had been enjoying his own Prince Albert, etc. He was delighted when I said I planned to give serious consideration to getting one for myself.

(2000)

STEPHANIE BROWN (1961–)

Commencement Address

I have no more to say about throwing up or causing myself to get diarrhea there's nothing heroic about it though the movies on TV want us to endure quietly and cry appropriately. It's a wonderful role for any young actress to place herself in some dead household where the dialogue is sexual between all of them including dead grandparents who are still alive in theory and very much inside everyone's bodies, clucking away like old geezers with huge inflated egos bruised by the failure of their children to spend each moment worshipping their self-created sun. So the girl you see who opens her legs to the idea of fucking everyone who says hello but also wants to feel like a nun with vaginal orgasms rather than the ones his kisses and teeth cause which seemed to come to e.g., Saint Thérèse the Little Flower just from prayer in her cloister for hours which made the girl, the subject of this poem, cry for its truth and its nakedness. Because how could it be good to have that curly-haired boy put his face between your legs nearly every afternoon who will not even say he loves you and this is what your parents don't like about it: he will not spend his money on you or take you places in his car. But of course we have to learn to live inside fences and to sweep and clean lower our heads until in the end it is this which gives me flutters I do not need his teeth and lips at my sacred entrance I find release in order and demure discipline the needle and thread tongue-tied when you accept that you do not have this choice if you become a slut, after you see the error of your ways, you renounce them, you become someone who will live easily within his four walls where he keeps you like the flame of love inside his body there's no need to find the way out this is the way it will be and always was: all the mirrors around you say sacrifice order and love.

(1998)

DENISE DUHAMEL (1961–)

❧

A Nap on the Afternoon
of My 39th Birthday

(June 13, 2000)

A man sits between my husband and me in the movies, then puts his hand on my breast and says, "Let's go." I say, "Excuse me, I'm with my husband . . ." But my husband hushes me and points to the screen. The man says, "Your wife and I will meet you in the lobby," and without looking up, my husband says, "OK." The man pushes me against a wall—he has some kind of coarse beard and his pubic hair is all prickly like a scouring pad. I'm screaming for my husband, but he never comes. I don't do anything to save myself—no karate chop, no biting, no clawing. I want to be saved by my husband, but I'm not.

The bearded man takes me to a rodeo and says, "This is how it's done." The big animals are fucking and the females are screaming— they aren't bulls or cows, but something fiercer and weird-looking. I say to the man, "You are my nightmare." Then the same man is buying me ice cream and we're friends, maybe even married. My real husband never comes to get me which probably has nothing to do with the real-life him, but instead has everything to do with my anxiety. It may even be a basic lesson how I have to save myself. Or a primitive fantasy that I want to be taken, no matter how brutal.

In a hallway I meet up with two women who have been scorned, and we storm into a man's apartment. I'm going to help them do what— kill him? We are dressed like Charlie's Angels and the man is the same man who raped me, who then bought me ice cream. He is watching some kind of pornography—women with snakes. We toss the TV on top of him. His feet curl up, a la the Wicked Witch, while the TV smokes and our clothes evaporate. Then we are, all three of us, transformed into women with big round butts and tiny waists. We prance around wearing only gossamer wings, the height of desire on a 19th century sepia gentleman's postcard.

(2001)

CHRISTOPHER EDGAR (1961–)

❧

In C

Loosen focus, trees move. A weekend becomes a fortnight. Aspects of leaves float supine, assume the horizontal positions of pirogues and barques skirting air. Greasy plaits and tiny shoulders form the outline of a young girl. Reverse perspective and the basic facts become memoirs of an amnesiac lost among nuns. These exercises are clear from the verandahs of the modest bungalows dotting the peninsula. Natives dream in bergamot and bougainvillaea. And why not? Let it slide. The life of forms in art is short, pathological then normal, the distance between which the eye abolishes. An awareness of surface covers the dirty dog which is in fact curved, and we are all oriented toward a single point, skating harpy-like down a rivulet of pond scum to a spiral jetty in a giant ravine. Here the placid lake lay, until discovered upside-down in the 1840s by a group of brown studies. Some years later, Dirk "Poussin" Bouts halted discourse and the vanishing-axis rode off into the sunset. Evidence of cause and effect was ample, a staircase the foreshortened River Jordan must climb. Painterly waves converged into a plastic and solid mountain of water that in fact framed him. Enraged, he created a doctrine reflecting optical unity. Man-mountains became mountain men, and "water mountains" became bodies in space, "space boxes" tied together for better or worse, richer or poorer, with scotch tape. The necessary verso of the entire plane became largesse, weather more clement, a hollow body made of felt, *mutatis mutandis,* as with an uncertain decisiveness he shimmered forth toward the flat bank, behind which she disappeared on a funicular.

(1999)

278

∾

The Prose Poem

On the map it is precise and rectilinear as a chessboard, though driving past you would hardly notice it, this boundary line or ragged margin, a shallow swale that cups a simple trickle of water, less rill than rivulet, more gully than dell, a tangled ditch grown up throughout with a fearsome assortment of wildflowers and bracken. There is no fence, though here and there a weathered post asserts a former claim, strands of fallen wire taken by the dust. To the left a cornfield carries into the distance, dips and rises to the blue sky, a rolling plain of green and healthy plants aligned in close order, row upon row upon row. To the right, a field of wheat, a field of hay, young grasses breaking the soil, filling their allotted land with the rich, slow-waving spectacle of their grain. As for the farmers, they are, for the most part, indistinguishable: here the tractor is red, there yellow; here a pair of dirty hands, there a pair of dirty hands. They are cultivators of the soil. They grow crops by pattern, by acre, by foresight, by habit. What corn is to one, wheat is to the other, and though to some eyes the similarities outweigh the differences it would be as unthinkable for the second to commence planting corn as for the first to switch over to wheat. What happens in the gully between them is no concern of theirs, they say, so long as the plough stays out, the weeds stay in the ditch where they belong, though anyone would notice the windsewn cornstalks poking up their shaggy ears like young lovers run off into the bushes, and the kinship of these wild grasses with those the farmer cultivates is too obvious to mention, sage and dun-colored stalks hanging their noble heads, hoarding exotic burrs and seeds, and yet it is neither corn nor wheat that truly flourishes there, nor some jackalopian hybrid of the two. What grows in that place is possessed of a beauty all its own, ramshackle and unexpected, even in winter, when the wind hangs icicles from the skeletons of briars and small tracks cross the snow in search of forgotten grain; in the spring the little trickle of water swells to welcome frogs and minnows, a muskrat, a family of turtles, nesting doves in the verdant grass; in summer it is a thoroughfare for raccoons and opossums, field mice, swallows and black birds, migrating egrets, a passing fox; in autumn the geese avoid its abundance, seeking out windrows of toppled stalks, fatter grain more quickly discerned, more easily digested. Of those that travel the local road, few pay that fertile hollow any mind, even those with an eye for what blossoms, vetch and timothy, early forsythia, the fatted calf in the fallow field, the rabbit running for cover, the hawk's descent from the lightning-struck tree. You've passed this way yourself many times, and can tell me, if you would, do the formal fields end where the valley begins, or does everything that surrounds us emerge from its embrace?

(1999)

LINH DINH (1963–)

∾

Fish Eyes

My son won't eat anything but fish eyes. At the fishmonger's, if my wife wants to buy a sturgeon that has already lost its set of eyes, she would also have to ask for two eyes plucked from a catfish, or even an eel, just so my son will have his fish eyes that evening. At home, these eyes are inserted into their new sockets.

If a boy who eats chicken legs all the time will most likely turn into a drunkard, and a boy who eats chicken wings will become a poet, what will become of my son, who never eats anything but fish eyes?

(1999)

The Most Beautiful Word

I think "vesicle" is the most beautiful word in the English language. He was lying face down, his shirt burnt off, back steaming. I myself was bleeding. There was a harvest of vesicles on his back. His body wept. "Yaw" may be the ugliest. Don't say, "The bullet yawed inside the body." Say, "The bullet danced inside the body." Say, "The bullet tumbled forward and upward." Light slanted down. All the lesser muscles in my face twitched. I flipped my man over gently, like an impatient lover, careful not to fracture his C-spine. Dominoes clanked under crusty skin: Clack! Clack! A collapsed face stared up. There was a pink spray in the air, then a brief rainbow. The mandible was stitched with blue threads to the soul. I extracted a tooth from the tongue. He had swallowed the rest.

(2000)

CLAUDIA RANKINE (1963–)

Intermission in Four Acts

THE THING IN PLAY (ACT I)

A world outside this plot prevents our intermission from being uninvolved—a present, its past in the queue outside the toilet, in each drink dulling the room. Hence our overwhelming desire to forgive some, forget others. Even so, we are here and, as yet, I cannot release us to here, cannot know and still go on as if all the world were staged. Who believes, "Not a big mess but rather an unfortunate accident arrived us here." Our plot assumes presence. It stays awkward, clumping in the mouth: I shall so want. And this is necessary time. Only now do we respect (or is it forget) the depths of our mistakes. There often rises from the fatigue of the surface a great affection for order. Plot, its grammar, is the linen no one disgorges into. Excuse me. From that which is systemic we try to detach ourselves; we cling to, cellophane ourselves into man-made regulations, so neatly educated, so nearly laid: *He maketh me to die down.* But some of us have drowned and coughed ourselves up. The deep morning lifts its swollen legs high upon the stage. Some wanting amnesia float personified abstractions. Some wash ashore, but not into the audience, not able to look on. Help me if who you are now helps you to know the world differently, if who you are wants not to live life so.

STILL IN PLAY (ACT II)

On the street where children now reside, the speed limit is 25. Green owns the season and will be God. A rain, that was, put a chill in every leaf, every blade of grass. The red brick, the asphalt, cold, cold. The front step, the doorknob, the banister, the knife, the fork. A faucet opens and the woman, Liv, arrives as debris formed in the sea's intestine, floating in to be washed ashore and perfumed. In time she opens her mouth and out rushes, "Why is the feeling this? Am I offal? Has an unfortunate accident arrived me here? Does anyone whisper *Stay*

282

awhile, or the blasphemous *Resemble me, resemble me?*" Those watching say with their silence, That is Liv, she has styes on her eyes, or she needs to forget the why of some moment. She doesn't look right. She is pulling the red plastic handle toward her, checking around her. She's washing, then watching hands, feet and shouting *Assemble me. Assemble me.* She is wearing shoes and avoiding electrical wires, others, steep drops, forgotten luggage. Those are her dangers. She cannot regret. A hook out of its eye, she's the underside of a turtle shell. Riveted, and riven, the others stare, contemplating the proximity of prison to person before realizing the quickest route *away from* is to wave her on. They are waving her on. Liv is waved on. Everything remains but the shouting. A cake is cooling on a rack. Someone is squeezing out excess water. Another is seasoning with salt. The blacker cat is in heat. A man sucks the mint in his mouth. The minutes are letting go. A hose is invisible on the darkened lawn.

MUSICAL INTERLUDE (ACT III)

A certain type of life is plot-driven. A certain slant in life. A man sucking his mint lozenge. He is waiting for the other foot to drop: his own, mind you. In a wide second he will be center stage.

His song will be the congregation of hope. He will drain his voice to let Liv know she cannot move toward birth without trespassing on here: To succumb to life is to be gummed to the reverberating scum seemingly arrested.

Erland knows Liv is as if in a sling, broken in the disappeared essence, the spirit perhaps: catfoot in a moist soil, at the lowest altitude or simply streamside, though seeming fine.

He knows he too, sometimes, is as if below, pained, non-circulatory, in an interval, the spirit perhaps in an interval. But then frictionized, rubbed hard—

sweet-life-everlasting, he is singing softly beneath his meaning in the sediment of connotation where everyone's nervously missing, so missed. His melody is vertical, surrendering suddenly to outcome, affording a heart, recalling, after all, another sort of knowing because some remainder, some ladder leftover, is biddy-bop, biddy-bop, and again. His voice catches. It feels like tenderness beckoning and it is into her voice, rejoicing.

IN MORTAL THEATER (ACT IV)

blessedly the absolute miscarries

and in its release this birth pulls me toward that which is without comparison. in the still water. of green pasture. Lord and Lamb and Shepherd in all circumstances. daylight in increase. always the floating clouds. ceaseless the bustling leaves. we exist as if conceived by our whole lives—the upsurge. its insides. in all our yesterdays. moreover

asking and borne into residence. the life that fills fills in a world without synonym. I labor. this is the applause. This—mercy grown within complexity. and in truth these lies cannot be separated out: I see as deep as the deep flows. I am as willing as is recognized.

I am.

am almost to be touching

(2001)

284

GABRIEL GUDDING (1966–)

∿

A Defense of Poetry

> *The test of such poetry*
> *is that it discomfits.*
> — *Charles Bernstein*

1. The lake trout is not a furious animal, for which I apologize that you have the mental capacity of the Anchovy.

2. Yes the greatest of your sister's facial pimples did outweigh a Turkey.

3. I was eating Vulture Beast Cream, I was eating Lippy Dung Corn, and I said "Your ugly dog is very ugly," for he is.

4. And that is when I turned and a snowflake banged into my eye like a rusty barge and I killed your gloomy dog with a mitten.

5. For I have bombed your cat and stabbed it. For I am the ambassador of this wheelbarrow and you are the janitor of a dandelion. Indeed, you are a teacher of great chickens, for you are from the town of Fat Blastoroma, O tawdry realtor. For I have clapped your dillywong in a sizeable door.

6. You have an achy knee which is where I clubbed your achy and pompous knee. I shoot your buffalo, may you be hanged by the upper lip and somehow burned in a canoe.

7. Is your butt driving through traffic

   that it should toot so at the world? I am averse to urine, yet I shake your hand upon occasion;

8. I have made a whiskey of your tears—and Joe-Bob made a flu-liqueur of your night-mucus;

9. That some of your gas has been banging around the market like a small soldier carrying a table. God booby.[1]

---

1. Just as the fog is shackled to the dirty valley stream and cannot go out loosely to join the loopy clouds who contain hollering eagles and whooshing falcons but must stand low and bound and suffer the scratch of a bush and the round poop of deer and the odd black spoor of the American black bear or the bump of a car on a road or the sick crashes of paintings thrown from a rural porch, so also is your mind bound to the low reach of trash and the wet wan game of worms and the dripping dick of a torpid dog— and unlike the clouds above you you do not feel swell but clammy and pokey and sweaty: a leaf-smell follows you, odd breezes juke your brook-chaff, lambs and rachel-bugs go up and forth in you, and when a car passes through you, windows down, the car-pillows in that car get puffy, absorbing water in the air, and those pillows become bosoms, gaseous moving bosoms, and that is the nearest you come to bosoms.

10. I overlook your titties. Your sneeze erased the blackboard and your cough knocked a dog into loneliness;

11. For you remind me of a dog hurled over a roof—yapping to no effect. And furthermore the habitual peristalsis in your bowels sounds like a barfight in a whale. In addition, that as a boy you lassoed storks with a petty friend named Jerry.

12. And just as you swallowed a cherry's stone and produced a tree, you recently ate a burger and found a bull honking among your feces.

13. For I would more expect a Pigeon to tote a rifle.

14. than a wise syllable issue from your cheesepipe.

15. And as your nose is packed with Error I advise you to pick it often.

16. For you are a buttock.

Indeed you are the balls of the bullock and the calls of the peacock; you are the pony in the paddock near the bullock and the peacock; you are the futtock on the keel and the fetlock (or the heel) of the pony in the paddock:

17.   Indeed you are the burdock on the fetlock and the beetle on the burdock and the mite on the beetle on the burdock on the fetlock of the pony in the pad-dock and the padlock of the gate of the paddock of the bullock and the peacock.

18.   Thus with you I am fed-up. For you are Prufrock and I am Wild Bill Hickok at a roadblock with the wind in my forelock and a bullet in my flintlock. You are Watson I am Sherlock.

19.   For you are the hillock and I am the hill; I am Hitchcock, O But-tock. You—are Cecil B. De Mille.

20.   Yes he hath thrown a squirrel at me which came flapping through the air like a disjointed hairbrush.

21.   The fact that the sequins on your dress caused you to look like the instrument panel of an airliner during a three-engine flame-out did not escape any-one's attention;

22.   That your heart is a colostomy bag[2] and your brain is the Peanut of Abomination.[3] And

---

2.   For these reasons and more, Dolores rightly asked as you walked by, "What is that smell that smells so much it is audible, is it a spoor?" I said it is the smell of a dillywong slammed in a door.

3.   Or the Dingleberry of Reason.

that the cake frosting you just
ate is actually earwax.

23. And since suing you would be
like suing a squirrel, and since I
would rather eat a mixture of
powdered mummy and water
than talk with you again[4], I will
try to punch your head hard
enough[5] so that you will not
dare chase me, but not so hard
that others will hunt me.

24. For you have killed my family[6]
and I have killed your dog, your

---

4. Some have called your mouth Bippy-Swingset,
and someone who seemed to resemble your
physician called the orifice in question the birth-
hole of a Raven, whereas it is common knowledge
all Ravens are born in burning forests, for the
beast is a charred contraption, well-cooked and
near dead. Some say that Crows are born out of a
sail's white leeward wall, others that thun Crow is
as an millet-corporal to the Raven's brook-
colonel, that a pelican has goiter and that a Crow
is in truth the silhouette of a gull knocked loose
from that gull, which can happen in the case of an
Sudden Explosion, where, in the afterclap and
initial desolation, gulls will breach the sky with
such celerity their silhouettes break free and fall
like dark packs to the ground, which is why the
crow is a kind of angry bird, being now without
grace and having a charred voice. Some insist the
crow is in fact a drunk, though at which saloon he
find his beer or how he should pay for it, or
whether he have beer, port, or an highball, these
"poets" will not aver: either way he follows not
the Doctrine of Christ and is a derisive and con-
demnable bird and ought therefore to be avoided
and never frighten a gull. Another annoying beast
can be the Squirrel. For he is midget blowhard.

5. And like a pipe thrown at an eagle I will send you
folding to the humpy.

6. I heard you once enquiring how you were born
and told you then that you were created because

289

bird, and the mouse of your daughter;

25. Your cousins Rosie, Yolanda, Amelia, Harriet, Johanna, and Carol have all been decapitated.

26. But we pushed Judy over a cliff.[7]

---

your mother subjected her privates to the attentions of a bull, which is why you have insisted that a cow says Ma when it is clearly saying Moo.

7. For: There was an Bee, who, flinging himself against his shadow in a Brooke, did drown, and so washed of his own Enmity, he did sail like a dark and brittle Bubble, to the general amphitheater of the Sea, where he was drowned a second time. Thus first he was sunk from life and second from the Known; and now lies twice dead. Like this captious Bee, you will drop from the world and sink to oblivion.

(2000)

JOE WENDEROTH (1966–)

◠

Twelve Epistles from *Letters to Wendy's*

AUGUST 19, 1996

Today I was thinking that it might be nice to be able, in one's last days, to move into a Wendy's. Perhaps a Wendy's life-support system could even be created and given a Wendy's slant; liquid fries, for instance, and burgers and Frosties continually dripped into one's vegetable dream locus. It would intensify the visits of the well, too, to see that such a care is being taken for their destiny.

AUGUST 26, 1996

Very high on marijuana brownies, I could not speak today at the register. I kept stepping aside for other customers and staring hard at the menu. I was overwhelmed by the chicken sandwich pictured there, but had no words for it. I kept saying, "*there,* that one . . . the man dressed like a woman." It's hard to get served when one understands the signifier as a process.

AUGUST 27, 1996

Still high on those brownies, but coming down. I've eaten, in the past twenty-four hours, so very many burgers and chicken sandwiches. The Sea of Coke is heavy today with meat—its cold swells with the meaty goodness that objects to language. Some kids drift by, talking. One of them says, "that sucks dead donkey dicks," and the other agrees. Imagine.

SEPTEMBER 5, 1996

Naturally I think about smashing the skulls and the rib-cages of the other customers. They stand in line so smug—like they were safe, *outside* the desires of or for an other. It's as if, for them, there is no *other's* desire—as if desire was one thing, and was *ours.* Restraining myself is not *dishonest*. It's a way of maintaining a keen sense of the unforeseeable injuries which shall certainly reunite us.

OCTOBER 8, 1996

It would bring me to despair to think that I could get a Frosty in my own kitchen. I need believe that a Frosty can only be gotten *outside* of where I ordinarily dwell. To be *constantly* in the place of real Frosties — this is unthinkable, somehow unbearable. The fact is: to be a subject of language is to desire an Event, and an Event needs a nothing to move out of, to seem to begin.

NOVEMBER 17, 1996

I eavesdrop on people at Wendy's. I notice they never talk about their assholes. It's not that I think an asshole, as an abstract (as Platonic form if you will), is so interesting. It's *specific* assholes that are interesting — my asshole as compared with Nick's, yours as compared with Ted's or Mary's. How one experiences another's asshole speaks volumes — it seems selfish not to make these volumes readily available.

NOVEMBER 25, 1996

This idiotic notion that one should love the other customers. Love here really only means: *agree, for the time being, not to attack.* People pretend, though, that each customer is an irreplaceable piece of some priceless puzzle — like the death of each customer is significant for every other customer. It's just not true; one cannot love what one does not know, and — fortunately — one knows very little.

DECEMBER 27, 1996

I can say without hesitation that if Wendy's ever started to "deliver" I would end my life. And in a way, my suicide would mimic Wendy's decision to "deliver." That is, I would decide that my blood, which, in my body, made sense, should flow out in to the dust, where it makes just more dust. *Our homes are dust?* you ask. Yes, our homes are dust. Don't pretend you are surprised.

JANUARY 3, 1997

I've been sort of hesitant to mention this, but I believe that one of your employees—you *must* know the one I speak of—is a beaver. It's impossible to look into her face, to hear the sounds she makes, and to see the way she moves, the way she carries bits of wood, and to not feel that *this is a beaver.* I've not mentioned this before because, obviously, beavers are powerful creatures.

JANUARY 19, 1997

These fucking teeny-bopper cunts—they'll steal your man as soon as look at you. Even if you don't have a man, they'll steal him. They'll steal him and they'll take him back to their fucking teeny-bopper bedroom. Then they'll suck his dick *real slow* as though they've never sucked a dick before and they'll say, "it's so big!" even if it isn't. And then afterwards they'll act like they never said it was big at all.

MARCH 14, 1997

As I look around the restaurant at all the beautiful folks enjoying themselves, I wonder what catastrophe awaits each one. Young man, will your heart explode? Will your intestines fill with blood? Perhaps a seizure on a boat in the middle of a lake. The sun shining down. The stars concealed once and for all. I always feel less anxious when I recognize that the collision is already well under way.

JUNE 28, 1997

My previous statements were made in haste. I was hungry and confused, and I longed for purpose. I wanted to seem like I was in the process of focusing in on something important. I wanted to feel purpose rising like an ancient city from the excavator's pick and shovel. I wanted this so much that I rushed—I swung my pick wildly, and I brought a great delicate city to the dust it had always verged on.

(2000)

LISA JARNOT (1967–)

∾

Still Life

Where we finally move closer, but instead we don't move closer at all, we just have an understanding that we want to move closer, which is a form of moving closer, or at least something to think about, that it was an idea, moving closer, though not ultimately satisfying, though something, on one or two or three occasions, during a single night, moving closer, and the sands accumulate into sand paintings, that are colorblind, and filled with raccoons, and the steps of the sand toward the pyramid of sand are altered, wearing pumpkins on their heads, wishing to be loved, in the steps of the sand, terrified, or not terrified, moving closer, identifying with raccoons, on certain evenings, that maybe to go from there, because obviously, the sand and raccoons accumulate, taking years, listening to the traffic, saying is it quiet where you live, near the sand and the raccoons, in a quiet room, near the sounds of all the traffic that moves closer, on the periphery, that the thing is this, accumulating, getting closer, to the raccoons and the traffic that moves closer, having moved, having said that moving closer is ideal, having said thank you, and so forth, that the so forth is moving closer, forward, toward what in most of the universe would have been a scene, where the sand is forgotten, and the raccoons, and the accumulation of pyramids, and clothing items, and various identifications, and so forth, but instead, one by one, or one, or two or three times awkwardly, there is news, and there are raccoons, and the raccoons are screeching in the yard, as if to say something about the grains of sand, at opposite sides of the universe, screeching, with their suits and ties, bringing news, like Tom Brokaw, colorblind, reliable, and standing in the sand, and the news, which should not be true, but is, that there are raccoons, screeching, outside, in the traffic, near the sand, and on the news, and the curious figure that is him, there, who is reliable, and like the sand, accumulating, rightly, while how wrong it is, the news, that there is a rightness about him, the news of the raccoons, so close enough, and safely in the sand.

(2001)

Ode

For let me consider him who pretends to be the pizza delivery man and is instead the perfect part of day, for the fact he is a medium, for the eight to twelve inches of snow he tends to be, for he who covers the waterfront, for he that was handmade in a tiny village in japan, for that he is more than just an envelope or inside-out balloon, for that he can always find the scotch tape, for that he resembles a river in mid-December muddied over, for that he has seen the taxi cabs on fire in the rain, for that he is like the heat beneath the desk lamp, for that he is not a tiny teal iguana, for that it is he who waits for me inside cafes, for that he has hands and legs, for that he exceeds the vegetable, for that he is the rest of the balance continuing huge.

(2001)

KAREN VOLKMAN (1967–)

⌒

It Could Be a Bird

It could be a bird that says summer, that says gather no late failing harvest in a wealth of arms. Lost weed, still you remember, in a storm-suit, the sky came down to walk among us, oh to talk. Such grey conviction, cracked calculus, chasm. Black earth repeating, I was never him, and so many green words of schism, that and this. If a tree could say, if a tree could say, what are you? to my dim attention, to my wayward random shape. Suit, suit, you're a cold suit, your stitched rain shivers and splinters, what web is this? Unnumbered mesh of other, kill, kiss.

(2001)

When Kiss Spells Contradiction

When kiss spells contradiction it spills an ocean of open clothes. I gave me to one who hung hearts so high it was a mast in mute blue weather, the clang and strop of it, the undercover wet. Said are they sails your impenetrables that only winds can jibe them, the arc and the rip and the rush of all that flood. But his were slow words, more a storm than a sending, what his hands knew of tack and tumble I will not tell.

If kiss were conquest, were conclusion, I might be true. In the bluebit, heartquit leaping I might be binded. But tongue, lip, lap are brim beginning, a prank of yet. I waxed for a man all hum and hover and stuttered must, what he'd read of snowlight and sunder I'll never pearl. I said, Are they moons, that they bleach in your fingers, and so much wrack at the socket, and rune and run. (Like a moon he was sharp when new and blunt when done.)

If kiss were question, were caution. What he knew of. Trice and tender. I'll never. *None.*

(2001)

༈

Two Poems from "Blasted Fields of Clover Bring Harrowing and Regretful Sighs"

gu7i

Favored lambs mentioned in a personal ad bend forward onto their knees as a peon carries the wrong box away. His employer emerges from a hole with his tan seersucker muddied holding galleys and leading a greener trainee. The spectator's disruption drew a reprimand. Distance to the beach in relation to time of departure conveyed in a series of double-jointed hand signals wasted on recruits. One shoved another flirtatiously. Water just off the porch did not suffice. Suspended above it the chef's diorama betrayed him with silk flowers. The man who played wolf in the film version lived next door and perfect sand lay just over the crest where no one made excuses for skin upon skin or lip balm crushed into a cap. Again the lambs' complaints drift on a pink foam from the hollow. A magazine a wrong night a chance meeting what is owed biting at elbows and ropes.

anm-amn

As a shopping cart careened the football team scattered. Next year they'll find changes of clothes in the woods. When Donald the Dandy rode his horse-drawn carriage through the W. Village (1969) he was roundly egged. The feathers of his headdress destroyed. His little dogchild keening mommy&daddy over and over would mind no one but him. D. denied raiding Sarduy and Woolf as he nursed the whiny cur. Each headshot a different era the nipple still surprised. Those along the canal tried to keep windows clean. Friends on the phone in the same room hardly knew. Another back turned to a picture window. One man in Confederate garb fingered Julia's necklace and grazed her breast. Thus was his gall not unlike that of an older queen who'd sprung out of a hedge nude from the waist down. Who was pushed in first. Teeter on a narrow strip of grass. Here little dogchild here.

(2001)

RICHARD BLANCO (1968–)

❧

Mango, Number 61

Pescado grande was number 14, while *pescado chico* was number 12; *dinero,* money, was number 10. This was *la charada,* the sacred and obsessive numerology my *abuela* used to predict lottery numbers or winning trifectas at the dog track. The grocery stores and pawn shops on Flagler Street handed out complimentary wallet-size cards printed with the entire *charada,* numbers 1 through 100: number 70 was *coco,* number 89 was *melón* and number 61 was *mango.* Mango was Mrs. Pike, the last *americana* on the block with the best mango tree in the neighborhood. *Mamá* would coerce her in granting us picking rights—after all, *los americanos don't eat mango,* she'd reason. Mango was fruit wrapped in brown paper bags, hidden like ripening secrets in the kitchen oven. Mango was the perfect house-warming gift and a marmalade dessert with thick slices of cream cheese at birthday dinners and Thanksgiving. Mangos, watching like amber cat's eyes; mangos, perfectly still in their speckled maroon shells like giant unhatched eggs. Number 48 was *cucaracha,* number 36 was *bodega* and mango was my uncle's *bodega,* where everyone spoke only loud Spanish, the precious gold fruit towering in *tres-por-un-peso* pyramids. Mango was mango shakes made with milk, sugar and a pinch of salt—my grandfather's treat at the 8th street market after baseball practice. Number 60 was *sol,* number 18 was *palma,* but mango was my father and I under the largest shade tree at the edges of Tamiami Park. Mango was *abuela* and I hunched over the counter covered with classifieds, devouring the dissected flesh of the fruit slithering like molten gold through our fingers, the pigmented juices cascading from our binging chins, *abuela* consumed in her rapture and convinced that I absolutely loved mangos. Those messy mangos. Number 79 was *cubano*—us, and number 93 was *revolución,* though I always thought it should be 58, the actual year of the revolution—the reason why, I'm told, we live so obsessively and nostalgically eating number 61s, *mangos,* here in number 87, *América.*

(2000)

JENNIFER L. KNOX (1968–)

∽

Hot Ass Poem

Hey check out the ass on that guy he's got a really hot ass I'd like to see his ass naked with his hot naked ass Hey check out her hot ass that chick's got a hot ass she's a red hot ass chick I want to touch it Hey check out the ass on that old man that's one hot old man ass look at his ass his ass his old man ass Hey check out that dog's ass wow that dog's ass is hot that dog's got a hot dog ass I want to squeeze that dog's hot dog ass like a ball but a hot ball a hot ass ball Hey check out the ass on that bird how's a bird get a hot ass like that that's one hot ass bird ass I want to put that bird's hot ass in my mouth and swish it around and around and around Hey check out the ass on that bike damn that bike's ass is h-o-t you ever see a bike with an ass that hot I want to put my hot ass on that bike's hot ass and make a double hot ass bike ass Hey check out that building it's got a really really really hot ass and the doorman and the ladies in the information booth and the guy in the elevator got themselves a butt load of hot ass I want to wrap my arms around the whole damn hot ass building and squeeze myself right through its hot ass and out the other side I want to get me a hot ass piece of all 86 floors of hot hot hot hot ass!

(2001)

❦

Requiem

Rocky Marciano leans into a lucky one. Takes a fall. But it's early in his career. He staggers back after the punch, shakes his head left, then right. This is years before million dollar purses and ESPN. But Marciano isn't Jake LaMotta either: bloated, eyes dulled, Scorsese filmed-in-black-and-white. Let's make this an allegory. LaMotta will be capitalism—slowing, slowed, unable to speak through a shattered mouthguard and broken teeth. No, that's not right either.

Let's go to the videotape.

There, Marciano leans into it—he wanted that punch, maybe to make himself angry enough to win: angrier than a million dollars, angrier than the nightly news.

Cut to commercial.

[Are your breath, armpits, eyebrows fetid? Febrile? Feral? Do you hanker after lo-cal, low sodium, low maintenance? Is your hunger the insatiable need to fill the unfillable? What defines you? Localize. Itemize. Narcotize. Intensify, intensify.]

The universe expands, except for a black hole, which swallows—not even light escapes. I once knew someone who swallowed light. Could make each noontime as bleak and cold as a Russian bunker, where friends and loved ones would be trapped for years, etching out their names with hardened, uncut fingernails. For two years after the war ended, six

soldiers were trapped in a Soviet bunker. No light, no way to move the corpses as the men died off one by one. Only two made it out, one falling dead as the light glinted off his ashen flesh when he stepped out into the sun after that long, long stay. Rocky Marciano hits the canvas, blinks as the ref makes the count. Rocky Marciano leans into a lucky one. Or is it lucky? Maybe Marciano staggers back a bit; maybe he sees stars, or hallucinates, sees himself as a thirteen year old boy watching police boats drag the Hudson River. It's nighttime and Marciano flattens against the barroom wall. He isn't drunk, but maybe he should be. Two decades as a prize fighter and anger gets boring—

becomes too familiar, rage *a priori*—a buzzing that he doesn't quite hear anymore. Like people who live near the trainyard and can sleep through the night. You know those people when you meet them, their voices carrying over everything else, voices raw and thin from yelling all day. A Camaro in the passing lane shakes with bass, with Led

Zeppelin's "Whole Lotta Love" looped and a hiphop vocal track added. What's that anger? It's a kind of violence you hear, a violence that fills everything you see. Inside the ear. What's more intimate than that? Rocky Marciano leans into a lucky one and his ear swells up. He's stone deaf within the year. No buzz, no bell to end the round— just the vast echo of finitude reaching out past the ropes at the edge of the ring.

(2000)

ANSELM BERRIGAN (1972–)

The Page Torn Out

Curtains open to a page being torn out of a notebook

PAGE: I am the page torn out!

NOTEBOOK: That felt wonderful! Tear out another one!

A second page is torn out

SECOND PAGE: I am the page torn out! I cause pleasure being torn!

FIRST PAGE: No, I am the page torn out!

SECOND PAGE: You are merely a precedent! I am the page torn out!

UNIVERSE *(lying on a yellow bedsheet decorated with cows):* Yawn.

NOTEBOOK: ". . . and the universe lay on a yellow
bedsheet covered with cows,
yawning . . ."

*The universe shrieks after reading the words in the notebook, & tears
out the page upon which they were written*

THIRD PAGE: I am the page torn out!

*A curtain behind the stage raises to reveal countless pages standing in
a vast stretch of desert wearing Roman slave garb & screaming "I am
the page torn out!"*

Curtains fall

(1999)

KATHERINE LEDERER (1972–)

∽

According to the Appetites

Let birds—let fly—that it was good. There was a night and then a
day—and every living creature, moved—was good.

   The light was good—the air—the man—the man became a living
thing—and there he put the man who formed—the earth—no rain,
no no.

               When you touch delight, you will not die.
               The door—the door—is hard to bear.

   I shall be hidden—nothing sweet—your days—your face—and
now you might—and at the east—which he—was taken—turned
away—and heard—the voice.

   I am—open—I am—out—the firstlings—and the seedlings.

(1998)

ANDREW ZAWACKI (1972–)

❧

Two Poems from *Masquerade*

4

Return was a myth departure coined as incentive: we didn't believe it, bracken and twig, but moved ahead anyway. Negotiating winter's frisk and what remained of its pane, worn away by powerlines and barns the rain brought down, we kept to where the sun revamped its reach: upholstered clouds and amassings of geese, making their exodus vocal, mountains that seemed to change their position, ruptures in the road the crews ignored, before defaulting to some other damage control. It would not have been false to conjure transparence or zero, to coax the sight of scaffolds ghosting white pine, ilex, tea tree, birch. The metabolism of snowshoe and compass: nothing could stall it or usher it onward, not when it had already been stated, and called us so we came.

12

Asleep on the shattered surface of a cinematic, lunar creek, one of us dreamt the silhouette of a dog, yet found upon waking it hadn't strayed. Such were the spells of a landscape that couldn't be trusted although we'd devised it ourselves, if only to attribute otherwise: a zone where no one believed any longer the hollows that brought them this far, where flowers were blooming again, without any scent.

(2001)

∾

An American Story

Two possums dressed as children (their mother raised them as such) were crying when their father (not a possum) came home. Their mother (not a possum either) was already there. She stayed home with the children everyday and kept house (though actually they lived in a bog swamp). There was a family dog too but it doesn't come up until later (when it dies). Now the mother had sent the children outside to play so she could get some cleaning done (an optimistic thought in a bog swamp). The children sat under a tree and ate the apples that had fallen to the ground (they were rotten). The ripe apples were still hanging from the boughs but the children were not allowed to climb the tree because they hung from their tails (which disturbed their parents to no end). As the children stuffed their mouths with the brown, sticky fruit, their dog, Ernest (a Laplander), bounded across the street to join them and was struck by a car. Now I'd like to tell you the dog died quickly, so I will, but actually it was a long, agonizing death involving hours of grueling pain and convulsions. The children were devastated. They ran into the house bawling, which is how their father found them when he came home (with the money he had stolen from the bank). He was a raccoon and a master thief. He and his accomplice had been planning the heist for weeks. His wife had known nothing about it (although she knew his accomplice all too well). He was a dashing possum with a broad toothy grin and a weakness for tragic women.

(1999)

MATTHEA HARVEY (1973–)

∾

The Crowds Cheered
as Gloom Galloped Away

Everyone was happier. But where did the sadness go? People wanted
to know. They didn't want it collecting in their elbows or knees then
popping up later. The girl who thought of the ponies made a lot of
money. Now a month's supply of pills came in a hard blue case with
a handle. You opened it & found the usual vial plus six tiny ponies of
assorted shapes & sizes, softly breathing in the Styrofoam. Often they
had to be pried out & would wobble a little when first put on the
ground. In the beginning the children tried to play with them, but the
sharp hooves nicked their fingers & the ponies refused to jump over
pencil hurdles. The children stopped feeding them sugar water & the
ponies were left to break their legs on the gardens' gravel paths or
drown in the gutters. On the first day of the month, rats gathered on
doorsteps & spat out only the bitter manes. Many a pony's last sight
was a bounding squirrel with its tail hovering over its head like a halo.
Behind the movie theater the hardier ponies gathered in packs amongst
the cigarette butts, getting their hooves stuck in wads of gum. They
lined the hills at funerals, huddled under folding chairs at weddings.
It became a matter of pride if one of your ponies proved unusually
sturdy. People would smile & say, "This would have been an awful
month for me," pointing to the glossy palomino trotting energetically
around their ankles. Eventually, the ponies were no longer needed.
People had learned to imagine their sadness trotting away. & when
they wanted something more tangible, they could always go to the
racetrack & study the larger horses' faces. Gloom, #341, with those big
black eyes, was almost sure to win.

(2001)

SARAH MANGUSO (1974–)

❧

Nepenthe

Van Gogh said he agreed with Courbet, that he couldn't paint angels
because he'd never seen one—and then painted them as he saw them
in paintings by the Italians.

Another of my friends is dead. His parents are doctors. There is no
way to ensure your children will outlive you.

The Greeks believed in a potion to make them forget grief and suf-
fering.

A friend writes: *My grandparents are 88 now and that makes them
very quiet.*

I didn't believe in my death until last night. There was no reason to
believe in it until then. There is still no reason to believe in it.

I like it when we believe in something like *to the stars by hard ways.*

But where is the Aldebaran that I can only get to with grief?

The doctors invite me to an interminable meeting with joy,

but I'm on my knees in the music room, driving the brush tip into
my open eye.

I am painting myself a bridge. I can almost see it . . .

(2002)

What We Miss

Who says it's so easy to save a life? In the middle of an interview for the job you might get you see the cat from the window of the seventeenth floor just as he's crossing the street against traffic, just as you're answering a question about your worst character flaw and lying that you are too careful. What if you keep seeing the cat at every moment you are unable to save him? Failure is more like this than like duels and marathons. Everything can be saved, and bad timing prevents it. Every minute, you are answering the question and looking out the window of the church to see your one great love blinded by the glare, crossing the street, alone.

(2002)

JENNY BOULLY (1976–)

~

He appeared then, wearing the clothes in which we left him. "Please get in. Come with me," he said. But my mother had warned me about this before. *Do not go,* she said. *Do not go with those who have gone before us. They will take you where you are not ready to belong.* So I shook my head and said no, but offered to follow instead. And so, with great purpose and determination, I pulled the cord and started the red lawn mower and gathered white flowers in my pocket. Smoke trailed behind his black car, emptying like all of the past, those dresses which we cloak time with, and through the miles, on dirt roads, highways, wooden bridges, I pushed the lawn mower along until it finally succumbed to its natural loss. He drove on, without me trailing behind. It grew dark. People with crooked fingers clung to wire fences, whispering. They passed cigarettes of tobacco and marijuana back and forth through the chainlink. They said, "Here, come smoke some of this." I did not recognize any of them to bear the faces of the dead, but still I declined, saying, "I must fix this machine" (which was leaking green fluid and sputtering half-held coughs). "I cannot stop. There is someone I've promised to meet. I must catch up. He is still moving in wait."

(2000)

NOTES ON CONTRIBUTORS

Agha Shahid Ali was born in New Delhi in 1949. He grew up Muslim in Kashmir, and was educated at the University of Kashmir, Srinagar, and the University of Delhi. He earned a Ph.D. in English from Pennsylvania State University and an MFA from the University of Arizona. His volumes of poetry include *Rooms Are Never Finished* (W.W. Norton & Co., 2001) and *The Country Without a Post Office* (W. W. Norton & Co., 1997). He taught at Hamilton College and the universities of Massachusetts and Utah. He died on December 8, 2001.

Nin Andrews was born in Charlottesville, Virginia, in 1958, and grew up on a farm, the youngest of six children. She attended Hamilton College and received her MFA from Vermont College. The author of *The Book of Orgasms* (Cleveland State University Poetry Center, 2000) and *Spontaneous Breasts* (Pearl Editions, 1997), she lives in Poland, Ohio.

Rae Armantrout was born in Vallejo, California, in 1947. Her most recent books of poetry are *The Pretext* (Green Integer, 2001) and *Veil: New and Selected Poems* (Wesleyan University Press, 2001). She has written a memoir called *True* (Atelos, 1998). She teaches writing at the University of California, San Diego.

John Ashbery was born in Rochester, New York, in 1927. His recent books include *Chinese Whispers* (Farrar, Straus and Giroux, 2002), *As Umbrellas Follow Rain* (Qua Press, 2001), and *Your Name Here* (Farrar, Straus and Giroux, 2000). "Whatever It Is, Wherever You Are," and "Haibun 6" are from *A Wave* (Viking, 1984); "A Nice Presentation," "Disagreeable Glimpses," and "Meet Me Tonight in Dreamland" from *As Umbrella Follow Rain*. Ashbery made a point about the suitability of prose as a medium for verse when he called his 1972 book of meditative prose *Three Poems* (Viking, 1972). He was the guest editor of *The Best American Poetry 1988*. He made "L'Heure Exquise," the "postcard collage" featured on the cover of this anthology, in 1977.

Margaret Atwood was born in Ottawa, Ontario, in 1939. Among her recent publications are the novels *Alias Grace, Cat's Eye*, and *The Robber Bride*, as well as *Eating Fire: Selected Poems, 1965–1995* (Virago Press, 1998). Her prose poems are gathered in her books *Murder in the Dark* (1983) and *Good Bones* (1992), both from Coach House Press in Toronto. She was guest editor of *The Best American Short Stories* in 1989. She lives in Toronto, Canada.

B.J. Atwood-Fukuda was born in New York City in 1946 and grew up in Tennessee, Illinois, and Cape Cod. She has a JD from Cardozo Law School and an MFA from New School University. She is working on a novel entitled *Secrets*. Recently back from three years in Singapore, she lives in Spuyten Duyvil, New York. "The Wreck of the *Platonic*" appeared in *American Letters & Commentary* in 1999. It was her first published piece.

W. H. Auden was born in York, England, in 1907. Educated at Oxford University, he became the most celebrated poet of his generation. In 1939 he left England for the United States, a move for which some of his British compatriots never forgave him. He became an American citizen in 1946. "Caliban to the Audience," a long prose oration in the manner of Henry James, was his own favorite among his poems. His books include *Collected Poems* (1976) and *The English Auden* (1977), both from Random House. As judge of the Yale Younger Poets Series, he chose the first books of Adrienne Rich, W. S. Merwin, John Ashbery, James Wright, and John Hollander. He died in Vienna in 1973.

Michael Benedikt was born in 1935. He edited *The Prose Poem: An International Anthology* (Dell, 1976). He was poetry editor of *The Paris Review* in the 1970s. "The Doorway of Perception" is from his fourth book, *Night Cries* (Wesleyan, 1976).

April Bernard was born in 1956. She is the author of three collections of poetry: *Blackbird Bye Bye* (Random House, 1989), *Psalms* (W. W. Norton & Co., 1995), and *Swan Electric* (W. W. Norton & Co., 2002). She has also published a novel, *Pirate Jenny*. She teaches at Bennington College. "Exegesis" appeared originally as part 10 of the poem "Lamentations and Praises" in *Psalms* (1993).

Charles Bernstein was born in New York City in 1950. His most recent books include *With Strings* (2001) and *My Way: Speeches and Poems* (1999), both from the University of Chicago Press, and *Republics of Reality: 1975–1995* (Sun & Moon, 2000). He is the editor of *Close Listening: Poetry and the Performed Word* (Oxford University Press, 1998). He has a home page at the Electronic Poetry Center (epc.buffalo.edu).

Anselm Berrigan was born in Chicago in 1972. He is the author of two books of poetry, *Integrity & Dramatic Life* (1999) and *Zero Star Hotel* (2002), both from Edge Books. "The Page Torn Out" appeared in *The Hat* in 1999.

Mark Bibbins was born in 1968. He lives in New York City and teaches poetry workshops at the New School, where he cofounded *Lit* magazine. His first collection of poems, *Sky Lounge*, will be published by Graywolf in 2003.

Frank Bidart was born in Bakersfield, California, in 1939, and educated at the University of California at Riverside and at Harvard University. His early books are collected in *In the Western Night: Collected Poems 1965–90* (Farrar, Straus and Giroux). His most recent volume, *Desire*, was published by Farrar, Straus and Giroux in 1997. He lives in Cambridge, Massachusetts, and teaches at Wellesley College.

Elizabeth Bishop was born in Worcester, Massachusetts, in 1911, grew up in New England and Nova Scotia, and was educated at Vassar College. She won the Pulitzer Prize for *A Cold Spring* (1955), the National Book Award for *Questions of Travel* (1965), and the National Book Critics Circle Award for *Geography III* (1976). Her *Complete Poems: 1927–1979* (1983) and *Collected Prose* (1984) were published by Farrar, Straus and Giroux. She died in 1979.

Richard Blanco was born in Madrid, in 1968, where his family had gone in exile from Cuba, and was raised and educated in Miami. His first book, *City of a Hun-*

dred Fires, won the Agnes Lynch Starrett Poetry Prize and was published by the University of Pittsburgh Press in 1998. He lives in Alexandria, Virginia.

Robert Bly was born in Minnesota in 1926. He is editor of *The Fifties, The Sixties, The Seventies*, and, more recently, *The Thousands*. His first book was *Silence in the Snowy Fields* (Wesleyan University Press, 1962) and his most recent book is *The Night Abraham Called to the Stars* (HarperCollins, 2001). He was the guest editor of *The Best American Poetry 1999*.

Jenny Boully was born in Korat, Thailand, in 1976, to a Thai mother and American father. She grew up in San Antonio, Texas, and has studied at Hollins University and the University of Notre Dame. *The Body* was published by Slope Editions in 2002. She lives in Texas.

Catherine Bowman was born in El Paso, Texas, in 1957. Two collections of poems have appeared: *1–800–HOT-RIBS* (1993) and *Rock Farm* (1996), both from Gibbs Smith Publishers. She reports on poetry for the NPR program "All Things Considered" and is the editor of *Word of Mouth: Poems Featured on NPR's All Things Considered* (Vintage Books, 2003). She teaches at Indiana University.

Joe Brainard was born in Salem, Arkansas, in 1942, and grew up in Tulsa, Oklahoma. He moved to New York City and became friends with many of the writers and artists associated with the New York School. His books include *I Remember* (1975) and *29 Mini-Essays* (1978). The poems anthologized here appeared originally in the "one line poems" issue of *Roy Rogers*, edited by Bill Zavatsky (1974). His paintings, collages, drawings, and assemblages are in the collections of the Museum of Modern Art and the Whitney Museum. He died in New York City in May 1994.

Stephanie Brown was born in Pasadena, California, in 1961, and grew up in Newport Beach. She is the author of a collection of poetry, *Allegory of the Supermarket* (University of Georgia Press, 1998). She has made her living as a public librarian since 1989. She is the mother of two elementary-school-age sons and lives in San Clemente, California.

Michael Burkard was born in Rome, New York, in 1947. His books of poetry include *Unsleeping* (2001) and *Entire Dilemma* (1998), both from Sarabande, and *My Secret Boat* (W. W. Norton & Co., 1990). He teaches in the graduate writing program at Syracuse University and at the Fine Arts Work Center in Provincetown. "A Conversation about Memory" appeared in his book *In a White Light* (L'Epervier Press, 1977).

Fran Carlen was born in 1954. She is the author of *The Adorable Quandary* (Adventures in Poetry, 1999), a chapbook of prose poems. Her work has appeared in *Shiny, The Germ*, and *Sal Mimeo*. She lives in Paris, France.

Anne Carson was born in Toronto, Canada, in 1950. Her most recent books are *The Beauty of the Husband* (Knopf, 2001), which received the T. S. Eliot Prize, and *If Not, Winter* (Knopf, 2002), translations of the fragments of Sappho. She is a professor of classics at McGill University and lives in Montreal.

Maxine Chernoff was born in Chicago in 1952. She is the author of six books of poetry, most recently *World: Poems 1991–2001* (Salt, 2001). The prose poems anthologized here appeared in *Utopia TV Store* (Yellow Press, 1979). Her most recent novel is *A Boy in Winter* (Crown, 1999). With Paul Hoover she is the co-editor of *New American Writing*. She chairs the creative writing program at San Francisco State University and lives in Mill Valley, California.

Tom Clark was born in Oak Park, Illinois, in 1941. He was poetry editor of *The Paris Review* in the late 1960s. His many books of poetry include *Easter Sunday* (Coffee House Press, 1987) and *Cold Spring: A Diary* (Skanky Possum, 2000). He has written literary biographies of Jack Kerouac (1984), Charles Olson (1991), Robert Creeley (1993), and Edward Dorn (2002). Since 1987 Clark has been a member of the core faculty in poetics at New College of California.

Killarney Clary was born in 1953 and lives in Los Angeles. The prose poems here were published in *Who Whispered Near Me* (Farrar, Straus and Giroux, 1989). Her third collection of poems, *Potential Stranger*, will be published by the University of Chicago Press in Spring 2003.

Andrei Codrescu was born in Sibiu, Romania, in 1946. He is the editor of *Exquisite Corpse: A Journal of Life & Letters* (www.corpse.org) and of such anthologies as *American Poetry Since 1970: Up Late* (Four Walls Eight Windows, 1987). He is a regular commentator on NPR and the MacCurdy Distinguished Professor of English at Louisiana State University in Baton Rouge. The poems anthologized here are from his San Francisco period (1973–1974) and are in *Alien Candor: Selected Poems 1970–1995* (Black Sparrow Press, 1996).

Billy Collins was born in New York City in 1941. His collections of poetry include *Picnic, Lightning*, *Sailing Alone Around the Room: New and Selected Poems*, and, most recently, *Nine Horses* (Random House, 2002). He is a Distinguished Professor of English at Lehman College (CUNY) and is currently Poet Laureate of the United States. He lives with his wife, Diane, in northern Westchester County, New York.

Hart Crane was born in Garrettsville, Ohio, in 1899. He began writing verse as a teenager. His father, a candy manufacturer, tried to dissuade him, but Crane was determined. He moved to New York City and lived in Brooklyn. From the roof of his Columbia Heights building he saw a vista dominated by the Brooklyn Bridge: "It is everything from mountains to the walls of Jerusalem and Nineveh." He wrote *The Bridge*, among other celebrated poems. Volatile, self-destructive, he drank heavily. He committed suicide in 1932, at the age of thirty-three, by jumping from the deck of a steamship sailing back to New York from Mexico.

Edward Estlin Cummings was born in Cambridge, Massachusetts, in 1894. Educated at Harvard, he worked as an ambulance driver in France during World War I but was interned in a prison camp by suspicious French authorities. The experience informs his novel *The Enormous Room* (1922). After the war, he lived in Paris, took up painting, and published *Tulips and Chimneys*, his first book of poems (1923). He experimented with punctuation and syntax and achieved great popularity, especially among young readers, with his playful surfaces and signature lowercase style. He died in New York City in 1963.

Lydia Davis was born in Northampton, Massachusetts, in 1947. Her books include *Break It Down* (1986), *The End of the Story* (1995), and *Almost No Memory* (1997), all from Farrar, Straus and Giroux. She has translated numerous books from the French, including works by Maurice Blanchot, Michel Leiris, and Pierre Jean Jouve. She lives in upstate New York.

Richard Deming was born in Duluth, Minnesota, in 1970, and grew up outside Boston. He is a lecturer at Yale and is finishing his doctorate at SUNY Buffalo. With Nancy Kuhl he edits Phylum Press. "Requiem" appeared in *Quarter After Eight*. He lives in New Haven, Connecticut.

Edwin Denby was born in Tientsin, China, in 1903. His books of poetry include *In Public, In Private* (1948) and *Complete Poems* (Random House, 1986). He served as dance critic of the *New York Herald Tribune* from 1942 to 1945. Posthumously published, his collected *Dance Writings* (Knopf, 1986) won the National Book Critics Circle Award in criticism in 1988. A volume of *Dance Writings & Poetry* was published by Yale University Press in 1998. He died in 1983.

Linh Dinh was born in Saigon, Vietnam, in 1963, came to the United States in 1975, and now lives in Certaldo, Italy, with his wife. He is the author of a collection of stories, *Fake House* (Seven Stories Press, 2000), and several books of poems, including *All Around What Empties Out* (Tinfish, 2002). He edited the anthologies *Night, Again: Contemporary Fiction from Vietnam* (Seven Stories Press, 1996) and *Three Vietnamese Poets* (Tinfish, 2001).

H. D. (Hilda Doolittle) was born in Bethlehem, Pennsylvania, in 1886. She attended Bryn Mawr as a classmate of Marianne Moore and later befriended Ezra Pound and William Carlos Williams at the University of Pennsylvania. She traveled to Europe in 1911, intending to spend only a summer, but remained abroad for the rest of her life. She became one of Freud's patients. Her books include *Heliodora and Other Poems* (1924), *The Walls Do Not Fall* (1944), *By Avon River* (1949), and *A Tribute to Freud* (1956). She died in Zurich in 1961.

Rita Dove was born in Akron, Ohio, in 1952. Her books of poetry include *On the Bus with Rosa Parks* (1999), *Mother Love* (1995), *Grace Notes* (1989), all from W. W. Norton & Co., and *Thomas and Beulah* (Carnegie-Mellon University Press, 1986), which won the Pulitzer Prize. "Kentucky, 1833" appeared in *The Yellow House on the Corner* (Carnegie-Mellon University Press, 1980). She was guest editor of *The Best American Poetry 2000*. She has held Fulbright and Guggenheim fellowships and served as Poet Laureate of the United States from 1993 to 1995. She is Commonwealth Professor of English at the University of Virginia and lives in Charlottesville, Virginia.

Denise Duhamel was born in 1961. She is the author of *Queen for a Day: Selected and New Poems* (University of Pittsburgh Press, 2001). In 2001 she received a National Endowment for the Arts fellowship in poetry. She teaches at Florida International University in Miami.

Jamey Dunham was born in 1973 and is a graduate of the MFA writing program at Bennington College. "An American Story" appeared in *Key Satch(el)*. He teaches at Sinclair Community College and lives in Cincinnati with his wife.

Christopher Edgar was born in 1961 and is publications director of Teachers & Writers Collaborative, a nonprofit literary organization in New York City. He won the *Boston Review* poetry prize in 2000. He is an editor of *The Hat* and translator of *Tolstoy as Teacher: Leo Tolstoy's Writings on Education* (Teachers & Writers, 2000). "In C" appeared in *The Germ* in 1999.

Russell Edson was born in 1935 and lives in Connecticut with his wife, Frances. His books include *The Very Thing That Happens* (with an introduction by Denise Levertov; New Directions, 1964), *The Tunnel: Selected Poems* (Oberlin College Press, 1994), and *The House of Sara Loo* (Rain Taxi, 2002). "A Performance at Hog Theater" appeared in *The Childhood of an Equestrian* (Harper and Row, 1973); "The Pilot" in *The Intuitive Journey & Other Works* (Harper and Row, 1976); "The Taxi" in *The Reason Why the Closet-Man Is Never Sad* (Wesleyan University Press, 1977); "The Rat's Tight Schedule" in *The Wounded Breakfast* (Wesleyan University Press, 1985); "The Canoeing Trip" in *Verse* magazine in 1997; and "The New Father" in *The Tormented Mirror* (University of Pittsburgh, 2001).

Thomas Stearns Eliot was born in St. Louis, Missouri, in 1888. He attended Harvard University and settled in England in 1914. With Ezra Pound's assistance, "The Love Song of J. Alfred Prufrock" appeared in *Poetry* in 1915. *Prufrock and Other Observations* was published in 1917, *The Sacred Wood* (a volume of critical essays) in 1920, and *The Waste Land* in 1922. Eliot was the founding editor of *The Criterion* and became a director of the publishing firm of Faber & Faber. *Four Quartets* appeared in 1943. His verse dramas include *Murder in the Cathedral, The Family Reunion*, and *The Cocktail Party*. He died in London in 1965.

Lynn Emanuel was born in Mt. Kisco, New York, in 1949. She is the author of three books of poetry: *Hotel Fiesta, The Dig*, and *Then, Suddenly* (University of Pittsburgh Press, 1999). She is a professor of English at the University of Pittsburgh.

Ralph Waldo Emerson was born in Boston in 1803. After studying at Harvard, he entered the ministry. His essays and addresses—"Self-Reliance," "Nature," "Experience," "The Poet," and others—are among the seminal documents in the history of American poetry. The "Sage of Concord" regarded himself as a poet. He acknowledged that he wrote mostly in prose. "Still am I a poet in the sense of a perceiver & dear lover of the harmonies that are in the soul & in matter." The prose sonnet in this anthology dates from 1839. In his journals, he wrote, "After thirty a man wakes up sad every morning excepting perhaps five or six until the day of his death." He died of pneumonia in 1882.

Aaron Fogel is the pen name of Jim Dolot, who was born in 1947. His work includes a collection of poems, *The Printer's Error* (Miami University Press, 2001); a book of criticism, *Coercion to Speak: Conrad's Poetics of Dialogue* (Harvard University Press, 1985); and numerous articles in journals, including *Repre-*

sentations, Western Humanities Review, and *Mosaic.* He has received a Guggenheim Fellowship and he teaches at Boston University.

Carolyn Forché was born in Detroit in 1950. Her first poetry collection, *Gathering the Tribes* (Yale University Press, 1976), won the Yale Younger Poets Award. Subsequent books include *The Country Between Us* (HarperCollins, 1982), *The Angel of History* (HarperCollins, 1994), which was chosen for the *Los Angeles Times* Book Award, and the forthcoming *Blue Hour* (HarperCollins, 2003). She teaches at George Mason University.

Michael Friedman was born in New York in 1960, grew up in Manhattan, and now lives in Denver. The prose poems anthologized here are from *Species* (The Figures, 2000). Since 1986 he has edited the influential journal *Shiny.*

Amy Gerstler was born in San Diego in 1956. *Medicine,* her most recent book of poems, was published by Penguin Putnam in 2000. Her previous books include *Bitter Angel* (Carnegie-Mellon University Press, 1998), *Crown of Weeds* (Penguin, 1997) and *Nerve Storm* (Penguin, 1993). She teaches in the graduate writing program at Bennington College and at Art Center College of Design in Pasadena, California. She lives in Los Angeles.

Allen Ginsberg was born in Newark, New Jersey, in 1926. He attended Columbia College. When he read "Howl" at a group reading in San Francisco's North Beach in 1956, he uttered the battle cry of the Beat movement. The poem, banned, became a cause célèbre. Other poems of this period, such as "America" ("America I'm putting my queer shoulder to the wheel") and "Kaddish," his elegy for his mother ("Get married Allen don't take drugs"), were key works in the countercultural literary uprisings of the 1960s. His books include *Collected Poems: 1947–1980* (Harper and Row, 1984), *White Shroud: Poems 1980–1985* (Harper and Row, 1985), and *Cosmopolitan Greetings: Poems 1986–1992* (HarperCollins, 1994). Ginsberg died of a heart attack on April 5, 1997.

John Godfrey was born in Massena, New York, in 1945. He studied at Princeton and Columbia and has lived in New York City's East Village since the 1960s. Among his six poetry collections are *Where the Weather Suits My Clothes* (Z Press, 1984), which includes "So Let's Look at It Another Way," and *Private Lemonade* (Adventures in Poetry, 2002). He works in Brooklyn as a community health nurse, specializing in pediatric infectious diseases.

Gabriel Gudding was born in Anoka, Minnesota on Bloom's Day, 1966. Raised in Minnesota, North Dakota, and Washington, he was educated at the Evergreen State College, Purdue and Cornell universities, and has begun creative writing programs in two prisons. He teaches at Illinois State University. *A Defense of Poetry* won the Agnes Lynch Starrett Poetry Prize and was published by the University of Pittsburgh Press in 2002.

Barbara Guest was born in Wilmington, North Carolina, in 1920. She grew up in Los Angeles, was graduated from the University of California at Berkeley, and lived for many years in New York City. She has published twenty-six books, twenty-three of them poetry, including *If So, Tell Me* (Reality Street, London,

1999); *Rocks on a Platter: Notes on Literature* (Wesleyan University Press, 1999); and *Symbiosis* (Kelsey St., 2000). "Color" appeared in *The Confetti Trees* (Sun & Moon, 1999). She wrote a biography of the poet H. D. under the title *Herself Defined* (Quill, 1984). She lives in Berkeley, California.

Carla Harryman was born in 1952. Her books include two volumes of selected writing, *There Never Was a Rose without a Thorn* (City Light Books, 1995) and *Animal Instincts* (Sun & Moon Press, 1989). Known for her genre experiments and gender irreverence, Harryman, a native Californian, now lives in the Detroit area and teaches English at Wayne State University.

Matthea Harvey was born in 1973 and is the author of *Pity the Bathtub Its Forced Embrace of the Human Form* (Alice James Books, 2000). She is the poetry editor of *American Letters & Commentary* and lives in Brooklyn, New York.

Robert Hass was born in San Francisco in 1941. His books of poetry include *Sun Under Wood: New Poems* (Ecco Press, 1996); *Human Wishes* (Ecco Press, 1989); and *Field Guide* (1973), which Stanley Kunitz selected for the Yale Younger Poets Series. His prose poems are in *Human Wishes* (Ecco Press, 1989). He has also cotranslated several volumes of poetry with Czeslaw Milosz. He served as Poet Laureate of the United States from 1995 to 1997 and was guest editor of *The Best American Poetry 2001*. He lives in California and teaches at the University of California, Berkeley.

Lyn Hejinian was born in the San Francisco Bay Area in 1941 and lives in Berkeley. Her recent books include *Slowly* (Tuumba Press, 2002), *The Language of Inquiry* (a collection of essays, from the University of California Press, 2000), and *A Border Comedy* (Granary Books, 2001). She is also the author of *My Life* (1987) and *The Cell* (1992), both from Sun & Moon Press. She is codirector (with Travis Ortiz) of Atelos, a literary project commissioning and publishing cross-genre work by poets.

Ernest Hemingway was born in Oak Park, Illinois, in 1899. At seventeen he joined the *Kansas City Star* as a reporter, then volunteered to serve in the Red Cross during World War I. After the war he settled in Paris and wrote the novels that made him famous (*The Sun Also Rises, A Farewell to Arms*) and the short stories (*in our time, Men Without Women* that caused a revolution in prose style). "Montparnasse" was written in Paris in 1922. The italicized prose that divides the stories in *in our time* (1925)—fifteen "chapters" plus an envoi—has been claimed for the province of the prose poem. Hemingway won the Nobel Prize in literature in 1954. He took his life in Ketchum, Idaho, in 1961.

John Hollander was born in New York City in 1929. He has published eighteen books of poetry, the most recent being *Figurehead* (Knopf, 1999) and a reissue of his *Reflections on Espionage* with added notes and commentary (Yale University Press, 1999). His books of criticism include *The Work of Poetry* (Columbia University Press, 1997) and *The Poetry of Everyday Life* (University of Michigan Press, 1998). He is Sterling Professor of English at Yale University. He was guest editor of *The Best American Poetry 1998*. Of "The Way We Walk Now," he has commented that the poem is "about prose, as well as about life after verse."

Fanny Howe was born in Buffalo, New York, in 1940. She grew up in Boston and raised her three children there, but much of her life has been spent in California. Her most recent collections of poems are *One Crossed Out* (Graywolf, 1997) and *Selected Poems* (University of California Press, 2000). Her most recent novel, *Indivisible*, was published by Semiotexte/MIT Press in 2001. A new collection of poems and a new collection of essays are expected from the University of California Press in 2003.

David Ignatow was born in Brooklyn in 1914 and spent most of his life in the New York City area. His many books of poetry include *Living Is What I Wanted: Last Poems* (BOA Editions, 1999), *At My Ease: Uncollected Poems of the Fifties and Sixties* (BOA, 1998), and *Against the Evidence: Selected Poems, 1934–1994* (Wesleyan University Press, 1994). He was president of the Poetry Society of America from 1980 to 1984. He died in 1997 at his home in East Hampton, New York. "The Story of Progress" was published in *Verse* and was selected by Robert Bly for *The Best American Poetry 1999*.

Mark Jarman was born in Mount Sterling, Kentucky, in 1952. His recent collections of poetry, both published by Story Line Press, are *Unholy Sonnets* (2000) and *Questions for Ecclesiastes* (1997), which won the 1998 Lenore Marshall Poetry Prize. He has two book of essays on poetry: *The Secret of Poetry* (Story Line Press, 2001) and *Body and Soul* (University of Michigan Press, 2002). Story Line Press will publish his book of prose poems, *Epistles*, in spring 2004. He teaches at Vanderbilt University.

Lisa Jarnot was born in Buffalo, New York, in 1967. "Still Life" and "Ode" appeared in her *Ring of Fire* (Zoland Books, 2001). She lives in New York City and is completing a biography of Robert Duncan.

Louis Jenkins was born and raised in Oklahoma and now lives in Duluth, Minnesota. His books of poetry include *An Almost Human Gesture* (Eighties Press and Ally Press, 1987), *Nice Fish: New and Selected Prose Poems* (1995), *Just Above Water* (1997), and *The Winter Road* (2000), the last three named all from Holy Cow! Press. The Thousands Press released a CD recording of Jenkins reading his poems, *Any Way in the World*, in 2000.

Peter Johnson was born in 1951 and has published two books of prose poems: *Miracles & Mortifications* (White Pine Press, 2001), which received the James Laughlin Award from the Academy of American Poets, and *Pretty Happy!* (White Pine Press, 1997). He is the editor of *The Best of the Prose Poem: An International Journal* (White Pine Press, 2000).

Jennifer L. Knox was born in Lancaster, California ("where everyone's got a hot ass"), in 1968. Her work appeared in *The Best American Poetry 1997*. She teaches at Hunter College, lives in Brooklyn, and is finishing her first book, *A Gringo Like Me*.

Kenneth Koch was born in Cincinnati, Ohio, in 1925. He received a doctorate from Columbia University and taught there for many years. His recent books of poetry are *A Possible World* (2002), *Sun Out: Selected Poems 1952–1954* (2002), and *New Addresses* (2000), all from Knopf. Also published recently were two books about poetry: *The Art of Poetry* (University of Michigan, 1996) and *Making Your Own Days* (Scribner, 1998). "On Happiness," "The Allegory of Spring," and "The Wish to Be Pregnant" are all from *Hotel Lambosa* (1993). He died on July 6, 2002.

Yusef Komunyakaa was born in Bogalusa, Louisiana, in 1947. His books of poems include *Pleasure Dome: New & Collected Poems, 1975–1999* (Wesleyan University Press, 2001); *Talking Dirty to the Gods* (Farrar, Straus and Giroux, 2000); *Thieves of Paradise* (Wesleyan University Press, 1998). *Neon Vernacular: New & Selected Poems 1977–1989* (Wesleyan University Press, 1994) received the Pulitzer Prize and the Kingsley Tufts Prize. He is on the faculty of Princeton University.

Ruth Krauss was born in Baltimore, Maryland, in 1901. A prolific author of children's books, whose titles include *The Carrot Seed* and *Charlotte and the White Horse*, she collaborated with illustrator Maurice Sendak on eight books between 1953 and 1960. Nearing sixty, she took Kenneth Koch's course in poetry writing at the New School. "News" appeared in the avant-garde magazine *Locus Solus* in 1961. She died in Westport, Connecticut, in 1993.

Emma Lazarus was born in New York City in 1849, growing up in a prominent fourth-generation Jewish family. A volume of her *Poems and Translations* was published in her teen years (1867). Her work attracted the attention of Ralph Waldo Emerson, with whom she had a lifelong correspondence. In 1883 she published "The New Colossus" for an auction to benefit the Statue of Liberty, which was erected in New York Harbor three years later. "The Exodus (August 3, 1492)" is from *By the Waters of Babylon* (1887). Emma Lazarus was thirty-eight when she died of cancer in 1887. Not until 1903 were her famous lines from "The New Colossus" added to a bronze plaque at the base of the statue.

Katherine Lederer was born in New Hampshire in 1972. Educated at the University of California at Berkeley and the Iowa Writers' Workshop, she is the author of *Winter Sex* (Verse Press, 2002). She lives in New York City.

Amy Lowell was born in Brookline, Massachusetts, in 1874. She published her first book of poems in 1912. In London in 1913 she joined Ezra Pound as one of the founders of the Imagist Movement, which put a high value on "sharp and precise" imagery, common speech, the "*exact*" word, not the merely decorative word," freedom in choice of subject matter, the omission of needless words, and a goal of "poetry that is hard and clear, not blurred and indefinite." Lowell and Pound inevitably quarreled, and after he withdrew from the group she became its chief spokesperson. Her posthumous volume, *What's O'Clock*, won the Pulitzer Prize in 1926. She died in 1925.

Sarah Manguso was born in 1974, grew up in Wellesley, Massachusetts, and was educated at Harvard University and the University of Iowa. She is the author of *The Captain Lands in Paradise* (Alice James Books, 2002). She lives in Brooklyn, New York.

Dionisio D. Martínez was born in Cuba in 1956. He is the author of *Climbing Back* (W.W. Norton & Co., 2001), selected by Jorie Graham for the National Poetry Series; *Bad Alchemy* (W.W. Norton & Co., 1995); and *History as a Second Language* (Ohio State University Press, 1993). He lives in Florida.

Harry Mathews was born in New York City in 1930. He divides his time between France and Key West, Florida. His most recent books are *The Way Home: Selected Longer Prose* (Atlas Press, London, 1999) and *Sainte Catherine*, a novella written in French (Éditions P.O.L, Paris, 2000). *20 Lines a Day*, an experiment in daily writing, was composed in 1983 and 1984 and published by Dalkey Archive Press in 1988.

Bernadette Mayer was born in Brooklyn, New York, in 1945. Her books include *Two Haloed Mourners: Poems* (Granary Books, 1998), *The Desires of Mothers to Please Others in Letters* (Hard Press, 1994), *The Bernadette Mayer Reader* (New Directions, 1992), and *Sonnets* (Tender Buttons Books, 1989). She has taught writing workshops at the Poetry Project at St. Mark's Church in New York City for many years, and she served as the Poetry Project's director during the 1980s.

Campbell McGrath was born in Chicago in 1962. He is the author of five books of poetry, most recently *Florida Poems* (2002) and *Road Atlas* (1999), a collection of prose poems, both from Ecco/HarperCollins. He has received the Kingsley Tufts Prize as well as fellowships from the Guggenheim and MacArthur Foundations. He lives in Miami and teaches at Florida International University.

James Merrill was born in New York City in 1926, the son of financier Charles E. Merrill, one of the founders of the brokerage firm Merrill Lynch & Co. A graduate of Amherst College, he published his *First Poems* in 1951.The epic poem begun in *Divine Comedies* (1976) and extended in two subsequent volumes was published in its entirety as *The Changing Light at Sandover* (Atheneum, 1983). The three poems anthologized here are from "Prose of Departure," a sequence appearing in *The Inner Room* (Knopf, 1988). Merrill's *Collected Poems* (2001) and *Collected Novels and Plays* (2002), edited by J. D. McClatchy and Stephen Yenser, were recently published by Knopf. He died on February 6, 1995.

W. S. Merwin was born in New York City in 1927, and has lived in Spain, England, France, and Mexico. His recent books include *The Pupil* (2001), a translation of Dante's *Purgatorio* (2000), and *The River Sound* (1999), all from Knopf. His prose collections *The Miner's Pale Children* (1970) and *Houses and Travellers* (1977) were reprinted by Henry Holt in 1994. He lives in Haiku, Hawaii.

Czeslaw Milosz was born in Szetejnie, Lithuania (then under the domination of the Russian tsarist government) in 1911. In 1931 he cofounded the Polish avant-garde literary group "Zagary." He spent most of World War II in Nazi-occupied Warsaw working for underground presses. After the war, he came to the United States as a diplomat for the Polish communist government. In 1950 he was transferred to Paris, and the following year he requested and received political asylum. He moved to the United States to teach Polish literature at the University of California at Berkeley in 1960. He has written virtually all of his poems in his native

Polish, although his work was banned in Poland until after he won the Nobel Prize in 1980. His recent books include *Road-Side Dog* (1998), in which "Be Like Others" appears, and *To Begin Where I Am: Selected Essays* (2001), both from Farrar, Straus and Giroux.

Thylias Moss was born in Cleveland in 1954. "Infected with the spirit of a cosmologist, [she] continues to do much writing and thinking, attracted to the inexplicable, the quirky, the contradictory, the apparently aberrant." Her most recent book of poetry is *Last Chance for the Tarzan Holler* (Persea Books, 1998). Soon to be published is *Slave Moth*, a narrative in verse. She teaches at the University of Michigan.

Harryette Mullen was born in Florence, Alabama, and grew up in Fort Worth, Texas. She is the author of six poetry books, most recently *Blues Baby: Early Poems* (Bucknell University Press, 2002) and *Sleeping with the Dictionary* (University of California Press, 2002). She teaches African-American literature, American poetry, and creative writing at UCLA.

Alice Notley was born in 1945. She grew up in Needles, California, and was educated at Barnard College and the University of Iowa. She lived for many years in New York City. Her books include *Disobedience* (2001), *Mysteries of Small Houses* (1998), and *The Descent of Alette* (1996), all from Penguin, USA. Since 1992 she has lived in Paris. "Untitled" appeared in the magazine *Courier* in 2002.

Frank O'Hara was born in Baltimore in 1926. He served in the navy in World War II. In 1951 he joined his Harvard friends John Ashbery and Kenneth Koch in Manhattan, and the New York School was on the way. O'Hara wrote for *Art News* and worked his way up from postcard clerk to associate curator at the Museum of Modern Art. His monograph on Jackson Pollock appeared in 1959. His books of poems include *Meditations in an Emergency* (Grove Press, 1957), *Lunch Poems* (City Light Books, 1964), and the posthumous *Collected Poems* (Knopf, 1971). He died in July 1966, having been hit by a dune buggy on Fire Island. Edwin Denby said O'Hara was "everybody's catalyst." The painter Phillip Guston called him "our Apollinaire."

Ron Padgett was born in Tulsa, Oklahoma, in 1942. His books include *New & Selected Poems, 1963–1992* (Godine, 1995), *The Straight Line: Writings on Poetry and Poets* (University of Michigan Press, 2000), and *You Never Know* (Coffee House Press, 2002). He is the translator of Blaise Cendrars's *Complete Poems*. In 2003 the University of Oklahoma Press will publish his memoir of his father, *Oklahoma Tough*. "Light as Air" appeared originally in *Boulevard*, "Album" in *Shiny*.

Michael Palmer was born in Manhattan in 1943. He has lived in San Francisco since 1969. He is the author of *The Lion Bridge: Selected Poems 1972–1995* (1998), and *The Promises of Glass* (2000), both from New Directions. The poem anthologized here appeared in *Sun* (North Point, 1988). Recent projects include *May I Now*, a collaboration with the Margaret Jenkins Dance Company.

Kenneth Patchen was born in Niles, Ohio, in 1911. His books include *Before the Brave* (Random House, 1936), *First Will and Testament* (1939), and *Journal of*

Albion Moonlight (1941), the latter two from New Directions. The three poems in this anthology appeared in *The Famous Boating Party* (New Directions, 1954). For more than thirty years, he lived with a severe spinal ailment that caused him almost constant physical pain. He died in 1972.

Wang Ping was born in Shanghai, China, in 1957, and came to the United States in 1985. Her publications include *Foreign Devil* (novel, 1996) and *Of Flesh and Spirit* (poetry, 1998), both from Coffee House, and *Aching for Beauty: Footbinding in China* (2000) from the University of Minnesota Press. She edited and cotranslated *New Generation: Poetry from China Today* (Hanging Loose Press, 1999). She teaches at Macalester College in Minnesota.

Edgar Allan Poe was born in Boston, Massachusetts, in 1809. Orphaned at the age of three, he was raised by a foster father in Richmond, Virginia. Gambling debts forced him to leave the University of Virginia. In 1827 he enlisted in the army and published *Tamerlane*, his first book of poems. He made his living as a writer of stories and reviews and later as a magazine editor in New York City and Philadelphia. Often condescended to—T. S. Eliot said Poe had the mind of "a highly gifted young person before puberty"—he was astonishingly inventive in ways that still inspire. He cannot be bettered as an author of macabre tales. With "The Murders in the Rue Morgue" in 1841, he created the detective story as a genre with nearly all its conventions in place. He exerted a profound influence on Baudelaire and Mallarmé, who translated him, and on French Symbolism in general. In his "Tomb of Edgar Poe," Mallarmé wrote that Poe's legacy was to "give a purer sense to the words of the tribe." Following his young wife's death from tuberculosis in 1847, Poe feuded, flirted, caroused, and eventually drank himself to oblivion. On October 3, 1849, he was found in a state of semiconsciousness in Baltimore and died four days later of "congestion of the brain."

Claudia Rankine was born in Kingston, Jamaica, in 1963. She is the author of *PLOT* (Grove Press, 2001), *The End of the Alphabet* (Grove Press, 1998), and *Nothing in Nature Is Private* (Cleveland State University Press, 1994). She is coeditor, with Juliana Spahr, of *American Women Poets in the 21st Century: Where Lyric Meets Language* (Wesleyan University Press, 2002).

James Richardson was born in Bradenton, Florida, in 1950. His recent books include *Vectors: Aphorisms and Ten-Second Essays* (Ausable Press, 2001), *How Things Are* (Carnegie-Mellon University Press, 2000), and *As If* (National Poetry Series, 1992). He teaches at Princeton University.

Kit Robinson has been active as a poet, teacher, and performer on the San Francisco Bay Area poetry scene for thirty years. He is the author of *The Crave, 9:45, Cloud Eight* (with Alan Bernheimer), *Democracy Boulevard, Balance Sheet,* and a dozen other books from such small presses as Atelos, Chax, Post-Apollo, Potes & Poets, Roof, The Figures, This, Tuumba, Whale Cloth, and Zasterle. He lives in Berkeley and works as a marketing executive in the information technology industry.

Mary Ruefle was born in McKeesport, Pennsylvania, in 1952. She is the author of seven books of poetry, including *Apparition Hill* (CavanKerry Press, 2002), which she completed in China in 1989, and *Among the Musk Ox People* (Carnegie-

Mellon University Press, 2002). A Guggenheim Fellow, she lives in Massachusetts. "Monument" appeared in *Seneca Review* in 2001.

Ira Sadoff was born in Brooklyn, New York, in 1945. His books include *Barter* (2003) and *Grazing* (1998), both from the University of Illinois Press. He is also the author of *The Ira Sadoff Reader* (poems, stories, essays) and *Uncoupling*, a novel. He teaches American literature at Colby College in Maine. "Seurat" is from his first book, *Settling Down* (Houghton Mifflin, 1975).

Leslie Scalapino has written more than twenty books of poetry, fiction, essays, and plays. *New Time* (poetry) and *The Public World/ Syntactically Imperma-nence* (poetry and essays) were published by Wesleyan University Press. Her newest book of poetry (from Post-Apollo Press) is *It's Go/In Quiet Illumined Grass/Land*.

James Schuyler was born in Chicago in 1923. *Freely Espousing*, his first collection of poems, did not appear until he was forty-six. His subsequent books include *The Crystal Lithium* (Random House, 1972), *Hymn to Life* (Random House, 1974), *The Morning of the Poem* (Farrar, Straus and Giroux, 1980), *A Few Days* (Random House, 1985), and the posthumous *Collected Poems* (Farrar, Straus and Giroux, 1993). *The Morning of the Poem* (1980) won the Pulitzer Prize. He was also the author of three novels, one of them, *A Nest of Ninnies*, in collaboration with John Ashbery. Schuyler died in New York City in April 1991.

Delmore Schwartz was born in Brooklyn, New York, in 1913. His first book was *In Dreams Begin Responsibilities* (New Directions, 1939). The title story caused a sensation when it appeared in *Partisan Review*. He later became an editor of that magazine, taught at Harvard, and wrote brilliant poems and essays as well as stories. In "Coriolanus and His Mother," Schwartz describes a performance of the Shakespeare tragedy as witnessed by Aristotle, Beethoven, Freud, Kant, and Marx. "Justice" is one of the prose poems that divide the acts. A volume of selected poems appeared in 1959 under the title *Summer Knowledge*. He died in the elevator of a seedy Times Square hotel in 1966.

Maureen Seaton was born in Elizabeth, New Jersey, in 1947. Her books include *Little Ice Age* (Invisible Cities Press, 2001) and *Furious Cooking* (University of Iowa, 1996). With Denise Duhamel she is coauthor of *Exquisite Politics* (Tia Chucha Press, 1997), *Oyl* (Pearl Editions, 2000), and *Little Novels* (Pearl Editions, 2002.) She teaches at the University of Miami.

Charles Simic was born in Belgrade, Yugoslavia, in 1938, and immigrated to the United States in 1954. As a poet and translator, he has published more than sixty books since 1967. He teaches at the University of New Hampshire. *Jackstraws*, a book of poems, and *Selected Early Poems* were published by Harcourt Brace in 1999. He was the guest editor of *The Best American Poetry 1992*. "The Magic Study of Happiness" appeared in his book on Joseph Cornell, *Dime-Store Alchemy*; "Contributor's Note" was published in *Verse* in 1997.

Gertrude Stein was born in Allegheny, Pennsylvania, in 1874, to wealthy German-Jewish immigrants. At the age of three, her family moved first to Vienna and then to Paris. They returned to America in 1878 and settled in Oakland ("no there there"), California. Stein attended Radcliffe College, where she studied with William James. She moved to Paris in 1903, and her apartment at 27 rue de Fleurus became a legendary international avant-garde salon. Picasso, Matisse, Ezra Pound, Hemingway, and Scott Fitzgerald were among the writers and artists who paid court. In 1907 she met Alice B. Toklas, who became her lifelong companion. *Three Lives* was published in 1909, *Tender Buttons* in 1914. Her writing earned her such sobriquets as the "Mama of Dada" and the "Mother Goose of Montparnasse." Of *Tender Buttons* she commented: "I struggled with the ridding of myself of nouns. I knew that nouns must go in poetry as they had gone in prose if anything that is everything was to go on meaning something." Stein told Hemingway that his was a "lost generation," and Hemingway repeated the line as the epigraph of *The Sun Also Rises. The Autobiography of Alice B. Toklas* (1933), which Stein wrote, became a best-seller. *Four Saints in Three Acts*, the opera she wrote in collaboration with Virgil Thomson, enjoyed a six-week run on Broadway in 1934. She died at the American Hospital at Neuilly on July 27, 1946, of inoperable cancer.

Mark Strand was born on Canada's Prince Edward Island in 1934. His books include *Blizzard of One* (1998), which won the Pulitzer Prize, and *Dark Harbor* (1993), both from Knopf. He served as Poet Laureate of the United States and was guest editor of *The Best American Poetry 1991*. "In the Privacy of the Home" and "Success Story" appeared in his first book, *Sleeping with One Eye Open* (Atheneum, 1964). "From a Lost Diary" and "Chekhov: A Sestina" are from *The Continuous Life* (Knopf, 1990). He teaches in the Committee on Social Thought at the University of Chicago.

James Tate was born in Kansas City, Missouri, in 1943. *Selected Poems* received the Pulitzer Prize for 1991. *Worshipful Company of Fletchers* won the National Book Award in 1994. Recent books include *Memoir of the Hawk* (Ecco Press, 2001) and *Dreams of a Robot Dancing Bee* (Verse Press, 2001). He was guest editor of *The Best American Poetry 1997*. He teaches at the University of Massachusetts, Amherst. Asked about *Memoir of the Hawk*, which consists of narrative "prose poems" *with* line breaks, Tate told Eric Lorberer that "early on I knew I was keeping my line breaks. Not that they're terribly significant either, so that's what's funny. And when *The Prose Poem* did away with mine, I wasn't upset in the least. I'm somewhere lost in this No Man's Land of the prose poem world."

Jean Toomer was born in Washington, D.C., in 1894, the son of a Georgian farmer. Though he passed for white during certain periods of his life, he was raised in a predominantly black community and attended black high schools. *Cane*, a book of poems and prose poems, was acclaimed when published in 1923. After *Cane* he came under the strong influence of the Russian mystic George Gurdjieff and conducted experiments in community living. Much of his work remained unpublished at the time of his death in 1967.

Paul Violi was born in New York in 1944. His most recent books are *Fracas* and *Selected Accidents, Pointless Anecdotes*, both from Hanging Loose Press, and *Breakers*, a selection of his long poems, from Coffee House Press. "Triptych" appeared in his book *Splurge* (Sun, 1982).

Karen Volkman was born in Miami in 1967. Her books of poetry are *Crash's Law* (W.W. Norton & Co., 1996) and *Spar* (University of Iowa Press, 2002). She teaches at the University of Chicago.

Anne Waldman teaches at the Jack Kerouac School of Disembodied Poetics at Naropa in Boulder, Colorado, a program she cofounded with Allen Ginsberg in 1974. Her books include *Marriage: A Sentence* (Penguin Poets, 2000), which includes "Stereo," and *Vow to Poetry: Essays, Interviews & Manifestos* (Coffee House Press, 2001). She was the director of the St. Mark's Poetry Project from 1968 to 1978. With Lewis Warsh she is coeditor of *The Angel Hair Anthology* (Granary Books, 2001).

Rosmarie Waldrop was born in Kitzingen, Germany, in 1935. Her most recent books of poems are *Reluctant Gravities* (New Directions, 1999), *Split Infinites* (Singing Horse Press, 1998), and *Another Language: Selected Poems* (Talisman House, 1997). She has translated works by Edmond Jabès, Jacques Roubaud, and Emmanuel Hocquard from the French and Friederike Mayröcker, Elke Erb, and Oskar Pastior from the German. *Lavish Absence: Recalling and Rereading Edmond Jabès*, a memoir, was published by Wesleyan University Press in 2002. With Keith Waldrop she is coeditor of Burning Deck Press. She lives in Providence, Rhode Island.

Joe Wenderoth, born in 1966, lives with his wife and daughter in Marshall, Minnesota, where he teaches at Southwest State University. His first two books of poems, *Disfortune* and *It Is If I Speak*, were published by Wesleyan University Press. *Letters to Wendy's*, excerpted here, appeared from Verse Press in 2000.

Tom Whalen was born in Texarkana, Arkansas, in 1948. His first prose poem was published in 1976. His books include *Roithamer's Universe* (a novel), *Winter Coat* (poetry), and, with Daniel Quinn, the comic fiction *A Newcomer's Guide to the Afterlife*. He lives in Stuttgart, Germany.

Susan Wheeler was born in Pittsburgh, Pennsylvania, in 1955. Her three books of poetry are *Bag 'O' Diamonds* (University of Georgia Press, 1994), *Smokes* (Four Way Books, 1998), and *Source Codes* (SALT Publishing, 2001). She has won a Guggenheim Fellowship, and teaches at Princeton University and at the New School in New York City.

Thornton Wilder was born in Madison, Wisconsin, in 1897. As a teenager he lived in China, where his father was consul-general. Educated at Oberlin, Yale, and Princeton, he also studied archaeology in Rome. In 1927 he won the Pulitzer Prize for his novel *The Bridge of San Luis Rey*. Two of his plays won Pulitzers: *Our Town* (1938) and *The Skin of Our Teeth* (1942). His 1955 play, *The Matchmaker*, was made into the musical *Hello, Dolly!* He died in Hamden, Connecticut, in 1975.

Tyrone Williams was born in Detroit, Michigan, in 1954. He has published *C.C.*, a book of poems, and coedited a collection of writings by the homeless in Cincinnati. "Cold Calls" appeared originally in the fall 2000 issue of *Hambone*. He is completing books on quotation in modern art and rap music and the public. He teaches at Xavier University in Cincinnati, Ohio.

William Carlos Williams was born in Rutherford, New Jersey, in 1883. He began writing poetry while a student at Horace Mann High School. He received his M.D. from the University of Pennsylvania and resolved to be a poet and practicing physician for the rest of his life. His major works include *Kora in Hell* (1920), *Spring and All* (1923), *Pictures from Brueghel* (1962), and the five-volume epic *Paterson* (1963). He wrote the prose improvisations of *Kora in Hell* on a daily basis. "So that scribbling in the dark, leaving behind on my desk, often past midnight, the sheets to be filed away later, at the end of a year I had assembled a fairly bulky ms." Later, he added "notes of explanation, often more dense than the first writing." He wasn't sure what to call the finished product. It was obviously not verse, but it was different from "the typically French prose poem." He decided there was "nothing to do but put it down as it stood, trusting to the generous spirit of the age to find a place for it." Williams's health began to decline after a heart attack in 1948 and a series of strokes, but he continued to write until his death in New Jersey in 1963.

Terence Winch was born in New York City in 1945. He has published three books of poems, *The Drift of Things* (The Figures, 2001), *Irish Musicians/American Friends* (Coffee House Press, 1986), and *The Great Indoors* (Story Line Press, 1995). He has recorded three albums with Celtic Thunder, an Irish band he started with his brother in 1977. His second album with the band, *The Light of Other Days* (Green Linnet Records), won the INDIE for best Celtic recording.

James Wright was born in Martins Ferry, Ohio, in 1927. He attended Kenyon College on the GI Bill and studied with John Crowe Ransom. *The Green Wall*, his first book, won the Yale Younger Series Prize (1957). Subsequent books include *Saint Judas* (1959) and *The Branch Will Not Break* (1963). He translated works by Pablo Neruda, Cesar Vallejo, and Georg Trakl. In 1972 he received the Pulitzer Prize in poetry. He died in New York City in 1980. The poems anthologized here are from the posthumously published *This Journey* (1982). *Above the River: The Complete Poems*, with an introduction by Donald Hall, was published in 1990 (Farrar, Straus and Giroux and University Press of New England).

John Yau was born in Lynn, Massachusetts, in 1950, shortly after his parents fled Shanghai. He received his BA from Bard College and MFA from Brooklyn College. His recent books are *Borrowed Love Poems* (Penguin, 2002), *My Heart Is That Eternal Rose Tattoo* (Black Sparrow, 2001), and a collaboration with the artist Archie Rand, *100 More Jokes from the Book of the Dead* (Meritage, 2001). He lives in New York City.

Andrew Zawacki was born in Warren, Pennsylvania, in 1972. He is the author of *By Reason of Breakings* (University of Georgia Press, 2002), coeditor of *Verse*, and editor of *Afterwards: Slovenian Writing 1945–1995* (White Pine Press, 1999). A doctoral student in the Committee on Social Thought at the University of Chicago, he won the Poetry Society of America's Alice Fay Di Castagnola Award for his prose poem sequence, "Masquerade," from which the two poems in this anthology were chosen.

ACKNOWLEDGMENTS

Heartfelt thanks go to Mark Bibbins for his valued assistance and to Michele Rosenthal for her help in the permissions process. I felt at times as if I had the benefit of a team of advisers, and that was a lucky thing, for no single reader can hope to keep up with the proliferation of prose poems out there. For their recommendations I'd like to thank Michael Anderson, Nin Andrews, Rae Armantrout, John Ashbery, Mary Jo Bang, Rachel Barenblat, Alan Bernheimer, Robert Bly, Catherine Bowman, Henri Cole, Jamey Dunham, Thomas Sayers Ellis, Amy Gerstler, Roger Gilbert, Laurence Goldstein, Stacey Harwood, Robert Hass, John Hollander, Peter Johnson, Steve Monte, Fred Muratori, Ron Padgett, Danielle Pafunda, Robert Pinsky, John Schertzer, Michael Schiavo, Charles Simic, Mark Strand, Susan Swenson, James Tate, Ed Webster, and Susan Wheeler. John Ashbery kindly allowed me to reproduce the collage that appears on the cover of this book. Martha Kinney, Allyson Salazar, and Gabrielle Zane wrote essays, still unpublished, that I found very useful. Danielle Pafunda did important research. I'm indebted as ever to Glen Hartley of Writers' Representatives and to Gillian Blake and Rachel Sussman at Scribner.

INDEX OF POEMS

339

341

INDEX OF POETS

031206

DATE DUE	ON LINE 5/03
DEC 0 9 2003	
GAYLORD	PRINTED IN U.S.A.